The Hardball Times Baseball Annual
2013

Featuring contributions by THT staff writers:
Brian Cartwright • Glenn DuPaul • Matt Filippi
Brandon Isleib • Chris Jaffe • Brad Johnson
Dan Lependorf • Jeff Moore • Dave Studenmund
Matt Swartz • Steve Treder

Plus contributions by FanGraphs staff writers:
Dave Allen • Dave Cameron • Carson Cistulli
Chris Cwik • Ben Duronio • Marc Hulet
Matt Klaassen • David Laurila • Eno Sarris
Eric Seidman • Bradley Woodrum • Jeff Zimmerman

With additional contributions by guest writers:
Evan Brunell • Craig Calcaterra • Adam Dorhauer
Vince Gennaro • Jack Marshall • Sean Smith

Produced by Dave Studenmund
Edited by Joe Distelheim, Greg Simons and Paul Swydan

The Hardball Times Baseball Annual 2013

A FanGraphs production

New content daily at hardballtimes.com and fangraphs.com

Edited by Joe Distelheim, Greg Simons and Paul Swydan
Stats developed by FanGraphs
Cover design by Summer Anne Burton
Typesetting by Dave Studenmund and Paul Swydan

Published by FanGraphs and The Hardball Times

ISBN-13: 978-1480273818
ISBN-10: 1480273818
Printed by CreateSpace

What's Inside

The 2012 Season

Commentary

History

Economics & Analysis

Et Cetera

Welcome to Our Book

Hello, baseball fan. Welcome to the ninth *Hardball Times Annual*. If you're a previous reader, welcome back. There have been a few changes. If you're a new reader, let me tell you what's in store.

Like our other *Annuals*, this one has four sections. First up is a review of the 2012 season, broken out by division. We've included a couple of other features: an overview of each team's farm system—including an intriguing prospect from each team—and a postseason recap that prominently uses a stat we call Championships Added. We think you'll find this an interesting way to remember the season just past.

The second section contains commentary on the season and baseball in general, beginning with our good friend Craig Calcaterra's humorous view of the season's events. Other subjects include an appreciation of Oakland's season by Dan Lependorf and a lament on Boston's by Evan Brunell. There's a lot of there there, but I particularly want to point out that Chris Cwik has contributed a new version of a *THT Annual* standard, the GM in a Box. This year, it's the White Sox's Kenny Williams on display.

Third, what is baseball without some contemplation of its history? Steve Treder presents an overview of Horace Stoneham's often-overlooked legacy, Sean Smith takes a new sabermetric look at Satchel Paige's career and Chris Jaffe ranks the entirety of major league umpires by how hitter- or pitcher-friendly they were. And those are just the highlights.

Fourth and finally, we've dedicated a section of the *Annual* to the economics of baseball, along with some extra analytic pieces. Dave Cameron considers the impact of the new Collective Bargaining Agreement. Vince Gennaro contributes an intriguing case study that he's been using at SABR conferences and competitions. Matt Swartz discovers which stats are most over-valued and under-valued in the free agent market. There are also a couple of cutting-edge analytical articles such as new insights on what batters should do with a runner on first, and the impact of Tommy John surgery on a pitcher's career.

There are no statistics in this year's *Annual*—you can find plenty of baseball stats at fangraphs.com—but there are a couple of new features that crop up randomly in the book. We've got multiple "case studies" of specific players who stood out this past season. In our case studies, you'll be asked to think about Kyle Lohse's newfound level of excellence on the mound or why Alfonso Soriano really was a better fielder last year, among other things.

Plus, Carson Cistulli has contributed a number of unique leaderboards to the *Annual*, based on many of the insightful stats collected and posted at Fangraphs.

Sure, you know who led the majors in batting last year, but do you know who led in Reckless Power?

These two features—really, the entire book—are the product of the Hardball Times' new partnership with Fangraphs. This past year, our two websites joined forces as a way of ensuring that we both continue to feature great new content and stats for our readers. We're trying out some new ideas this year, including the idea of self-publishing the *Annual*. Please let us know what you think.

We're also looking forward to creating great new baseball insights in the coming years. Keep your eyes on us—it should be fun.

The Hardball Times has been an eight-year labor of love for more people than I can count. The site has now posted over 14,000 articles with lots of great baseball analysis and commentary. We love watching baseball and we love talking about it. It's our obsession. I imagine you feel the same.

There are so many people to thank for our success. David Appelman and Dave Cameron of Fangraphs have been fantastic partners. We've had support from many friends in the sabermetric community over the years, such as Bill James, Tom Tango, SABR president (and THT author) Vince Gennaro and Sean Forman of Baseball Reference. John Dewan of ACTA Sports and Baseball Info Solutions has been a great friend. I could go on and on, but I just don't have the space.

This particular book is the result of a lot of hard work by the writers listed herein, crack editors Joe Distelheim and Greg Simons and, most of all, our new typesetter and all-around Book Guy Paul Swydan. My deepest thanks to all of you.

May first base rise up to meet you. May the wind be always at your back at bat. May the sun shine in the eyes of that outfielder trying to catch your pop fly.

This is not easy work, this creation, but our hope is that reading it is easy—and as pleasurable as watching Carlos Beltran float around the bases.

Happy Baseball,

Dave Studenmund

Read us all year long at...
hardballtimes.com
fangraphs.com

The 2012 Season

The American League East View

by Matt Filippi

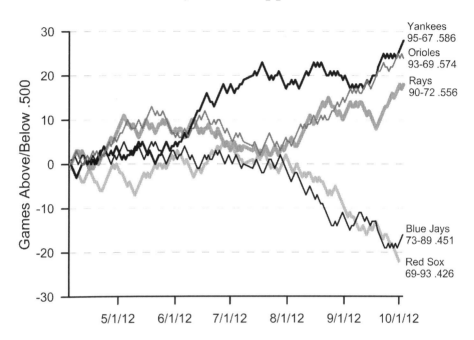

The American League East was supposed to be a four-dog race between the big-spending Yankees, the wisely-investing Rays, the recovering Red Sox and the emerging Blue Jays. The Orioles seemed to lack their own adjective ("sort of talented?") and generally were predicted to fall into last place. But that's why they play the games, right?

Boston Red Sox (Fifth Place, 69-93)

Things did not go according to plan in Boston, to put it mildly. Bobby Valentine was supposed to come in, impose the discipline that Terry Francona didn't, and take this talented roster back to the playoffs. Unfortunately, those plans didn't come to fruition. Not only was Valentine fired the day after the season ended, but the Sox gutted their roster mid-year and officially began rebuilding.

After 2011's infamous September collapse, Boston started the 2012 season with an 11-11 record. Despite the mediocre start, expectations were still high. Adrian Gonzalez, Jacoby Ellsbury, Dustin Pedroia and Kevin Youkilis made for a formidable lineup, and the rotation was led by Jon Lester and Josh Beckett, with Felix Doubront and Daniel Bard working into the mix. Plus, they were expecting Carl Crawford, Daisuke Matsuzaka and Andrew Bailey back from injury during the season as reinforcements. There definitely was reason to be optimistic.

But then things started to fall apart. Evan Brunell has all the horrific details elsewhere in this tome, but the first major fallout was a trade of Youkilis to the White Sox for two spare parts. Top prospect Will Middlebrooks replaced Youk, and did a fine job until an injury ended his season prematurely, but this move was only the start of things—the warning bell. A group of players met with upper management toward the end of July to complain about Valentine's antics, though Valentine wasn't the root cause of Boston's 2012 woes.

Ellsbury, Pedroia and Middlebrooks all experienced significant injuries, while Matsuzaka and Crawford were ineffective after returning. The best offense in the majors in 2011 managed a triple-slash line of only .260/.315/.415 and 734 runs in 2012, good for ninth in the majors. But even with these lowered expectations, you might still argue that the Sox should have been better.

That's until you look at the pitching. The Sox's starting rotation posted a 5.19 ERA, fourth highest in baseball. Lester gave up a career-high 25 homers, and his strikeout rate dipped by more than one per nine innings. Beckett's strikeout rate also dropped drastically as his ERA increased to 4.65. Clay Buchholz got off to a very rocky start, posting a 7.19 ERA through May, but settled down nicely, lowering that mark to 3.45 in his last 19 starts.

With the manager's position vacant again, and lots of money freed up due to a mega-trade that sent Crawford, Beckett, and Gonzalez to the Dodgers for prospects, the Red Sox are in a position to start rebuilding around their current pieces. There's always hope for next year, but first they'll have to wash that bad taste out of their mouths.

Toronto Blue Jays (Fourth Place, 73-89)

This was supposed to be a stepping-up year for the Blue Jays. They were young and talented, and maybe if things had broken the right way, they could have contended. Unfortunately, the injury bug bit the Jays too.

Starting pitchers Brandon Morrow, Kyle Drabek, and Drew Hutchinson, relievers Luis Perez, Jason Frasor, and Sergio Santos, and position players Brett Lawrie, J.P. Arencibia, and Jose Baustista were all on the disabled list for decent chunks of time. All teams deal with injuries, but this was an excessive total. The good news, however, is that this is still a very young team, and the Jays very well could come back strong next year.

One bright spot for the 2012 Jays was Edwin Encarnacion. The third-turned-first baseman-turned designated hitter had always shown good potential at the plate, and he finally put it together last year, blasting 42 homers and hitting .280/.384/.557, while playing 150 games. One of his more impressive batting feats was posting very similar strikeout and walk rates, 14.6 percent and 13 percent, respectively. This performance earned him a three-year extension, ensuring the long-term presence of another of Toronto's building blocks.

As bright as Encarnacion was though, starting pitcher Ricky Romero was that disappointing. Romero typically had walked around three batters per nine innings, and in the past had struck out more than seven per nine, but his walk rate rose above five in 2012, while the strikeout rate fell below seven. He gave up a career-high 116 earned runs, far above his previous high, and saw his ERA rise from 2.92 in 2011 to 5.77. With all the injuries the staff suffered, you can't say a better Romero would have made much of a difference, but his performance must have left front office staff members scratching their heads.

The Jays are still a very young team with a great farm system and a bright future. This past season was ugly, and the concerns about Romero are real, but they'll have just about every one of the players they lost to injury in 2012 back to health early in 2013.

Tampa Bay Rays (Third Place, 90-72)

The Rays were one of the favorites to win the division, and rightfully so given the starting pitching they sport. After barely squeaking into the postseason in 2011, however, it was felt that this year would be extra competitive, especially if you believed the Blue Jays would improve and the Red Sox would rebound, as many did. Most of the script was rewritten in Tampa's favor, as the Jays suffered countless injuries, and the Red Sox spent the season in baseball purgatory. Tampa indeed won 90 games, but it wasn't enough to reach the playoffs.

Just because there was no October baseball at Tropicana Field doesn't mean the rotation didn't come through, however. Rays starters led the majors with a 3.34 ERA, and had four pitchers make more than 30 starts. David Price had arguably the best year of his career, while James Shields and Jeremy Hellickson solidified the middle of the rotation, each contributing ERAs in the 3.00s. Matt Moore and Alex Cobb also had very nice rookie campaigns, with Moore striking out almost a batter per inning. Yet he won't get the Rookie of the Year consideration many thought he would, due to the rapid emergence of Mike Trout, and to a lesser extent, Yu Darvish and Yoenis Cespedes.

The story of this team however wasn't the rotation, but rather the bullpen, featuring lead character Fernando Rodney. Heading into 2012, Rodney was known as a flame thrower without much command, as his 18.7 percent walk rate led to him flaming out of Orange County. The Rays signed him to a one-year deal with an option, anticipating he would work in the back end of the bullpen, and he rewarded them and then some. Rodney saved 48 wins and posted a 0.60 ERA, allowing only five earned runs the entire year. His ERA set the record for the lowest ever recorded by a reliever. Fellow relievers Jake McGee, Wade Davis, and Joel Peralta all had nice years as well, but Rodney was the headliner.

The offense was, and for the most part always has been, the problem with the Rays. As a whole, the hitters were essentially league average in 2012. Batting .240/.317/.394, they lacked sufficient firepower to support the hurlers. Their biggest bat, Evan Longoria, was hurt for much of the year with a hamstring injury, though he still contributed an OPS close to .900 in his limited time. After that, Ben Zobrist and B.J. Upton were their most productive players, Zobrist for his versatility and his .377 on-base percentage, and Upton for his defensive skills in center field and his 28 homers. Other than that, there weren't really any hitters of any note besides Jeff Keppinger and Matt Joyce, who put up decent numbers.

One would have to think the Rays will be right back near the top of the division next year, but there are a couple of hanging issues. With Shields' contract bumping up to $9 million next year, there are cheaper options—such as Chris Archer—who can take his place, so Tampa may look to trade him for a package of less expensive players. Also, the team may lose Upton in free agency, and he'll be tough to replace. Regardless of how these issues are resolved, you cannot rule out this team for 2013.

Baltimore Orioles (Second Place, 93-69)

According to essentially every media outlet and baseball personality out there, the O's were doomed to another last-place finish. Yet, with the help of both young players and castaways, they were able to win 93 games and competed for the division title until the very last game of the season. It was a magical year for all the O's fans and players, as Baltimore played meaningful baseball in October for the first time since 1997.

The question that hung over the Orioles all year was whether (or even when) or not they were for real. For most of the season, they flirted with a negative run differential (meaning they allowed more runs than they scored) which, if you talk to statisticians, meant that their winning record was unsustainable. But they were able to counter the negativity with a great back-end of the bullpen and timely hitting.

The Orioles won a lot of close games because of how solid they were in the late innings. Jim Johnson broke out as the closer, saving 51 games, but he had a strikeout rate below six per nine innings. He was able to use a lethal sinker/slider combination to yield a lot of weak contact and plenty of ground balls (62.3 percent), which made him very effective (2.49 ERA).

The O's also had fireballer Pedro Strop in the bullpen; Strop walked a ton of guys (over five per nine innings), but he also racked a lot of strikeouts and didn't give up very many homers. Other than that, it was all Buck Showalter being able to play the matchups, using Luis Ayala for righties and Troy Patton for lefties. Brian Matusz and Tommy Hunter helped out down the stretch, as well.

The starting rotation was very average on the whole. Jason Hammel was fantastic, reinventing himself with two mid-90s fastballs and a big-time slider, though he missed most of the second half with a knee problem. Wei-Yin Chen was also solid in his debut season, though he was homer prone. Chris Tillman, Joe Saunders, Miguel Gonzalez, and Steve Johnson all pitched well enough in limited action. The young guys Baltimore was hoping would step up—Jake Arrieta, Brian Matusz, and Zach Britton—all struggled to keep their jobs. Keeping this in mind, it was truly remarkable what the Orioles were able to do.

Overall, the Baltimore offense was around league average, hitting .247 with a .311 on-base percentage, but they did blast 211 homers, good for second-best in the league. What's more, their hitting was timely, as they posted the fourth-highest league OPS in high-leverage situations.

The offense was led by emerging star center fielder Adam Jones, who paced the team with an .839 OPS. Nick Markakis also had a strong year with an .834 OPS. Chris Davis and Nate McLouth found new homes and resurrected their careers—Davis hit 33 long balls and McLouth posted a .342 on-base percentage in the second half in Baltimore. It was a year in which a new guy played hero every night.

The O's do have a nice core of young players, but there are worries. Their rotation is a little messy, and they benefited from a number of "out of nowhere" performances, so it's hard to project exactly what they'll do next year. However, for one year at least, the Orioles reminded us how much fun baseball in Baltimore can be.

New York Yankees (First Place, 95-67)

The Yanks came into this season considered by many the favorites to win the division, but they had a lower profile than usual. The spotlight was on the Red Sox and their collapse, along with the Rays and even the Jays. As a result, the Yankees were kind of overlooked, something you don't often see from a team that had won 97 games the year before.

During the offseason, general manager Brian Cashman signed free-agent veteran Hiroki Kuroda to a one-year deal, while shipping top prospect Jesus Montero to Seattle for Michael Pineda, a young pitcher who was coming off a great debut season. Kuroda, 37, made a smooth transition from the National League West and posted a 3.32 ERA over 219.2 frames and 33 starts, with the latter two figures being career highs. Pineda, on the other hand, suffered a torn labrum in his right shoulder and didn't throw one meaningful pitch with his new team.

The rotation still held up strong, anchored by Kuroda and CC Sabathia, who finished with a 3.38 ERA (though he failed to compile at least 230 innings and 33 starts for the first time since 2006). Phil Hughes settled in right around where he was in 2010 (16-13, 4.23 ERA vs. 18-8, 4.19), which was good enough to be a solid back-end piece. But, for Yankee fans, the best part of the starting rotation had to be the effective return of Andy Pettitte.

The Yankees were also supposed to have one of their better bullpens until something awful happened. While shagging fly balls during batting practice before a game in Kansas City in May, Mariano Rivera fell down and didn't get up. He was taken to the hospital, and it was learned later that he had torn the anterior cruciate ligament in his right knee, and was out for the season. This was a man who had been automatic for about 16 years as the closer, and had almost never been hurt. Rivera's loss was especially worrisome because he was in his contract year and, at age 42, there obviously was talk of retirement. Luckily, Rivera very much wants to return in 2013.

In his absence, the other bullpen arms stepped up, starting with Rafael Soriano. He wasn't particularly popular with the fans because he had signed a big contract and had shown some attitude problems in the past. But Soriano saved 42 games for the AL East champs, while posting a 2.26 ERA in 69 appearances. He was helped by setup men David Robertson and Boone Logan, along with limited work from Joba Chamberlain and David Phelps. Scrap-heap signings Clay Rapada, Cody Eppley and Derek Lowe all had solid contributions in middle relief, as well.

Offensively, the Yankees once again led the majors with 245 homers, though their overall slash line was down a bit at .265/.337/.453. Although not much press surrounded him, Robinson Cano had another fantastic season, hitting .313 with a career-high 33 homers, while playing a very good defensive second base. Derek Jeter also picked up right where he left off at the end of 2011 by racking up a major-league-best 216 hits. Injuries did take their toll in the second half as Alex Rodriguez and Mark Teixeira both missed chunks of time, as did Brett Gardner, who only played in a handful of games due to an elbow injury.

The Bombers reportedly plan to get their payroll below $189 million by 2014 to meet the luxury tax threshold, and if they're serious about that, they have some big questions coming up this offseason. They're going to have to get creative to get that payroll down, while still putting a winning product on the field.

The American League Central View

by Matt Klaassen

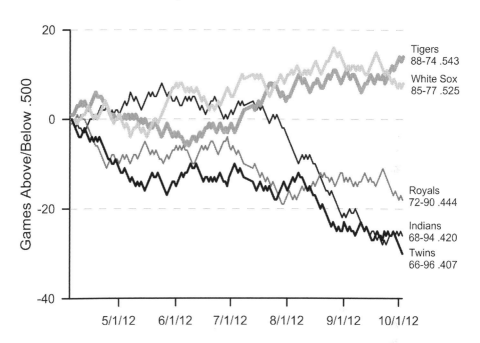

The 2012 American League Central was supposed to be pretty easy to figure out. The Detroit Tigers were already the favorites to win a division full of supposed rebuilding teams even before they added Prince Fielder. The question most were asking was not whether or not the Tigers would win the division, but by how many games.

While the Tigers did end up winning the Central, it was anything but the cakewalk nearly everyone expected. Along the way, one player accomplished a feat that had not been performed in 45 years. Additionally, plenty of other memorable events took place that were not at all *panthera tigris*-related.

Minnesota Twins

Remember how the Twins would "magically" win the Central every year, and respected, saber-friendly writers would write paens to the genius of manager Ron Gardenhire? Who else but Gardy in 2010 would have thought of telling Justin Morneau to hit like Albert Pujols in his prime, Jim Thome to hit the best he ever had at 39, and Francisco Liriano to have a Cy Young-contending season out of nowhere? That's just what great managers do.

Somehow, Gardy forgot to do stuff like that in 2011, and Minnesota finished last in the division at 63-99. His memory failed again in 2012, and the Twins finished 66-96. It was strange that the same writers who called Gardenhire the best manager in baseball when the Twins won did not call for his head when the Twins lost. Well, Minnesota did avoid 100 losses, so that's something he can put on his resume. By the time you read this, Joe Posnanski will have finished at least one 3,000-word blog post titled "Gardy Time, 2012 Edition: the Triumph of the Will(ingham)."

Actually, free agent import Josh Willingham had a very nice year for Minnesota, hitting .260/.366/.524 with 35 home runs while the hitter he effectively replaced, Michael Cuddyer, was middling for Colorado and missed a third of the season. Joe Mauer was another bright spot for the Twins in 2012, as he bounced back to hit .319/.416/446 after a 2011 season marred by injuries and poor hitting. On the downside, Mauer played about as many games at first base and designated hitter as he did at catcher, which is not a great sign given that he turns 30 in April and the Twins owe him about $140 million through 2018. The Twins were so bad all year, they really do not fit into any other storyline.

Pretender Time

Pretty much everyone knew the Twins were going to be terrible. Much more interesting tales of (eventual) futility took place in the pseudo-contending teams housed in Kansas City and Cleveland.

The Royals did not seem likely to contend going into the season given their poor starting rotation. However, even after closer Joakim Soria was lost for the season during spring training, they had an impressive and deep bullpen that might have made up for some of the rotation's deficiencies. More significantly, what recently had been hailed as the "Best Farm System Ever" delivered promising players like Eric Hosmer, Mike Moustakas and Salvador Perez to the big leagues in 2011. Along with Alex Gordon, Billy Butler and a revived Jeff Francoeur, the offense looked promising. If the starting pitching could be something approaching adequate—and luck went the Royals' way—that young talent could shoot them right into division title contention. The Royals' marketing slogan for the season reflected a certain bravado: "Our Time."

Fast forward to April 13, the Royals' home opener. They came into the game 3-3 after starting the season on the road and were facing division rival Cleveland. In the top half of the first inning of the Royals' 2012 home opener, starting pitcher Luke Hochevar gave up seven runs, which was all the more remarkable considering he gave up no home runs. The Royals went on to lose, 8-3.

One game is just one game, no matter how humiliating, and it would be wrong to emphasize a certain narrative of that one inning putting the team "on edge." But from the fan's perspective, the home opener presaged what came next, as the Royals were swept by Cleveland at home. Then Detroit brought the brooms to town, and, finally, Toronto did the same thing. Kansas City did not win again until the second game of its next road trip, and when all was said and done, the Royals had a 12-game losing streak, with the first 10 coming at home.

The season was not all gloom and doom for the Royals, however. Billy Butler hit 29 home runs, the most by any Royals player since Carlos Beltran in 2002. Alex Gordon had another good year both at the plate and in the field. Shortstop Alcides Escobar was solid, and catcher Salvador Perez came back in the second half from a spring injury to produce strong results, making the long-term pact KC gave him look a stellar bargain. The bullpen was quite good, even without Soria. Luis Mendoza was something less than terrible, not that a 97 ERA+ or 5.6 strikeout-per-nine innings from a starter is anything to brag about. The Royals might have only gone 72-90, but they finished third. That counts as progress (of a sort) in Kansas City.

In other, more meaningful ways, the season was awful. The best thing you can say about the starting rotation is that "Luis Mendoza was something less than terrible." Jeremy Guthrie put up good numbers after he came over in a trade that sent the apocalyptically lousy Jonathan Sanchez to Colorado. Danny Duffy and Felipe Paulino each were good for short time, but both ended up having season-ending Tommy John surgery. Hochevar's season was the usual combination of a few good starts combined with many more terrible ones, and Bruce Chen's luck simply ran out.

The offense, which was supposed to be the bright spot of the team, was mostly disappointing. Third baseman Moustakas played good defense, but after a promising first half at the plate, he totally fell apart in the second half. That was better than Eric Hosmer, supposedly the organization's next superstar, who hit even worse. Even if you think he is a Gold Glove defender, .232/.305/.359 is not enough from a first baseman, no matter how young. Hosmer might have been one of the worst everyday position players in baseball in 2012 were it not for the superlatively lousy efforts of Francoeur.

In a fitting gesture, the first firing of the season was not a coach, but the marketing firm that came up with the "Our Time" slogan. Yeah, those marketing consultants were definitely the problem with the 2012 Royals.

The "Our Time" slogan also had a certain resonance elsewhere. After the Indians beat up on the Royals for the second game in a row during the Royals' losing streak in Kansas City, a game that included multiple bench-clearing incidents and ejections, Cleveland closer Chris Perez tweeted: "Huge team win tonight; time for a sweep to tell the Royals it's not 'Our Time,' it's #TribeTime."

The 2012 season indeed was intended to be "Tribe Time." Cleveland was supposed to have a fighting shot at a division title. After finishing 80-82 in 2011, the Indians decided they were on the brink. They had traded prospects for Rockies pitcher Ubaldo Jimenez to bolster a rotation fronted by Justin Masterson. They had hitting prospects like Jason Kipnis and Lonnie Chisenhall ready to supplement the offensive core of Shin-Soo Choo, Carlos Santana and Asdrubal Cabrera. They brought in veteran pitcher Derek Lowe to solidify the back of the rotation. Hey, anything can happen, right?

Cleveland was actually in first place as late as June 23. Sure, the Indians were outplaying their run differential, but hey, so were the Orioles, and the Indians had outperformed their Pythagorean expectation by five games in 2011. Unlike the Orioles, however, Cleveland started losing. The Indians went 12-15 in June and 11-15 in July. By the end of July, the Indians were in third place, but at six games back, there remained at least had a glimmer of hope. Then August came, and Cleveland went 5-24, and "Tribe Time" ended with a whimper.

If there was a nail-in-the-coffin series for Cleveland, it probably was the first weekend in August in Detroit, when the Indians were swept by a combined score of 26-13. Fittingly, it was the supposed top part of the Cleveland rotation that was rocked in the first two games, with Masterson giving up seven runs in four innings in that Friday's 10-2 shellacking and Jimenez giving up six runs in 5.1 frames in a 6-1 Saturday loss.

Overall, very little went right for Cleveland. Even the relative bright spots were marred. Decent (if unspectacular) seasons by players like Kipnis, Choo, and Santana simply were not enough to overcome the many glaring negatives, with the predictable frailties of Grady Sizemore being just the tip of the iceberg. Chisenhall was supposed to take over at third base, but injuries limited him to 151 plate appearances. Maybe the team was right to give up on Matt LaPorta as the first baseman of the future, but the stopgap replacement, Casey Kotchman, was one of Jeff Francoeur's few rivals at the bottom of the Terrible Everyday Players heap.

All this negativity, and we've not yet delved into what really went wrong in Cleveland: the rotation. It is one thing for a stopgap like Lowe to fail—that happens. The rotation was a question mark going into the season, but the hope was that Masterson's 2011 breakout would be sustainable, and Jimenez would regain the form that made him one of the best pitchers in baseball in 2009 and 2010. Instead, Masterson reverted to his pre-2011 form against left-handed hitters, and his ERA ballooned from 3.21 in 2011 to 4.93 this past season.

After managing a 2.88 ERA in baseball's toughest park for pitchers in 2010, Jimenez's 2011 ERA went up to 4.68 in a season split between Colorado and Cleveland. However, his walk and strikeout rates were basically the same in both seasons, so the idea that he could regain his top-of-the-rotation form (especially after getting away from Coors Field) was not totally crazy, at least not at the season's outset. In 2012, however, Jimenez's strikeouts went down, and his walks and home runs allowed went up. His 5.40 ERA was hardly fit for a No. 5 starter, much less an ace.

Cleveland's bullpen was actually pretty good, with Perez and (the probably superior) Vinnie Pestano leading the way. However, if a team is getting blown out in the fifth inning due to lousy starting pitching, the bullpen effectiveness is muted. Perez did keep talking, blowing up to the press about ownership being cheap and not going after players like Josh Willingham in free agency. Manager Manny Acta was fired before the end of the season. Cleveland may have finished fourth, but actually had the worst run differential not just in the division, but in the American League.

The Real Race

If Minnesota was the team that no one believed in, Detroit was the overwhelming favorite, and Cleveland and Kansas City were fashionable-if-foolish darkhorse picks, where did that leave Chicago? Perhaps fittingly, given the departure of manager Ozzie Guillen, the White Sox seemed, well, boring. Maybe not for rabid fans of new manager Robin Ventura—who had zero major- or minor-league coaching or managing experience before 2012—but pretty boring to most onlookers.

The Tigers didn't find the White Sox boring, however. Chicago actually spent 126 days in first, compared to Detroit's 46. The White Sox finished the season with a Pythagorean record one game better than Detroit's. Yes, in the end, Detroit ended up winning the division, while the White Sox did not even make the playoffs, but it was a wild ride along the way.

The Tigers outclassed the White Sox in top-end talent. Center fielder Austin Jackson quietly had a great year for Detroit, hitting .300/.377/.479 with surprising power. Prince Fielder managed to smack 30 home runs despite moving into an American League park that tends to be hard on left-handed power hitters. And, of course, the Tigers had baseball's best hitter in 2012 in Triple Crown winner Miguel Cabrera.

On the pitching side, the Tigers also seemed stronger. They had the erratically brilliant Max Scherzer, who produced a dreadful April, but was one of the better pitchers in baseball after that. Doug Fister, their No. 2 who came over in a 2011 trade with Seattle, featured good control and a knack for keeping the ball on the ground. And Detroit made a good trade for Anibal Sanchez at the deadline. Oh, and they also had perhaps baseball's best pitcher, Justin Verlander. Let's not overlook him.

The 2012 White Sox did not have quite the guns to compete with the best pitcher and best hitter, but they did receive some very good, if unexpected, performances. At 36, Paul Konerko was not quite the force he had been in previous years, but he had a nice year. Still, the White Sox were carried by a number of players who many left for dead. Adam Dunn looked, well, done in 2011, and while in 2012 he tailed off after a strong start, he did manage to hit 41 home runs. Catcher A.J. Pierzynski, perhaps the most disliked player in the majors, somehow managed to hit a career-high 27 home runs in 2012—nine more than he had hit in any single season previously. Alex Rios had a disastrous 2011, but—perhaps refreshed by a move from center to right field—he hit .304/.334/.516 with 25 home runs.

The rotation had its problems: John Danks endured a season-ending injury before Memorial Day, and Gavin Floyd had his poorest season in a while. Philip Humber pitched a perfect game on April 21, yet still ended the season out of the rotation with a 6.44 ERA.

It wasn't all doom and gloom though, as a couple of starting pitchers really put Chicago in the thick of things. Jake Peavy, who had his best season since 2007 with the Padres, gave the White Sox a 3.37 ERA over 219 innings (more than he had pitched in the two prior seasons combined). Even better, though, was Chris Sale, who was converted from a reliever to a starter in spring training, despite concerns about his ability to handle the workload. He ended up as perhaps the best pitcher in the American League (3.05 ERA over 192 innings) not named Verlander.

The division race was very important, as both Wild Card teams (Baltimore and Texas) ended up having more wins than the AL Central champion. Even the Angels and Rays, who did not make the playoffs, had more victories. It was apparent, even as the season wound down and the race remained close, that there was no backup for getting into the final tournament.

It is strange, in a way, to pick out certain series as "key" in this race, as each team blew opportunities to put the other away for good down the stretch. One series between the teams does stand out, though. From Aug. 31 to Sept. 2, Detroit hosted Chicago, sweeping the Pale Hose to knot up the division. Yet the Tigers could have been ahead had they not blown the three previous games at home to the lowly Royals, all three one-run contests, including one in which Verlander gave up eight runs in 5.2 innings.

Yet, by Sept. 10, Detroit was three back again after a 6-1 loss to Chicago. The Tigers won the next two against the White Sox, then later fell to the ChiSox in a makeup game on Sept. 17. Neither team seemed to want to take hold of the division. During the last weeks of the season, Chicago, after leading for most of the season, simply fell short, going 13-18 in September and the first few days of October, while Detroit went 18-13. Chicago's last gasp came when it hosted Tampa Bay at the end of September, a series in which it lost three of the four games. Perhaps the most devastating defeat was on Sept. 29, when Sale—who had been so good all year—gave up five runs in 3.1 innings to an unimpressive Rays offense.

———————————

For the Tigers, a season that began as a big disappointment after so many predictions of success turned itself around, as they not only came through to win the division, but did so behind a historic campaign from Cabrera. It was a tough way to end the season for a White Sox team that looked like it was headed to the playoffs right until the season's last couple of weeks. Prior to the season, Chicago had been neither denigrated nor celebrated, but simply ignored. Either of those fates, of course, is preferable to being mired in rebuilding, or being a team whose "Time," despite all the best intentions, did not come.

The American League West View

by Glenn DuPaul

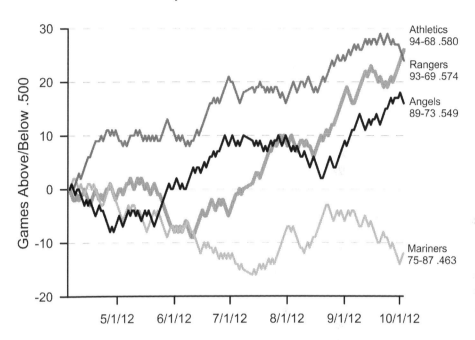

The American League West has been baseball's smallest division since 1994, sporting just four teams. Next season, with the addition of the Houston Astros, the AL West will no longer bear that distinction. The final season for the AL West with just the Los Angeles Angels, Oakland Athletics, Seattle Mariners and Texas Rangers could quite possibly have been its most exciting.

Two Titans Rise in the West

From 2004 to 2009, the Angels owned this division, winning the title in five out of six seasons. In recent years, the Rangers seized supremacy from Los Angeles, as they won the West in 2010 and 2011 before ultimate defeat in the World Series both years.

In the offseason, Angels owner Arte Moreno and his newly reformed front office, headed by general manager Jerry Dipoto, set out to end Texas' recent string of AL West dominance. They did so in a swift and overtly aggressive manner. The Angels stole the show at the Winter Meetings when they signed quite possibly the best hitter ever to become a free agent, Albert Pujols, and the best starting pitcher on the market this past offseason, C.J. Wilson, to massive contracts.

The combination of back-to-back seasons ending in heartbreak and the Angels' big additions almost necessitated a reaction from Texas. Its response was to invest over $110 million in Japanese superstar Yu Darvish. The electric Darvish was brought over to replace the gap left by Wilson at the top of the Rangers rotation.

The two teams shifted baseball's focus to the West. Texas and Los Angeles were labeled the game's new "superpowers," and their rivalry was set up to be as great as Boston and New York in terms of their talented rosters and bloated payrolls.

Suppressing Safeco and the End of an Era

The Mariners finished 2012 in the cellar of the AL West for the third straight season with a record of 75-87. Seattle's offense averaged the fewest runs per game (3.8) in the AL for the fourth straight season.

Their offseason addition of hitting prospect Jesus Montero was not nearly as successful as they may have hoped. Montero split time between designated hitter and catcher and hit just .260 with an on-base percentage below .300 and just 15 home runs.

Another former top hitting prospect, Mariners first baseman Justin Smoak, continued to be a disappointment. He ranked last among qualifying first basemen with a .654 on-base-plus-slugging (OPS), despite finishing strong with a .341 average and five home runs in September. Seattle's shortstop, Brendan Ryan, who is a wizard with his glove, and disgraced utility man Chone Figgins both hit well below .200 in over 650 combined plate appearances.

The Mariners' continued offensive struggles were not the story of their 2012 campaign, however; instead two moments were enough to define their season.

For almost half of a decade, Felix Hernandez and Ichiro Suzuki have served as the dual faces of the Mariners franchise. On July 23, Ichiro left that title solely in Hernandez' hands, as Suzuki was traded to the New York Yankees just months before his contract would expire.

After spending over a decade with the Mariners, the legendary leadoff man played his first game in a different MLB uniform, though it was still at Safeco Field, against his former team. Witnessing Ichiro play in Seattle against the Mariners in a Yankees uniform was by far one of the more surreal moments of the 2012 season.

With the departure of Ichiro, King Felix was left to rule Seattle by his lonesome, and the big right-hander did not disappoint.

Less than a month after Ichiro's departure, Hernandez made baseball in Seattle exciting and relevant again when he pitched baseball's 23rd perfect game. Hernandez has already won an AL Cy Young Award and inked a large contract extension with Seattle, but his perfect game performance was one of those career-defining moments that Mariners fans will never forget.

Amazingly, of the seven no-hitters thrown in 2012, three occurred in Safeco Field, and two were of the perfect-game variety. Since Safeco opened in 1999, the stadium has had a reputation as a "pitcher's park." The three no-hitters and continued lack of runs scored by the Mariners offense may have been the last straw for the Mariners organization. Plans have been announced to move the fences in to more hitter-friendly dimensions for the 2013 season. It will be interesting to see how much of an effect these changes actually have on the run environment in Safeco.

Trout Season

In April, the eyes of the baseball world rested on Pujols, as "El Hombre" began a new journey in Anaheim. During his time in St. Louis, Pujols had garnered a reputation for being a machine. The hitter never lacked composure and went about his business of demolishing baseballs. For this reason, many figured Pujols wouldn't be affected in any way by an attempt to justify the 10-year contract he had just signed for over one quarter of a billion dollars.

Whether he was trying to live up to expectations or not, to say that Pujols struggled to begin his Angels career would be the understatement of the season. In April, Pujols hit for a miserable triple-slash line (batting average/on-base percentage/slugging percentage) of .217/.265/.304, with zero home runs and just four RBI. It took Pujols until May 6 to hit his first home run.

Pujols' slow start was contaminating the rest of the team. On April 27, the Angels sat nine games behind the Texas Rangers, with a record of 6-14. The next day, in a bold move, Los Angeles released veteran outfielder Bobby Abreu and called up baseball's No. 1 prospect, 20-year-old Mike Trout. Trout struggled in his first game, going 0-for-4 with a strikeout. After that initial game though, the struggles for Trout were few and far between, as he sparked life into the Angels and did everything in his power to save their season.

The Angels went 83-59 after calling up the rookie outfielder. Trout's season will go down in history as quite possibly the greatest rookie season of all time. The lead-off hitter excelled in every facet of the game, with spectacular wall-scaling grabs, lighting speed on the basepaths and jaw-dropping home runs.

Trout finished the year with a batting line of .326/.399/.564, 30 home runs and 49 steals while playing Gold Glove defense in center field. He became the first player in the history of the game to hit at least 30 home runs, steal 45 bases and score 125 runs.

Trout, with help from a resurgent Pujols, who finished his campaign with a Pujolsian stat line, led the Angels to the top of every offensive and defensive advanced leaderboard.

Yet the Angels, with the best offense and defense in baseball, finished the season outside the playoff picture. How was this possible?

Their starting pitching completely failed them.

Coming into 2012, the Angels boasted one of the best, if not the best, rotations on paper. Wilson, Jered Weaver and Dan Haren all were considered aces, and Ervin Santana was as good a No. 4 starter as one could find in the game. Baseball is not played on paper, though, and the 2012 Angels can attest to that.

Weaver was the only pitcher to perform as advertised, as among other things, he tossed a no-hitter in early May. Wilson did not live up to his billing as the top starter in his free agent class, and Haren and Santana both gave up way too many home runs to succeed.

As the trading deadline neared, the Angels front office realized its current rotation would not be enough to send the team to the playoffs. Thus, Los Angeles went out and made yet another huge splash with the addition of Zack Greinke.

Greinke pitched well for the Angels, striking out 78 batters in 89.1 innings with a 3.53 ERA, but his efforts would not be enough as the Angels rotation ranked 17th in baseball in park-adjusted ERA, a total letdown for a starting staff that was pegged as one of game's best.

The Angels added Greinke, Pujols and Wilson, had the best offense and defense in baseball, and received one of the greatest seasons of all time from a player who began the year in the minor leagues, yet they did not make the postseason.

So, which AL West teams did?

A Texas Three-Peat?

The defending AL champions got off to a blistering start in 2012, winning 13 of their first 16 games, building a large early lead on the rest of the AL West. Much of the Rangers' start could be credited to their star outfielder, Josh Hamilton, who hit .395 in April with nine home runs. Hamilton's torrid pace continued in May as he hit 12 more home runs, including an incredible performance in which he went deep four times in one game.

Hamilton's bat would cool off, but Texas held the AL West lead almost the entire way. Below are listed the Rangers' leads over the second-place AL West team at the end of each month from April to September:

Month	Lead
April	6.5
May	5.5
June	6.5
July	3
August	4
September	2

Texas' lineup has been great for years, and 2012 was no different. Hamilton's contributions, as well as an MVP-caliber season from Adrian Beltre, made this lineup among the best in baseball. Every player in Texas' lineup was above average offensively, except one.

Long-time Ranger and 2012 utility man/designated hitter Michael Young was one of the worst players in baseball. Ron Washington refused to take the veteran out of the lineup despite a month's worth of games (May 27—June 26) where Young accumulated only three extra-base hits and zero home runs. Not only was Young left in the lineup, but he continued to hit in major spots in the order, primarily third and fifth. Among hitters with at least 500 plate appearances, Young was in the bottom 10 in every advanced hitting metric.

Texas has had consistently good offensive teams over the last decade, but the Rangers' recent team success can be attributed primarily to their pitching.

The top of Texas' rotation was just fine, as Darvish proved to be a great investment. The Japanese import struck out over a batter an inning while posting an ERA below 4.00 in over 190 innings. Matt Harrison also enjoyed a career year at the top of their rotation. Texas' bullpen was led by offseason acquisition Joe Nathan, and Alexi Ogando was very solid as well, but issues with the back end of the rotation were the team's Achilles' heel.

Injuries to Colby Lewis and Nefalti Feliz caused Texas to make some desperate moves, namely the additions of veteran starters Ryan Dempster and Roy Oswalt. In 128 innings, Oswalt and Dempster combined for an ERA of 5.41, much worse than the Rangers were expecting to receive for the prospects and salary they surrendered.

Moneyball Part II: A Decade Later...

Rebuilding. That word has been synonymous with the Athletics for years, and 2012 was supposed to be no different. With both Anaheim and Texas shaping up to be superpowers, Oakland's current budget and roster almost certainly could not compete.

A's general manager Billy Beane was well of aware of this fact and began yet another rebuilding plan during the offseason by trading All-Star starters Trevor Cahill and Gio Gonzalez, as well as All-Star closer Andrew Bailey, for younger, cheaper players. Oakland also let outfielder Josh Willingham walk in free agency.

Then, in an extreme case of cognitive dissonance, Oakland began acquiring veteran talent. Beane brought in or retained 29-year-old Seth Smith, 32-year-old Coco Crisp, 34-year-old Grant Balfour, 39-year-old Bartolo Colon and 40-year-old Manny Ramirez. Somehow, these moves weren't even Oakland's largest head scratcher of the offseason.

That move came when Beane gave highly touted Cuban prospect Yoenis Cespedes a four-year, $36 million contract. Many teams were rumored to be in on negotiations for Cespedes' services. Oakland outspent the rest of the league, which is about as close as you can get to a baseball oxymoron, to make the toolsy outfielder its highest-paid player before he had ever played a game on U.S. soil!

Coming into the season, Oakland's rebuilding plan seemed non-cohesive and in many ways, uncertain. The movie, "Moneyball," based on the book of the same name that chronicled the 2002 Athletics, created a stereotype that Oakland's front office (or, more generally, sabermetrics) regarded getting on base as of primary importance. Getting runners on base is extremely valuable to a successful baseball team, but it is nowhere close to everything.

At the end of June, the plan wasn't working. Oakland was really struggling offensively, with a team OBP barely over .300, and sat 13 games behind the Rangers for the division lead.

CoolStandings.com gave Oakland a 1.1 percent chance of winning the AL West and only a 10.8 percent chance of getting a Wild Card spot. The pitiful Houston Astros were fewer games behind the first-place team in the National League Central than Oakland was from the West division lead.

The season was proceeding according to expectations. Oakland's young team looked like it would finish well off the pace set by the Angels and Rangers and again would have to look towards the future.

There's a memorable scene in "Moneyball" in which Brad Pitt, portraying Beane, explains to the Athletics owner that despite where Oakland currently stood in the standings, they still had a shot, because the Athletics' record did not, in fact, reflect the team's true ability. In 2002, the Athletics stayed the course and reaped the benefits of that strategy, and 10 years later the 2012 team took a page out of its predecessor's book.

Oakland would go 19-5 in July and claw right back into the playoff race, including an incredible string of five straight one-run victories over the class of the AL, Texas and the New York Yankees. Oakland's magic could not be stopped through August, and the A's entered September just four games behind the Rangers in the west, and were all alone in first place in the AL Wild Card race.

Oakland's team on-base percentage rose to .319 after June 30, but it took more than getting on base to fuel such a miraculous comeback. Oakland's true success was built around pitching and defense. A former first base prospect, Sean Doolittle, and All-Star rookie Ryan Cook helped anchor a no-name bullpen. After multiple injuries to ace Brandon McCarthy and a performance enhancing drug suspension ended Colon's season, Tommy Milone, a 25-year-old rookie, became the oldest member of the A's rotation.

The younger the starter, the better he seemed to perform for Oakland, as the 23-year-old Jarrod Parker, the main piece in the Cahill deal, was the Athletics' ace on a team that set the major league record for most wins by rookie pitchers with 54.

The O.co Coliseum is a cavernous ballpark that warrants a defense that can cover a ton of ground. The Athletics covered more than enough ground, as they ranked near the top of the league in most advanced defensive metrics.

Oakland's combination of starting pitching depth, good defense and unlikely contributions from players like Brandon Moss and Josh Reddick was enough to make the club a contending team.

It seems clear that the risky signing of Cespedes was what put Oakland into October baseball. The Cuban outfielder wasn't always healthy, but he put up some big numbers (.292 average with 23 home runs and 82 RBIs), and in the games he started, the Athletics had an incredible record of 82-46.

With nine games left in 2012, Oakland sat five games behind Texas. The chances of winning the division were slim (4.8 percent), but the A's had a Wild Card spot nearly locked up (70.2 percent). Oakland would continue its torrid pace until season's end, while Texas' lack of starting pitching depth finally came back to bite the Rangers.

Texas would lose six of its last eight games, while Oakland won seven of its final eight. This incredible stretch of games set up an AL West showdown between Oakland and Texas on the season's final day. The winner would take the AL West, while the loser would have the unfortunate luck of entering the new "coin-flip" round that is the AL Wild Card play-in game.

On that day, the team of destiny continued to be just that. Texas blew an early 5-1 lead, in part because of a crucial dropped fly ball by Hamilton, and Oakland cruised to a 12-5 victory.

Oakland's struggles in recent seasons had caused the O.co. Coliseum to be consistently empty, but on the final day of 2012, a sell-out crowd stayed well after the game to watch its team celebrate a division victory that no one thought it could win.

Coming Attractions: American League

by Jeff Moore

While we all enjoy looking forward, this is not a book specifically dedicated to prospect analysis. Still, we like to whet our beaks. So in the pages that follow, you will find a brief overview of each Amercian League team's farm system, as well as analysis of one interesting prospect per team. They aren't necessarily the prospects who get a lot of ink throughout the year, but they are all noteworthy in their own special way.

American League East

Baltimore Orioles

The Orioles farm system isn't deep, but they entered the season with a top-five prospect both in the field and on the mound. Dylan Bundy and Manny Machado both made it to the majors this season, and Machado is unlikely to return to the minors. Bundy got only a brief stint at the end of the season, so he could easily return to Double or Triple-A to begin 2013, but he won't be there long.

Still Far Away: Nick Delmonico, 1B/2B

Delmonico, drafted as a third baseman in 2011, had to deal with a position switch while being thrown into full-season ball to begin his career—two tough tests for a 19-year-old. He handled both reasonably well, playing 95 games at Low-A Delmarva after extended spring training, splitting time between first and second base. Delmonico hit just .249, but showed a plus eye at the plate as well as good pop, hitting 11 home runs. He may need to return to Delmarva, and is still a ways from the majors, but he's off to a nice start.

Boston Red Sox

For years, heavy spending in the draft has kept the Red Sox farm system stocked with talent despite their willingness to include prospects in trades. That philosophy won't work anymore with the new draft restrictions, but the effect hasn't been felt yet, and the Sox farm system remains deep.

Big Leap: Jackie Bradley, OF

In his first full professional season, Bradley established himself not only as a legitimate prospect, but as a true all-around threat. Between High-A and Double-A, he batted .315/.430/.482 with great plate discipline. Even though Bradley hit just nine home runs, his 42 doubles allowed him to use his speed on the bases and project that there could be even more power in his frame.

New York Yankees

The Yankees have done a nice job developing their hitting talent over the past few years, but have not been nearly as good on the mound. They also took a blow to their system when they traded top prospect Jesus Montero to the Mariners right before the season began, leaving them without any impact bats near the majors.

Big Leap: Tyler Austin, OF

Austin took well to full-season baseball, as he hit .320/.405/.598 in his first half-season in Low-A ball and earned a promotion. He performed well in Tampa, although his power didn't completely make the trip with him, but he showed he could handle the Florida State League. A jump to Double-A could be in Austin's very near future.

Tampa Bay Rays

The Rays' model of constantly restocking their farm system to provide young talent for their major league ballclub has served them well, but it's becoming more difficult as they draft later in the first round. Still, they've done well to stockpile draft picks and make up for quality with a quantity of first-rounders over the past few years.

Still Far Away: Taylor Guerrieri, RHP

The Rays traditionally take a slow approach with the development of their pitchers, promoting them one level per year, with few exceptions. Guerrieri appears to be on that same schedule. The 2011 first-rounder didn't pitch in his draft year, and only appeared in the short-season New York-Penn league in 2012. He dominated the league, posting a 1.02 ERA despite having his innings limited. Guerrieri should head to Low-A ball next season, but expect the slow pace of his development to continue.

Toronto Blue Jays

The Blue Jays have been increasingly active in the international market over the past few years, and the fruits of that activity are beginning to show. Adeiny Hechavarria made his first appearance in the majors this season, and there's more coming over the next few years.

Big Leap: Justin Nicolino, RHP

Nicolino took well to his first taste of full-season ball, pairing with Aaron Sanchez in a tandem system, throwing 124 1/3 innings with a 2.46 ERA and almost a strikeout per inning. The Blue Jays should take Nicolino off his leash next season in the Florida State League to see what he can really do.

American League Central

Chicago White Sox

Trades and promotions have left the White Sox with even less talent than their already shallow farm system had a year ago. The club has few prospects without significant holes in their games.

A Step Back: Nestor Molina, RHP

Molina was the main return from Toronto in the trade of 2011's closer, Sergio Santos, and was expected to be nearly major league ready. Instead, he spent most of the season at Double-A, where his strikeout rate dropped dramatically from the previous year, and his ERA nearly doubled. There have been questions about whether or not Molina can remain a starter, and he did little to put those worries to bed in 2012.

Cleveland Indians

Much of the depth the Indians had in their farm system was depleted through trades and poor drafts over the past few years. The emergence of 2011 first-rounder Francisco Lindor has helped give the Indians at least one legitimate prospect on whom they can dream.

A Step Back: Tony Wolters, SS

Some struggles were to be expected from Wolters in his first taste of full-season competition, but the lack of plate discipline was not. He had maintained a decent walk-to-strikeout rate in short-season leagues. That approach crumbled in the Carolina League however, as Wolters walked just 36 times in 537 plate appearances, while striking out 104 times. He doesn't get on base enough or have enough power for those types of strikeout numbers.

Detroit Tigers

The Tigers have seen their system slip over the years thanks to a willingness to trade prospects for major league help, but their playoff runs will also tell you that the strategy is working. Despite the moves, they still have some legitimate talent on the farm, some of which could be in Detroit soon.

Still Far Away: Danry Vasquez, OF

A Venezuelan free agent who signed for $1.2 million in 2010, Vasquez began the year in Low-A West Michigan, where he struggled, hitting just .162 over 29 games. Sent down to the New York-Penn League, Vasquez flourished, hitting .311 the rest of the way. He is still quite raw, but the Tigers like his tools. Vasquez will get another shot at the Midwest League in 2013.

Kansas City Royals

The Royals farm system that was considered to be historically deep not too long ago is not what it once was, thanks to major league promotions, but it still has a lot to offer. The hitting prospects have gone on to the next level, but there still remain a number of high-end pitching prospects, which the Royals must focus on developing with more consistency than they have in their past.

Still Far Away: Bubba Starling

You may have heard Starling's name this season because people were reminded that he's actually older than Bryce Harper, but that's not a knock on Starling so much as a reminder of Harper's talent. Starling is the ultimate athlete, but raw as a baseball player. He didn't get on the field until over a year after he was drafted, but when he did he showed both why scouts love him, but also why the Royals are taking it slow with his development. While Starling hit 10 home runs in 53 games in the Appalachian League, he also struck out 70 times.

Minnesota Twins

If the Twins are to return to prominence in the AL Central, it will have to be at the hands of their farm system aiding an aging major league roster. Luckily, they have some pieces in place to make that happen in a few years.

Big Leap: Jose Berrios, RHP

While Byron Buxton got all of the publicity, the Twins had a second pick at the end of the first round and used it on Berrios, who had a better debut than Buxton. The prep right-hander went 3-0 with a 1.17 ERA in 30 2/3 innings combined between the Gulf Coast and Appalachian Leagues. Even more impressive, Berrios struck out 49 batters during that time and walked just four. That performance may have earned him a trip straight to the full-season leagues to begin next season.

American League West

Los Angeles Angels

Mike Trout got all of the attention in the Angels farm system over the past few years, and rightly so. Unfortunately, he's gone, and there's not anyone like him coming anytime soon. Additionally, the Angels traded three of their better prospects to acquire Zack Greinke during the season, leaving the cupboard even more bare than it already was.

Big Leap: C.J. Cron, 1B

Cron went from polished collegiate hitter dominating inexperienced competition in 2011 to legitimate power prospect in 2012. He does however need to refine his approach. Cron hit .293/.327/.516 with 32 doubles and 27 home runs in 2012, but walked just 17 times in 557 plate appearances. Better pitchers will exploit that approach, and it remains to be seen how much of Cron's power was supplied by the hitter-friendly California League. He'll have to adjust accordingly next season.

Oakland A's

The A's greatly improved their organizational depth before the 2012 season, but then depleted it again by sporting a major league team made up of a ton of rookies. The move worked with their playoff run and left them with an interesting mix of players back down on the farm.

Big Leap: Addison Russell, SS

In his draft year, Russell went from being the 11th overall draft pick to one of the game's top prospects. It's not just that he played well in short-season leagues; Russell dominated them to the point that he was promoted to Low-A Burlington, where he hit .310/.369/.448 in 66 plate appearances. Russell will be 19 next season and could return to Burlington, but should he succeed he won't be there for long, and could be in Double-A before he turns 20.

Seattle Mariners

The Mariners have the pitching depth in their farm system to rival any organization in baseball, and even more impressive, most of it is close to the majors. The Mariners rotation at the end of 2013 almost certainly will look nothing like the one they had at the end of 2012.

Still Far Away: Victor Sanchez, RHP

Sanchez was the most expensive signee in the 2011 international market, and he made his first appearance in 2012, going 6-2 with a 3.18 ERA for short-season Everett. At age 17, Sanchez more than held his own against older competition, a trend that could continue for years in the Mariners farm system. With their depth, however, they won't rush him.

Texas Rangers

The Rangers' activity on the international market has kept them among the deepest organizations in baseball despite promoting prospect after prospect to the majors. The Rangers continue to replace departing free agents with young players, and that trend should continue as Jurickson Profar and Mike Olt work their way into the major league lineup.

A Step Back: Neil Ramirez

Ramirez was thought to be insurance for the major league rotation in case of injury as the 2012 season began, but he pitched so poorly at Triple-A that he was demoted. Even back at Double-A he went just 2-5 with a 4.20 ERA. The stuff is still there, but Ramirez clearly let the Pacific Coast League get the best of him in 2012, despite pitching adequately there the season before. He should return to the PCL in 2013 to get things straightened out.

The National League East View

by Ben Duronio

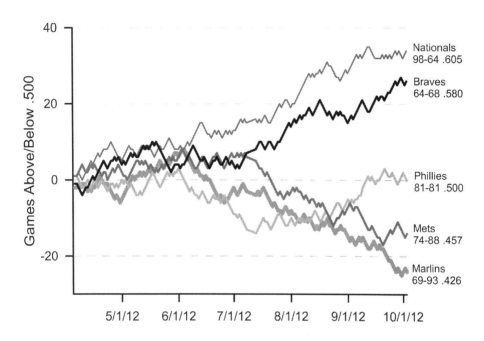

The big theme in the National League East this year was pitching. The division saw one of the best seasons of any knuckleballer in history, a reliever who recorded the highest strikeout percentage in baseball history, and a youthful star put together a tremendous season in his first full big league year before being shut down. Overall, the division featured three legitimate Cy Young candidates in R.A. Dickey, Gio Gonzalez, and Craig Kimbrel, with Stephen Strasburg and Kris Medlen having numbers worthy of the award, but lower inning totals due to recovery from Tommy John surgery. Bottom line, the team with the best pitching throughout the season won the division.

Nationals Put Baseball on Notice

After making the offseason acquisition of Gonzalez and the signing of Edwin Jackson—both deals made with the intent of bolstering their rotation—the Washington Nationals were seen as a dark horse to win the division. The bullpen was well built, the lineup was deep enough to compete and the youthful rotation had serious potential. To top it off, the Nationals were just about ready to showcase one of the top prospects the game has ever seen in Bryce Harper. Even though Harper started in the minors, he was a big early season favorite to win the NL Rookie of the Year Award, and he did not disappoint.

Harper served as a sparkplug to an offense that was often missing its 30-home run hitter from the year before in Michael Morse and its high-priced free agent acquisition from the previous year, Jayson Werth, due to injury. To top it off, the team's cornerstone player, Ryan Zimmerman, needed multiple cortisone shots to deal with a faulty shoulder that caused him to struggle during most of the season's first half.

Harper was not alone in maintaining the offense while some of their bigger names and bigger bats were injured, however, as first baseman Adam LaRoche and shortstop Ian Desmond put together career seasons to help pace the offense.

The offense was good, but starting pitching is what separated the Nationals from the rest of the pack in the NL East. Nationals starters recorded the lowest ERA in the NL, backed by a 2.89 ERA from Gonzalez, a 2.94 ERA from Jordan Zimmermann, and a 3.16 ERA from Strasburg. Even their back-end starters, Ross Detwiler and Jackson, recorded solid seasons with 3.58 and 4.03 ERAs, respectively.

The Nationals battled with the second-place Braves all the way up until the final week of the season, but once they took the NL East lead on May 22, they never let go. In one of the tougher divisions in baseball, Washington secured the top spot early and maintained the lead throughout the season.

The Braves Grab the Wild Card

While the Nationals won the division, the Atlanta Braves proved to be one of the NL's top teams throughout the year, finishing with 94 wins and the top Wild Card spot.

Entering the season, the Braves were thought to have one of the deepest pitching staffs in the league, featuring veterans Tim Hudson, Jair Jurrens and Tommy Hanson, along with young pitchers with massive potential in Brandon Beachy, Mike Minor, Julio Teheran and Randall Delgado.With a rotation that was expected to be seven deep, and also the ability to turn reliever Medlen into a starter at some point, the rotation was expected to be able to handle injuries and poor performance quite well. For the most part, this was true, but the group certainly had its issues throughout the year.

Minor got off to an absolutely horrible start, as he held a 6.20 ERA through his first 15 games. Beachy was tremendous at the beginning of the year and looked to be the budding ace of the staff, but an elbow ligament injury in mid-June caused him to undergo Tommy John surgery and miss the remainder of the year. Veterans Hanson and Jurrjens struggled immensely after returning from injuries that forced them to miss the tail end of 2011, so the rotation altogether faced many more problems than expected. To top it off, Teheran did not pitch well at Triple-A, essentially eliminating him from any hopes of contributing at the major league level, at least in 2012.

Despite all the struggles, the rotation still finished with the seventh-best ERA in baseball, thanks to a second-half resurgence from Minor and an absolutely dazzling stint from Medlen. The dimunitive right-hander put himself into Cy Young Award contention by posting a 1.57 ERA and 10-1 record over 138 innings pitched between the rotation and bullpen. Medlen, along with reliever Kimbrel, who set the major league record for strikeout percentage, were the key cogs in the pitching staff throughout the season and were easily the team's most valuable pitchers.

On the position player side, there were really three big storylines in Atlanta. The first, and without a doubt the biggest, was the retirement of Chipper Jones. The future Hall-of-Fame third baseman hit 14 home runs with a .377 on base percentage in his final season, making the All-Star Game in the process. He appeared in just 112 games as he battled injuries and age, but the season was a magical final year, and included two walk-off home runs against the rival Philadelphia Phillies.

Outside of Jones' dazzling final dance, the outfield production was the next-biggest storyline. Combining solid skills at the plate with great baserunning and defense, the outfield put together one of the better seasons of any outfield group in history. Their defensive ratings across the board were extraordinarily high, making all three Gold Glove contenders. Jason Heyward vaulted into the NL Most Valuable Player Award conversation with a 27-home run, 21-steal season after struggling in his sophomore campaign. Free-agent-to-be Michael Bourn hit nine home runs, set his career high in slugging percentage and nabbed 42 bases. Finally, left fielder Martin Prado hit 10 home runs, swiped a career-high 17 steals and played superb defense in both left field and third base, and made appearances at first base, second base, and shortstop when called upon.

The last offensive storyline, which potentially cost the team the division, was the lackluster performance of Dan Uggla and Brian McCann. The two former All-Stars put together their worst seasons as major leaguers, as Uggla hit just 19 home runs after hitting over 30 for five consecutive years, and McCann recorded the lowest batting average (.230) and on-base percentage (.300) of his career by a large margin. If either of them had hit like they have in the past, the season may have lasted longer than just one extra play-in game for the Braves.

Just When the Phillies Were Out, They Came Back

What really put the Philadelphia Phillies back this season was an awful June. The team entered the month with a record just above .500, and after winning five consecutive division titles, few doubted their ability to contend throughout the season. June changed things, however, as the Phils went just 9-19 and put themselves in a sizable hole behind Washington and Atlanta.

With a poor performance in the middle months of the season, the Phillies decided to act as sellers at the deadline, essentially abandoning any expectation of legitimate 2012 playoff contention. They traded Hunter Pence, Shane Victorino and Joe Blanton, but the team actually performed well during the tail end of the season, and in early September re-entered the fray for the second Wild Card. Philadelphia eventually fell too far behind the top contenders for the last playoff spot and finished the season with a 81-81 record, an accurate description of its season. It was not successful in the same stature as the Phillies have become accustomed to, but after being far out of the race at the trade deadline, they competed and got some solid performances to conclude a begrudgingly respectable season.

The Phillies rotation was partially to credit and to blame for the team's 2012 struggles. Roy Halladay had a very disconcerting season, as he posted a 4.49 ERA over 156.1 innings as he battled injuries. On the plus side, Cliff Lee pitched much better than his 6-9 record suggests—he compiled a 3.16 ERA over 211 innings—and Cole Hamels had another very impressive year with a 3.05 ERA and 17-6 record. The staff did not meet preseason expectations, as it fought against injuries that forced six starters to make more than 20 starts, but overall it was a solid group.

The problem was that the offense also battled injuries to core players and was not productive enough to balance the decline of the pitching staff. The Phillies still have a very solid roster, and also very expensive, so they should be able to compete with nearly the same overall quality they have displayed over the last half decade, assuming they are able to avoid or better prepare for injuries to key players.

Mets Start Hot, Fold in Second Half

In what has become somewhat of an annual story for the New York Mets, they surprised out of the gate and were competitive through the All-Star break, but ran into a wall after the midsummer classic and stumbled to the finish line. Despite the overall season being a disappointment given the productive first half, the club did have some historic performances.

The most notable single-game feat was Johan Santana's 134-pitch, eight-strikeout no-hitter against the Cardinals on June 1, the first no-no in franchise history. Santana would fade shortly after the no-hitter and would only make four second-half starts, but that couldn't sour a moment 51 years in the making for Mets fans.

The historic performances lasted all season long for Dickey, who produced one of the greatest seasons ever for a knuckleball pitcher.

Dickey's story and development as a knuckleballer have been inspirational, and his 20-6 record and 2.73 ERA, along with a NL-best 230 strikeouts show how far determination and creativity can go. Even in Dickey's book, he explained that he "will never lead the league in strikeouts." Guess it's time to produce a revised edition. His incredible season was even a surprise to himself, and Met fans were ecstatic during nearly every one of Dickey's 33 starts.

While Dickey was certainly a Cy Young favorite, the Mets also finished the season with an MVP Award candidate in David Wright. Wright had a superb first half with 11 home runs, 59 RBI, and a .351/.441/.563 batting line. Though he hit just .258 after the All-Star break, which coincided with the team's second-half struggles, Wright still finished with his highest OPS since 2008. The Mets' issue was the lack of talent surrounding Wright, specifically in the outfield, where the team cycled through a number of players due to injuries and poor performance. High-priced free agent Jason Bay continued his struggles in New York, and heavy-hitting prospect Lucas Duda showed why his best defensive position is likely designated hitter, though he also showed inconsistencies at the plate. Ike Davis proved to be a solid second man to Wright in the second half of the year, but his monumentally bad first half saw him finish the year with just a .227 batting average, despite hitting 20 home runs with an OPS just under .900 in the second half.

To top off the Mets' struggles, the anticipated improvements in the bullpen never materialized as planned. Frank Francisco's 5.53 ERA as the team's closer explains the bullpen issues rather well, though he was not the only reliever to be blamed for the frequent late-inning collapses. Entering 2013, the Mets will need to find ways to improve their defense, gain more production from the outfield and continue to look for solutions in the bullpen.

Marlins Fail to Meet Expectations

With a number of free-agent signings that were expected to bolster the lineup, defense, rotation and bullpen, along with the addition of a new manager and unveiling of a dazzling new stadium, the Miami Marlins were one of the preseason favorites to surprise in the NL East. The lineup was now even more dynamic in terms of both speed and power, the rotation featured a mix of veterans with high levels of success in the past, and the bullpen had solid match-up arms along with a proven closer thanks to the signing of Heath Bell.

Despite all of the offseason moves made to provide talent around Hanley Ramirez and Josh Johnson, the Marlins lacked consistency in a number of areas. To start the year, Bell blew save after save and eventually lost his role as the closer in the first few months of his first year in Miami. Additionally, the Marlins battled injuries in their outfield and a tremendous lack of production from first baseman Gaby Sanchez.

As the team continued to fall behind in the division, Miami made a desperation move, acquiring Carlos Lee to take over for Sanchez at first base. After dipping even further down in the standings just a handful of games after Lee's acquisition, the Marlins opted to sell off many assets to attempt to build for the future. They dealt off the starting infield, including Ramirez, and one of the best and most consistent home-grown starters the franchise has ever produced in Anibal Sanchez. As a team that entered the year with extremely high expectations, it did take courage to admit in the middle of the season that things were not going to work the way the Marlins had planned. Trading off those players ended any hopes at making a comeback in the division or in the Wild Card race in the team's first year in the new stadium, but focusing on acquiring young, cost-controlled talent was a wise decision, especially given the lackluster state of the team's farm system.

Jacob Turner came over from Detroit, and though he netted just a 1-4 record in seven starts, he did record a 3.38 ERA that was backed by a solid strikeout-to-walk ratio. Nathan Eovaldi put together just a 4.43 ERA in his 12 starts after coming over from the Dodgers in the Ramirez trade, but he did record a 3.72 ERA in five September starts, and gained solid experience against NL East opponents to finish the year. The season ended up going in a much different direction than Ozzie Guillen and the Marlins' front office hoped, but with Giancarlo Stanton continuing to improve (37 homers in 501 plate appearances), Jose Reyes putting together a very impressive second half (.312, eight homers, 20 steals), and Johnson having a healthy season as he enters his final season before free agency, the Marlins have some valuable top-end talent and are not as far away from competing as their record this year suggests. The front office will have to bolster the lineup a bit more and hope to find more gems like Justin Ruggiano, but all is not lost in Miami, even though 2012 certainly can be categorized as a lost season.

The National League Central View

by Bradley Woodrum

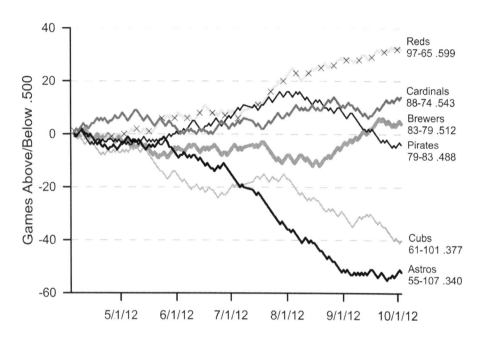

The league's only six-team division is no more. Founded in 1994, the National League Central division has had six teams ever since the Milwaukee Brewers joined the fray in 1998. In the interim 14 seasons, the St. Louis Cardinals took the NL Central crown six times, the Chicago Cubs and Houston Astros three times each, the Brewers and Cincinnati Reds once each, and the Pittsburgh Pirates not a single time.

In 2012, the Reds added their second tally to the division championship column, and posted the second-best record in the NL with a 97-win season. The Cardinals, on the merit of an 88-win season, nabbed the second Wild Card spot for the team's second consecutive Wild Card berth.

But the dominant story of the NL Central was not so much about the red stockings and red birds dominating, but more about the wave of high-profile roster turnover throughout the division. And no team had more well-known turnover than the Cardinals.

Life After Pujols

Because of trades, free agency departures, and injuries over the past season and a half, the Cardinals employed four new position player starters—Allen Craig, Daniel Descalso, Carlos Beltran and Rafael Furcal, who joined the team late in 2011. They also added three fresh names to the rotation in Lance Lynn, Joe Kelly, and Adam Wainwright, who missed all of 2011 (four if you want to count Shelby Miller, who made his first start at the end of the season). But the biggest change was that Albert Pujols was wearing a different shade of red for the first time. After signing a titanic 10-year, $254 million contract with the Los Angeles Angels of Anaheim, Pujols left the franchise that drafted him and he headed west.

Since the total value of Pujols' new contract ended up surpassing the gross domestic product of the Federated States of Micronesia, the Cardinals had to have a contingency plan. And when that contingency plan, Lance Berkman, went down with a series of injuries, they had to have depth.

The duo of Craig and Matt Carpenter combined to start 116 of the Cardinals' 162 games at first base. With steady numbers from both the 27-year-old Craig and 26-year-old Carpenter, St. Louis boasted a .291/.353/.480 slash at first base and an .833 OPS that ranked fourth in the league—not bad for a team relying on its third and fourth options.

When Furcal, the starting shortstop, went down with an elbow sprain during the stretch run, former first-round pick Pete Kozma came up from Triple-A and took the everyday shortstop duties. When Chris Carpenter's 37-year-old shoulder seized up with a pain that can only be described as exactly how painful thoracic outlet syndrome is, the Cardinals turned to youngsters Lynn, who won 18 games and posted a 3.78 ERA over 176 innings, and Kelly, who had a 3.53 ERA in 107 IP.

If the Cardinals achieved consistency from any of their starters, it came from Matt Holliday, who tallied a team-leading 688 plate appearances with a .295/.379/.497 slash line, and Kyle Lohse, who posted a career-best 2.86 ERA and 16-3 record despite a relatively pedestrian strikeout rate (16.6 percent compared to the NL starting pitcher average of 19.1 percent). These two men played major roles in producing 765 runs, fifth most in the majors, and allowing 648 runs, good for the second-best run differential in the NL.

And on Oct. 3, in Chris Carpenter's third and final start of the 2012 season, St. Louis clinched the second Wild Card spot and paved the way for yet another post-season run, doing so despite the fact that they lost the division to its new winning machine, the Reds.

The Big Red

If the story of the NL Central was one of roster turnover, then the Reds chapter begins with a righty named Latos. After the Reds finished the 2011 season with an undesirable 4.16 ERA and not a single pitcher over 200 innings pitched, the team made its rotation an offseason priority. The first step in that direction was acquiring the San Diego Padres' workhorse, 24-year-old Mat Latos.

The Latos trade sent the Padres a ransom of prospects and major league talent: Yonder Alonso, Edinson Volquez, Yasmani Grandal, and Brad Boxberger. But the reward of the trade converged with strong seasons from Johnny Cueto, Homer Bailey, and Bronson Arroyo to give the Reds four pitchers over 200 innings pitched, the only team to accomplish the feat. Gone were Travis Wood and Dontrelle Willis—and the need for backup starters.

On Aug. 18, 27-year-old Todd Redmond made his major league debut and pitched 3.1 innings against the Chicago Cubs. He departed with four earned runs on the board. The game was historic. Why? Because it was the only game started by a Reds pitcher other than Cueto, Latos, Bailey, Arroyo or Mike Leake.

Meanwhile, the bullpen, which led the league with a cheat-code-like 2.65 ERA, pitched the second-fewest innings in the league with 434.1 innings. They made about 70 fewer appearances than the average bullpen, and when they did appear, it was typically a foregone conclusion as to what would happen.

Aroldis Chapman, more a "Cuban Laser" than a "Cuban Missile," slung a team-leading 1.51 ERA with a gaudy 44.2 percent strikeout rate. And behind him were new acquisitions Sean Marshall (2.51 ERA), Alfredo Simon (2.66 ERA), and Jonathan Broxton (2.82 ERA), as well as the familiar faces of Jose Arredondo (2.95 ERA), Sam Lecure (3.14 ERA), and Logan Ondrusek (3.46 ERA).

With numbers like that, it is hard to believe the Reds play in a hitters' park. And that they had just let their long-time closer, Francisco Cordero, depart in free agency the preceding winter.

While the pitching staff was a relay of changing names, only two major changes occurred in the field. Ryan Ludwick took the starting left field job, and rookie Zack Cozart nabbed the starting shortstop gig.

For the Reds position players, the biggest offseason story had to be the extension of all-world first baseman Joey Votto. The 28-year-old left-handed batter missed about 50 days on the disabled list with various knees problems throughout the season, but despite playing in only 111 games and making just 475 PAs, he still led the league in walks.

Among players with at least 400 PAs, Votto's .474 on-base percentage was about 60 points better than the next-nearest hitter (Joe Mauer at .416). He may have missed almost a third of the season, but in the two-thirds he played, Votto made the case for being the best first baseman in the world.

Votto, Ludwick, Bruce, and the Reds' otherworldly, revamped pitching staff led them to their best season since 1976, but roster turnover did not treat the other teams in the NL Central so well—especially not the defending division-champion Brewers.

All Buck, No Bang

Judging by their $97.7 million payroll—second in the division only to St. Louis' $110.3 million payroll—one could reasonably think that the mid-market Brewers were prepared to defend their 2011 NL Central championship. One would be incorrect.

Despite winning 96 games the season prior, the Brewers managed just a paltry 83 wins in 2012, finishing only four games above the .500 mark. But the team that managed only 83 wins was not the same as the one that captured 96 victories the year prior.

Gone were Casey McGehee, Yuniesky Betancourt, and—most importantly of all—Prince Fielder. The 28-year-old heir of Cecil Fielder cashed in on his seven years with the Brewers in the form of a nine-year, $214 million contract with the Detroit Tigers. In the space left by these departures, the Brewers employed a hodgepodge of new and old names.

Corey Hart and Travis Ishikawa split the first base duties, while newly acquired Jean Segura shared playing time with the underwhelming Cesar Izturis, Cody Ransom and Alex Gonzalez at shortstop. Former Cubs infielder Aramis Ramirez added a solid season at third base, while Japanese veteran and MLB rookie Norichika Aoki took over right field in what may have been the best value acquisition of the offseason.

All told, the Brewers put together the best offense in the NL—they scored 776 runs—and the third-best in the majors. The problem, however, was that they allowed 733 runs. While Ryan Braun was putting on an impressive encore of his 2011 Most Valuable Player season, the Brewers bullpen spent 2012 reenacting the finer points of the Hindenburg disaster.

With a 4.66 ERA, no bullpen had worse results than the Brewers relief squad. Not even the Cubs 'pen, which mustered a league-low 28 saves, was as bad as the Brewers. Milwaukee relievers had a decent strikeout rate, placing sixth in the NL by punching out 23.2 percent of the batters they faced, but they could not keep a lid on the free-pass jar.

The leaky control may have been bearable, perhaps, if their 10.3 percent walk rate—third-worst in the majors—had come from low-leverage inning eaters. But when the closer, John Axford, has the fifth-most walks on the team with 39, the bullpen has no option but to fail. Axford, who led the 2011 season in saves and even garnered some Cy Young and MVP votes that season, finished the year with 10 home runs allowed, nine blown saves, eight losses, and an un-Axford-like 4.67 ERA.

The Brewers bullpen, which threw only about one-third of the team's innings, allowed almost 40 percent of the pitching staff's runs. The only bullpen remotely close to allowing 40 percent of its team's runs was the Rockies bullpen, which, because of Colorado's four-man rotation, was responsible for almost half the team's innings.

The poor performance from the Brewers bullpen may not excuse the fact that they had to use 11 different starting pitchers, that Randy Wolf had a 5.69 ERA before they traded him, or that Rickie Weeks had a down year, but it does go a long way to explain how Milwaukee won 13 fewer games in 2012.

The Pittsburgh Pendulum

If the Brewers' season was a letdown, then the Pirates' season was a kick in the mouth. On Aug. 8, the Pirates beat the Arizona Diamondbacks, 7-6, as Neil Walker clapped a first-inning home run and Kevin Correia battled through six innings to get his ninth win of the season. The Pirates, at the end of that August day, had a 63-47 record—fourth best in the NL—and looked like the surging favorites for at least a Wild Card spot.

The Pirates, on the merit of their strong first half, had positioned themselves not only for the franchise's first playoff appearance in two decades, but also for a chance at erasing the harsh memory of the 2011 season. Last season, the Pirates went from first place on July 25 to fourth place—for good—on Aug. 12. It took them 16 tormentous days to ruin the entirety of their 2011 campaign.

And then came 2012. From Aug. 9 to Sept. 3, the Pirates won only seven games. They went from 2.5 games behind the Reds to 11.0 games back, and from 16 games above .500 to only six games above .500.

The team again finished in fourth place, despite terrific seasons from Andrew McCutchen (.327/.400/.553), Garrett Jones (.274/.317/.516), and A.J. Burnett (3.51 ERA in 31 starts). The second collapse, however, is perhaps more remarkable than the first, because about the only thing that stayed the same between the seasons was the Pirates uniform.

Gone: Ryan Doumit, Lyle Overbay, Ronny Cedeno, Paul Maholm, Jose Veras, and Brandon Wood, all players who made major contributions in the 2011 campaign. In their place came Burnett, McGehee, Erik Bedard, Wandy Rodriguez and Clint Barmes.

But despite the infusion of new talent, McCutchen's breakout and Burnett's resurgence, the Pirates managed to score only 651 runs, tied with the Padres for seventh-worst in the majors, and San Diego has to play in Petco Park, where offense is little more than a rumor. While Pittsburgh's pitching and defense allowed only 674 runs—about league average—248 of those runs, about 42 percent, were surrendered in the final two months of the season.

For much of the season, it looked like the Pirates, with the fifth-smallest payroll in the majors at $63.4 million, had finally solved the equation of their struggles, but they once again turned cold with the weather and left their fans wondering if the season-sapping pendulum could be stopped.

Turnover from Top to Bottom

The Chicago Cubs and Houston Astros spent most the season fighting for the coveted top pick in the 2013 MLB amateur draft, but it was the Astros who finally won out with an astounding 107-loss performance that was sprinkled with some of the game's most historic defensive miscues. The Cubs had to settle for the second pick after tallying a 61-101 season.

If two franchises ever could write about the pains of rebuilding, it would be these two. During the offseason, both front offices installed sabermetric personnel at every level. Former Red Sox GM Theo Epstein took over as the Cubs' president of baseball operations while Padres GM Jed Hoyer moved to the Wrigleyville offices as the team's first sabermetric GM.

In Houston, Jim Crane, the new Astros owner, brought in Jeff Luhnow from the Cardinals scouting department. Luhnow promptly began acquiring free agent analysts from the sabermetric blogosphere, hiring Mike Fast and Kevin Goldstein away from Baseball Prospectus.

And while these two teams aggregated front office talent, they unleashed a flurry of trades that drained their on-field talent. The Astros, under Luhnow, executed 12 in-season trades during the season. They dealt away eight major leaguers who were either starters or key bullpen members, including Carlos Lee, Brett Myers, J.A. Happ and Rodriguez.

As a result of the team's various trades, Houston received 17 minor leaguers. According to J.J. Cooper of *Baseball America*, the Astros went from possessing "the least successful farm system in baseball" to one of the more promising systems in the league. Their seven affiliate teams throughout the domestic minor leagues posted the best overall record, going a combined 417-347, for a .546 winning percentage.

The Astros may have missed their final chance to capture the NL Central championship, but they have more than a good chance at taking the AL West title within the next 10 years.

But as Houston looks to future years, the Cubs are looking to future months. Despite their dismal performance in the 2012 campaign, the Cubs—who had an $88.2 million payroll—have only about $40 million committed to their 2013 roster. After the team traded away long-time Cubbies Sean Marshall, Ryan Dempster, Carlos Zambrano and Geovany Soto, they executed a slew of call-ups, including top prospects 22-year-old Anthony Rizzo, 22-year-old Josh Vitters, and 23-year-old Brett Jackson.

Of the young trio, only Rizzo performed to expectations (.285/.342/.463), and by the All-Star break, the team was 19 games under .500. By the end of the season, they had traded away 13 major leaguers in exchange for 19 players, most of them minor leaguers and prospects.

But the team has good reason to hope in the near future. Pitcher Jeff Samardzija had a breakout campaign (3.81 ERA through 174.2 innings), and Matt Garza is still under contract for at least one more season. The team also has a growing treasure of young pitching talent, headlined by 22-year-old Arodys Vizcaino.

And with impressive position prospects like Jorge Soler, Javier Baez, and Daniel Vogelbach pushing quickly through the Cubs' minor league system—and a 2013 free agent market rich with pitching talent—Cubs fans have already turned their expectations to medium-to-high for the 2013 and 2014 seasons. Which means it's about time for Cubs fans once again to say, "Maybe next year."

The National League West View

by Steve Treder

Every baseball season presents its share of surprises. That's really kind of the point, after all. If we knew in advance everything that was going to happen, then there wouldn't be much purpose in conducting the season. "That's why they play the games," goes the old saying, because those games have an uncanny way of defying outcomes expected on paper. The sport's unpredictability, one might say, is the only thing about it that's predictable.

But the 2012 National League West took that standard and super-sized it with turbocharged steroids. The division presented a whole lot more than its share of surprises; it presented surprises within surprises within surprising surprises. There's unpredictable, and then there's 2012 NL West kind of unpredictable.

Alas, space and time do not permit us to review them all. So we've taken the long, long list of surprising outcomes in the division and sorted and trimmed our way down to the very most arresting. Let's examine, then, The Top Ten List of Most Unpredictable Stories in the 2012 NL West.

No. 10: Pythagoras and the Snakes

In 2011, the Arizona Diamondbacks stunned everyone by vaulting from a 65-97, last-place 2010 finish to a runaway division flag at 94-68.

But closer inspection revealed that the 2011 D-backs, though they were a genuinely good team, had benefited from unusually good fortune in terms of run distribution. Scoring 731 and allowing 662, they "should" have come in at 88-74, yet their actual record was six wins better than that. This feat was achieved in particular because the Snakes put up a 28-16 mark in one-run games, the very best such margin in the major leagues.

In 2012, the D-backs, understandably pleased with their status, returned with the same manager (Kirk Gibson), and largely the same roster—the only major additions were outfielder Jason Kubel and starting pitcher Trevor Cahill. This unit delivered run production and run prevention at rates extremely close to those of the prior year: this time around—734 scored versus 688 allowed. That works out to a Pythagorean record of 86-76.

But this time around, the same manager and mostly the same players, dealing with essentially the same proportion of runs, fell far short of their projection, dropping to a distant third at 81-81. They pulled this off by putting up a 15-27 mark in one-run games, tying the 101-game-losing Chicago Cubs for the very worst such margin in the major leagues.

No. 9: What the Freak?

The notion that the Giants' Tim Lincecum would suffer a collapse in effectiveness in 2012 was hardly expected, but neither was it particularly shocking. Pitchers, after all, are inherently prone to sudden collapse, and the 28-year-old Lincecum is a pitcher who's handled a heavy workload for several years, and, yes, he's slightly built and has always featured an unorthodox quasi-gymnastic delivery.

So, for "The Freak" to encounter the first sustained rough patch of his career wasn't surprising in itself. But the sequence we've come to expect in these situations is as follows: (a) star pitcher falls into a bad slump, then soon (b) star pitcher is placed on the 15-day disabled list for "shoulder soreness," and finally (c) we fans freely speculate about what's really ailing, the star pitcher's shoulder or just his ERA?

But no such sequence unfolded in San Francisco. Lincecum insisted he felt fine, attributing his struggles entirely to "mechanics" and "rhythm" and "your guess is as good as mine," and the Giants took him at his word. Even as Lincecum's problems mounted—and they mounted very high; at one point he was 3-10 with a 6.42 ERA—manager Bruce Bochy never sat him out of a single turn.

Lincecum pulled it together reasonably well over the balance of the season, but he never regained his standard pre-2012 form. The result was a pitcher tying for the league lead in starts while leading the league in wild pitches, runs, earned runs, and losses.

No. 8: The Rockies' rotation

Any lucky devil placing a preseason bet predicting the 2012 Colorado Rockies would do what they would with their starting pitchers would have drawn exceptionally attractive odds. Because what the 2012 Rockies would do with their starting pitchers is, well, unprecedented in the history of Major League Baseball.

It was on June 19 that manager Jim Tracy announced the Rockies were abandoning the modern-orthodox five-man starting rotation. In its place, they were introducing a four-man cycle (old school!), but with a 75-or-so-pitch limit in each outing (never-before-seen school).

We won't debate the merits of the plan. But we will note that a theoretical advantage of the novel approach would be to focus the team's starts onto its four best starting pitchers while freeing up that fifth arm to assist with the increased bullpen workload. However, the Rockies didn't work it that way.

Of the 55 Colorado starts following the implementation of the new pitch limit, only 21 times was the Rockies' starter working on three days' rest, and when Jhoulys Chacin returned to the rotation on Aug. 21, they scrapped the plan altogether. Aside from those 21 games, Colorado pitchers threw on four days' rest or more—that is, just like every other team in the league—because Colorado didn't stick with any set of four starters, but instead shuffled a multitude of arms into and out of the mix. This raises the obvious question of the purpose of the extra-low pitch limit.

In any case, it added up to a stat sheet quite unlike any presented before. Only one pitcher on the entire 2012 Rockies staff threw as many as 100 innings (ironman Jeff Francis, at 113). Fourteen different pitchers made starts, nine of them with 10 or more starts. Alas, they combined to go 16-39 with a 6.11 ERA in the first half and 13-29 with a 5.43 ERA in the second. To the degree that that was an improvement, it was offset by a decline in effectiveness from the heavier-worked relievers: 17-13, 4.09 in the first half to 18-17, 4.92 in the second.

No. 7: The Padres' Second Half

The San Diego Padres came into the 2012 season with low expectations. They were the last-place team in 2011 and were entering the second year of a full-blown rebuilding phase, having traded away their most prized star (ace starter Mat Latos) in the offseason for a package of prospects.

And as 2012 progressed, the Padres took those low expectations and underperformed them. They were 7-17 in April and 10-18 in May, and looked every bit that bad. June was another loser, marking the 10th straight month of Padres baseball that failed to produce a winning record.

But at the outset of July, the woebegone Friars suddenly reeled off a six-game winning streak, the first time the franchise had managed such a feat in more than two years. They would forge a winning record in July, and again in August. Only a mini-slump in the season's final couple of weeks prevented a winning September.

The ballclub that had slogged to a 34-53 record in the first half of 2012 cruised at 42-33 the rest of the way, leaving the basement far behind.

The explanation is entirely simple: Overnight, the Padres discovered how to hit. San Diego run production soared from a measly 3.4 per game through the end of June to a boisterous 4.6 from that point forward. At the All-Star break, the team batting line was .234/.308/.358, and it was an unrecognizable .262/.332/.406 afterward.

No. 6: Chase Headley: RBI Champion

The leading contributor to San Diego's caterpillar-to-butterfly metamorphosis was 28-year-old Chase Headley. Coming into 2012, in four years as the primary Padres third baseman, Headley hadn't been bad, but he hadn't been especially good, either. His career high in home runs was 12, in RBIs, 64.

At the All-Star break in 2012, Headley had eight homers and 42 RBIs in 315 at-bats, with a rate stat line of .269/.342/.392, all close to his established career norms.

Then, in the second half, he hit .308/.386/.592 with 23 homers and 73 RBIs in 289 at-bats. That's 73 RBIs in 75 games.

No. 5: A.J. Ellis: Big League Regular

Through 2011, in nine years of professional baseball, A.J. Ellis had never spent a complete season at the major league level. An 18th-round draft pick, Ellis was organizational roster filler for the Los Angeles Dodgers, spending his first several years as a backup catcher in the low minors.

But Ellis developed the capacity to draw walks, and then he developed the capacity to hit for a good average. Gradually, he worked his way up the chain. In stretches of 2010 and 2011, Ellis tenuously clung to a backup catcher role for the major league club. Coming into 2012, his playing time in The Show amounted to 62 starts in 87 total games, and 244 plate appearances.

In 2012, at the age of 31, Ellis was the Dodgers' Opening Day starting catcher. He held the job all year long, hitting .270/.373/.414 in 128 starts (133 games) and 505 plate appearances. His 4.1 WAR tied him with Matt Wieters for sixth-best among all major league catchers.

No. 4: Now That's a Comeback

On May 25, 2011, Giants catcher Buster Posey suffered a severely fractured ankle in a home plate collision. The young star's season ended immediately, as he underwent surgery and began a long period of recovery and rehabilitation. While the prognosis was that Posey would be ready to play again by spring training of 2012, there was reasonable concern about just how complete his restoration would be, and, the rigors of catching being what they are, whether Posey's performance would be impacted.

The good news? Posey returned in 2012 and proved capable of handling a full workload, appearing in 114 games behind the plate, 29 at first base, and three at DH.

The better news was that Posey's performance over the first half was rock-solid. He hit .289/.362/.458 and was the starting NL catcher in the All-Star Game.

The astonishingly great news was that in the second half, Posey hit .385/.456/.646. He wound up with 8.0 WAR, tying him with Ryan Braun for second in the majors, behind only Mike Trout.

No. 3: Super Marco

On July 27, the Rockies traded veteran infielder Marco Scutaro, along with cash, to the Giants for minor league second baseman Charlie Culberson. Amid the clutter of deadline deals that week, this one attracted precious little attention. It was plainly a salary dump by the Rockies, hopelessly out of the race, finding a taker for the 36-year-old Scutaro. Colorado was even willing to toss some money the Giants' way to help cover Scutaro's cost, even though Culberson is not a top prospect.

Scutaro's performance for Colorado had been wholly uninspiring, as he compiled just 0.6 WAR in 95 games. The Giants didn't see him as anything more than infield depth. Since Pablo Sandoval was on the DL, they plugged in Scutaro at third base, but his projected role was just that of a utility player.

However, somebody forgot to tell Scutaro that he was washed up. Filling in for Sandoval, he hit well for a couple of weeks. When The Panda returned, the Giants gave Scutaro a shot at the second base job, and he promptly stole it from incumbent Ryan Theriot.

Scutaro never cooled off; he just got hotter and hotter. He hit .314 in August and .402 in September/October. In 61 regular-season games for the Giants, he hit .362 with 88 hits, 40 runs scored and 44 driven in, yielding 2.1 WAR. Then in the NL Championship Series, he hit .500 and was named MVP, and capped his season by driving in the winning run in Game Four of the World Series.

No. 2: The Mother of All Trades

On Aug. 25, 2012, the Los Angeles Dodgers and Boston Red Sox pulled off the largest-magnitude exchange in the history of waiver-wire deals. In a financial transaction of massive scope, the Dodgers took more than a quarter-billion dollars in contract obligations off of Boston's hands.

The wisdom of the exceptionally bold move can only be determined over the long run. But its immediate-term motivation, from the Los Angeles perspective, was obvious. The first base upgrade from James Loney to Adrian Gonzalez was expected to be sufficient to deliver the NL West title to the Dodgers. A helpful contribution from starting pitcher Josh Beckett would be appreciated as well, of course, but that wasn't the central point. Gonzalez was.

Though the Dodgers were in second place at the time the trade was executed, they were only a couple of games out, and they had been in first for more than a few days in August. In addition, their rival for the division flag (as we'll explore below) had just taken a vicious uppercut to the solar plexus. Los Angeles wasn't angling for a Wild Card slot on Aug. 25. This franchise was playing to win, and now.

The bombshell proved to be a dud. Not only would the Dodgers fail to win the division, they would lose 16 of their next 26 games following the trade and be eliminated from the race in less than a month. Gonzalez was an immediate-term flop, hitting an entirely Loney-like .243/.295/.369 over that span.

No. 1: Melky and the Giants

In 2010, Melky Cabrera's market value was such that he was flat-out released at the age of 26 by the Atlanta Braves. Scavenged by the bottom-feeding Kansas City Royals, Cabrera surprised everyone with an excellent all-around 2011 performance.

The Royals' confidence that Cabrera would sustain that performance was such that in November of 2011, they traded him for Jonathan Sanchez, an erratic 29-year-old southpaw with a career record of 38-46 and a 4.26 ERA, coming off a season in which he spent most of the second half on the disabled list. Cabrera then surprised everyone by not just sustaining his 2011 level of performance but dramatically exceeding it, delivering MVP-quality results for the 2012 San Francisco Giants, posting 4.6 WAR through 113 games.

Through Aug. 14, that is. To what degree Cabrera's surging level of play was a function of performance-enhancing drugs is, of course, unknowable. But what's certain is that he flunked a drug test and was suspended for the remainder of the regular season.

The Giants were left with no apparent means of coming close to replacing Cabrera's contribution. They were in a first-place tie with the Dodgers, but the San Francisco lineup minus Cabrera was less than equal to the Los Angeles lineup. And when, a week and a half later, the Los Angeles lineup received the addition of Gonzalez, it was clear to everyone that the Giants were in a world of serious hurt.

But the Giants never got that memo. The ballclub had 14 series left on the regular-season schedule to be played without Cabrera. Led by the spectacular hitting of Posey and Scutaro, they would win 12 of them. In all-important head-to-head show-downs against the Dodgers, the Giants swept three in Los Angeles on Aug. 20-22, and took two out of three in San Francisco on Sept. 7-9. By the middle of that final month, any semblance of a division race was kaput.

Coming Attractions: National League

by Jeff Moore

While we all enjoy looking forward, this is not a book specifically dedicated to prospect analysis. Still, we like to whet our beaks. So in the pages that follow, you will find a brief overview of each National League team's farm system, as well as analysis of one interesting prospect per team. They aren't necessarily the prospects who get a lot of ink throughout the year, but they are all noteworthy in their own special way.

National League East

Atlanta Braves

For the past few years, the strength of the Braves farm system has been its impressive pitching depth, especially those who were close to the majors. Many fans envisioned Julio Teheran and Randall Delgado securing established roles in the Atlanta rotation. Instead, Teheran struggled greatly in his second stint at Triple-A, while Delgado made 17 starts in the major leagues but didn't grab hold of a rotation spot the way many had hoped. Additionally, an injury to Arodys Vizcaino, followed by his trade to the Cubs, has completely removaed the luster from what was thought to be the future of the Braves rotation.

Still Far Away: Lucas Sims, RHP

A power-armed right-hander, Sims was the Braves' first-round selection in the 2012 draft, and offers a different kind of arm than the pitchers the Braves have previously chosen in the first round. Over the past few years, they've selected polished college arms like Mike Minor and Sean Gilmartin, who offered more certainty than projectability. Sims, on the other hand, throws in the mid-90s with a potential power slider that the Braves can dream on. Sims only saw action in rookie league after signing, so he's still got a ways to go, but he should reach the Low-A South Atlantic League at some point next season.

Miami Marlins

Part of the rebranding of a franchise has to happen within their farm system as well, and the Marlins have a few key pieces that got that process off to a good start. The Marlins never overpaid for draft picks the way many clubs did, so the new slotting system should help them select the best talent in the first round rather than a signable prospect. Their 2010 first-rounder, Christian Yelich, has become the exception, however, emerging as one of the best all-around prospects in the game.

A Step Back: Zack Cox, 3B

He's new to the Marlins organization, but Cox isn't new to prospect followers. The former 2010 Cardinals first-round pick looked to be on the fast track to the majors, but his struggles at the start of this season led to his inclusion in a midseason trade. In his first stint in Triple-A, Cox's plate discipline—which was never strong to begin with—broke down altogether, and he hit just .254/.301/.409 combined for the season. He's not a power hitter, so if Cox wants to be a major league hitter he'll need to get his average back near .300.

New York Mets

Years of low-spending drafts and misses on international prospects have left the Mets in a strange place. They have one impact prospect on the horizon in pitcher Zack Wheeler, but he was acquired in a trade, and a number of other flawed prospects that leave as many questions as anything else.

Big Leap: Wilmer Flores, 3B

After years of giving international prospects bonus credit for having mediocre seasons at advanced levels for their age, the Mets finally made Flores stay where he belonged until he mastered a particular level. He started 2012 at High-A St. Lucie—his third trip there—and finally became the hitter the Mets hoped he would be, hitting 10 homers in 64 games before a midseason promotion. The strong play carried over into Double-A, where Flores hit .311/.361/.494 in 66 games to end the season. The Mets finally moved him off shortstop, playing him primarily at third base, but the jury is still out on his ability to handle the hot corner. Where he ends up on the field will go a long way toward determining his value.

Philadelphia Phillies

Once a strong, deep farm system, the Phillies minor leagues have been depleted due to trades for veterans. They still have some talent, especially on the mound, but they're not nearly as deep as they've been in the past, and are virtually devoid of major league-ready bats.

A Step Back: Trevor May, RHP

May was considered the top pitching prospect in the Phillies system entering 2012, with a mid-level ceiling but a pro body and pro stuff. This season was a stumble for May, who has had them before, as he went 10-13 with a 4.87 ERA in Double-A, while battling his control. May doesn't have the stuff to get away with walking 4.7 batters per nine innings, so he'll have to get that reeled in, but he does still miss a lot of bats, even when he's struggling. May might repeat Double-A next season.

Washington Nationals

Between the graduations of Stephen Strasburg and Bryce Harper, as well as the prospects traded to acquire Gio Gonzalez, the Nationals farm system has been left without major league-ready impact talent, but for all the right reasons. They've still shown they're not afraid to take chances in the draft, however, always electing to take the player with the highest ceiling.

Big Leap: Alex Meyer, RHP

Another draft pick the Nationals took a chance on, Meyer has done everything he can to help quell the Nationals' apprehension. The concern with Meyer was his control, as his six-foot, nine-inch frame leads to a delivery that's hard to repeat, but he walked just 3.1 batters per nine innings this season while striking out 9.7. He began the season in Low-A, but received a midseason promotion and had no problem with the Carolina League. Meyer made just seven starts there, so he could head back to Potomac to begin the season, but he should be in Double-A by the end of 2013.

National League Central

Chicago Cubs

The Cubs are rebuilding everything, from their front office to their coaching staff to their organizational philosophy. Chicago has always had a strong presence in the international market, and that isn't likely to change.

Still Far Away: Dan Vogelbach, 1B

Vogelbach looks like a prospect from a different era in baseball. He's a big-bodied first baseman whose entire value resides in his bat. Luckily, Vogelbach can rake, and he has big-time power, which will have to play in order for him to have a shot. His combined .322/.410/.641 line between the Arizona Rookie League and short-season Northwest League is a good start.

Cincinnati Reds

As with many organizations with talented, young players in the majors, the Reds farm system doesn't offer much depth. Furthering that situation was their trade for Mat Latos before the 2012 season, which sent four of their top prospects to San Diego and furthered their all-in approach to the season.

Still Far Away: Robert Stephenson, RHP

The Reds' 2011 first-rounder finally got on the field and had no problem transitioning to professional baseball. Between Low- and High-A, Stephenson posted a 3.18 ERA, while striking out 10 batters per nine innings. The Reds kept the handcuffs on Stephenson pretty tightly, allowing him to average just 4 1/3 innings per start. That should change this year, and it should be fun to see what he can do once he's allowed to pitch deep into games.

Houston Astros

The Astros farm system has gone from the worst in baseball to one of the more intriguing thanks to the mass exodus of any major league talent the front office has executed the past two seasons. The result is a deep collection of prospects, ranging from high to low in terms of potential, but filling a lot of future needs at the same time.

Big Leap: Nick Tropeano, RHP

The former Stony Brook Seawolf made the leap from possible back-end starter who was a good senior signee to legitimate pitching prospect with one of the best change-ups in the minors. Tropeano didn't do much differently—he's always had a great change-up—but in 2012 he was able to prove it worked against better competition, as he posted a 3.02 ERA against Low- and High-A hitters.

Milwaukee Brewers

After cleaning out their farm system in trades for veterans like Zack Greinke, the Brewers found themselves on the other side of the equation this season, flipping Greinke himself for a trio of new prospects to help rebuild a weak system. They've also struck out in recent drafts, particularly in the first round.

A Step Back: Jed Bradley, LHP

One of two college pitchers selected by the Brewers in 2011, the former Goergia Tech left-hander couldn't get anybody out in the Florida State League, as he went 5-10 with a 5.53 ERA. He struck out just five batters per nine innings, an unsustainably low figure. Look for Bradley to repeat High-A in 2013, but he'll have to do much better in that pitcher-friendly league.

Pittsburgh Pirates

Picking in the top 10 in the draft for the better part of a decade is finally beginning to pay off for the Pirates. Gerrit Cole and Jameson Taillon headline their future pitching staff, and they used the old draft rules (or lack thereof) to sign over-slot talent late in drafts, which has helped them establish a deep farm system.

Still Far Away: Luis Heredia, RHP

Much was made out of Heredia, signing for a huge bonus at the age of 16 out of Mexico. He pitched in the short-season New York-Penn League this season, going 4-2 with a 2.71 ERA. Heredia struck out just 5.4 batters per nine innings, but that's not as big a red flag as it would be with most pitchers given that he was only 17 and was facing much older competition. Heredia will continue to grow into his body and gain more velocity, and the strikeouts will come.

St. Louis Cardinals

The Cardinals have a good mix of depth and impact talent, with Shelby Miller and Oscar Taveras among the best pitching and hitting prospects in the minors, respectively. Their pitching depth has allowed them to insert rookies right into major league spots where they can be effective, keeping their successful run in the NL Central going.

A Step Back: Jordan Swagerty, RHP

A spring training arm injury ended Swagerty's season before it ever began, and ultimately may have ended any chance he had of becoming a starter. The former college reliever was scheduled to work as a starter, but there were some who believed Swagerty always was destined for a bullpen role down the road. His missed time probably makes that decision easier for St. Louis.

National League West

Arizona Diamondbacks

The Diamondbacks used two first-round picks to give them the pitching depth that may be the envy of all other farm systems around baseball. Much of that depth began to manifest itself in the majors this season, with the promotion of prospects Tyler Skaggs and Pat Corbin.

Still Far Away: Socrates Brito, OF

Sporting one of the best names in the minors—and perhaps the entire country—Brito backed it up this year with a strong performance in the short-season Pioneer League. As a 19-year old, he hit .312/.357/.444 while splitting time between center and right field. Brito hasn't shown much power in terms of home runs, but his 15 doubles give the Diamondbacks hope that there is a little more pop in his bat than what he's shown. He should be ready for full-season ball in 2013.

Colorado Rockies

The Rockies have missed on many recent first-round picks, leaving their system in a strange place. They acquired some intriguing prospects in exchange for former ace Ubaldo Jimenez, but have had issues developing pitching prospects, something that has been a problem for them historically. Hopefully that will change with the development of 2011 first-rounder Tyler Anderson, but it remains to be seen how he deals with the high altitude.

Big Leap: Trevor Story, SS

Big things were expected out of Story, the team's supplemental first-rounder from 2011, but perhaps not so much so soon. He hit .277/.365/.505 in his first year of full-season ball, with an impressive 43 doubles and 18 home runs. It was an impressive power display, and the Rockies hope that even more of those doubles can begin to clear the fence. If they do, and Story can remain at shortstop, he could be a potential All-Star.

Los Angeles Dodgers

Under Frank McCourt, the Dodgers limited their spending in the draft and activity on the international free agent market, which ultimately weakened their farm system. That should change in the years to come, but for the time being, that effect—plus trades—has left Los Angeles without much impact talent.

A Step Back: Garrett Gould, RHP

After such a strong first full season in 2011, the Dodgers have to be disappointed by the 2012 season Gould turned in. The California League has that effect on pitchers. He got hit hard, going 5-10 with a 5.75 ERA, though he did still strike out nearly a batter per inning. Gould wasn't the first well-regarded prospect to get roughed up in the Cal League, and he won't be the last. He could return there next season to try to master it, or the Dodgers could elect to just send him to Double-A and move on.

San Diego Padres

Despite their well-documented first-round struggles, the Padres have built up an impressive collection of talent at all levels of the minor leagues. Trading veterans has greatly made up for their misses in the draft, and they've ended up with prospects they know much more about and with whom they have track records.

Still Far Away: Adys Portillo, RHP

Despite reaching Double-A this year, Portillo still has a lot of work to do before he's major league ready. The right-hander handled the Low-A Midwest League, but wanting to keep him from the California League, the Padres jumped him up to San Antonio in what turned out to be a disastrous move. Portillo's already questionable control escaped him altogether, and he stopped striking enough batters out. The Padres' desire to keep him out of the Cal League is understandable, but it may be unavoidable.

San Francisco Giants

A decade of picking at the end of the first round coupled with some trades to solidify playoff runs has left the Giants without a lot of top talent. The talent they do have, while not far from the majors, is hardly high-ceiling, impact talent, but they could have a few nice pieces to fit in with their already strong major league nucleus.

A Step Back: Gary Brown, OF

Brown entered the season coming off one of the great all-around minor league seasons of 2011, having fully exploited all that the California League had to offer hitters. He found the Eastern League a little more challenging, and even though he came around in the second half, Brown still posted just a .731 OPS and demonstrated little power. His plate discipline remained intact, but the power deserted him. Don't be surprised to see it return next season in the Pacific Coast League, with Brown's major league power numbers falling somewhere in between.

The Giants and Scutaro Win, as Does Valverde (Sort of)

by Brad Johnson

After the final day of the 2012 season, the St. Louis Cardinals were six games behind the Atlanta Braves in the Wild Card race. In years past, the Cardinals would have been dismissed as an inconsequential also-ran. Of course, in years past, there was no second Wild Card.

Not only did the Cardinals reach the postseason, but they played a role in many of the most interesting story lines. They pushed past the 94-win Braves amidst an umpiring debacle, bested the Washington Nationals in a heart-wrenching comeback, and drove the eventual World Series champion San Francisco Giants to the brink of elimination.

They say that in any given game of baseball, you will see something you have never seen before. This postseason offered a few blissfully unique moments. All four Division Series went to a fifth game for the first time ever. The highest-paid player in baseball, Alex Rodriguez, was pinch-hit for, then benched. And in a perfect storm of improbability, the two most fascinating plays of the postseason involved Cardinals shortstop Pete Kozma.

It is inconceivable to pen any retelling of the 2012 postseason without prominent mention of "The Infield Fly." In one of the most important games of the season, an umpire ruled that a ball Kozma didn't catch in the outfield was an automatic out in the infield. Thus, the world was reminded of a question that great philosophers have pondered for decades: What is an infield fly?

Philosophy was not the only discipline to be called upon. Hunter Pence and the Thrice-Struck Ball broke open the final game of the Natonal League Championship Series when it sliced past a bewildered Kozma. It was an improbable lesson in the physics of baseball, shattering bats and spin.

Beyond discussing rare plays, it is a THT tradition to evaluate postseason performances with a specially designed statistic—Championships Added (ChampAdded).

The math requires some explanation. Every game has two possible outcomes, a win or a loss. We assume that there is a 50 percent chance for either outcome. Once the game is over, one team has won (it has moved from 50 percent probability to 100 percent certainty) and the other team has lost (from 50 percent to zero percent). This is how Win Probability works, and you can read more about it in Dave Studenmund's article about the Orioles bullpen.

When two teams meet in the seventh game of the World Series, there is one full championship at stake. The team that wins the game will be the champion. As such, ChampAdded views this game as having a 1.000 value.

Of course, all other games are worth a fraction of a championship. For example, the seventh game of the NLCS is worth .500 championships. This is because the winner of the game advances to the World Series where it is assumed to have a 50 percent chance of winning. The loser goes home. The chart below shows the relative championship value of each possible playoff game.

Championship Value of Playoff Games										
	0-0	1-0	1-1	2-0	2-1	2-2	3-0	3-1	3-2	3-3
Wild Card Game	0.125	X	X	X	X	X	X	X	X	X
Division Series	0.094	0.094	0.125	0.063	0.125	0.250	X	X	X	X
Cham-pionship Series	0.156	0.156	0.188	0.125	0.188	0.250	0.063	0.125	0.250	0.500
World Series	0.313	0.313	0.375	0.250	0.375	0.500	0.125	0.250	0.500	1.000

Once you know the importance of each game in terms of championships, we can convert each play of a game into a share of a championship by simply multiplying the Win Probability impact of that play times the ChampAdded value of the game. The ChampAdded values reported below use this concept.

You can think of it this way: Since there were eight teams left after the Wild Card games, each team had a 12.5 percent chance of winning it all (one divided by eight is .125). Over the course of the postseason, players on the World Champion Giants contributed a total of .875 ChampAdded (1.000 minus .125 equals .875). Every other team's sum ChampAdded was -.125. It is a zero sum game.

Following each series recap, ChampAdded will be used to identify a series MVP, a series goat, and the biggest play of the series. The MVP was the biggest contributor to his team's championship hopes in a given series. The goat is the player who hurt his team the most. The biggest play is the play with the highest Champ WPA associated with it.

NL Wild Card: St. Louis Cardinals vs. Atlanta Braves

With just one game to get things right, Braves manager Fredi Gonzalez benched All-Star catcher Brian McCann in favor of David Ross. There were reasons: McCann was mired in a deep slump and playing through injury, and Ross was seen as the superior defender. Gonzalez was rewarded with an early 2-0 lead off the bat of Ross, but a handful of Braves errors later contributed to six Cardinals runs.

Trailing 6-3 in the eighth, the Braves had an opportunity to chip away at the lead. With runners on first and second, Andrelton Simmons popped up to shallow left field. Kozma appeared to line up the ball and then dodged out of the way, acting as though he thought Matt Holliday had called him off (he had not). At that same moment, left field umpire Sam Holbrook signaled the infield fly rule. The ball fell, the runners advanced, and Simmons was out.

After an extended delay to clear beer bottles thrown onto the field by disgruntled fans, the Braves loaded the bases but were unable to capitalize. The Cardinals held onto their 6-3 lead and moved onto the Division Series.

Game MVP: Holliday's home run in the top of the sixth turned out to be the eventual game-winning run, yet it was Ross who contributed the best game. His 3-for-4 effort included an early home run, two RBIs, and .037 ChampAdded.

Game Goat: By the numbers, Braves starter Kris Medlen, who allowed five runs (two earned) in 6.1 innings. His -.032 ChampAdded reflects those five runs allowed.

In truth, this honor was shared by Chipper Jones, Dan Uggla, or Simmons. All three made crucial errors in the field that led to runs. Simmons also made two of the most critical outs at the plate—including that infield fly.

Big Play: Ross opened the scoring with a two-run home run in the fourth. The play was worth .026 ChampAdded but wasn't enough to help secure a Braves victory.

AL Wild Card: Baltimore Orioles vs. Texas Rangers

On paper, the match-up of Yu Darvish vs. Joe Saunders did not favor the Orioles. In reality, the Orioles rode a 1-1 game into the sixth, when they proceeded to score the game-winning run. The game remained tight until the ninth, when the Orioles added a pair of insurance runs off Rangers closer Joe Nathan. The Orioles won 5-1.

Game MVP: One of the many beautiful things about baseball is that it so frequently offers up unlikely heroes. When the Orioles sent Saunders to oppose Darvish, many groaned that the Orioles would find themselves with an early deficit.

He appeared as though he would live up to that expectation when he allowed a first-inning run. Instead of collapsing, though, he managed 5.2 innings of one-run ball before handing the baton to the bullpen. His effort was worth .034 ChampAdded.

Game Goat: Josh Hamilton wins the ignominious honor with an 0-for-4 performance worth -.024 ChampAdded. He's entering free agency after a chaotic season that included a fast start to the season followed by a deep midsummer slump.

Big Play: In the Orioles' half of the sixth inning, Nate McLouth led off with a single. Chris Davis followed with the big play of the game. He grounded a single to right field that allowed McLouth to advance to third base. The play was worth .015 ChampAdded.

Most analysts would point to the next at-bat as the big play, when Adam Jones lofted a sac fly that scored McLouth. That was the eventual game-winning run, but the play itself had a slightly negative value according to ChampAdded.

NL Division Series: San Francisco Giants vs. Cincinnati Reds

Two games into the postseason, it looked like a quick exit from the playoffs for the Giants. The Reds decisively won those first two games of the series in San Francisco. They outscored the Giants by a total of 14-2.

With the Reds needing only one win at home, the Giants came back to reel off three straight victories. Game Three was a closely fought match. The Reds opened the scoring with a first-inning run which the Giants matched in the third. The score remained tied at 1-1 until the Giants added another run in the top of the 10th inning. Scott Rolen contributed an error that allowed Buster Posey to score.

The Giants cruised to their first easy victory in Game Four and an outburst of scoring in the fifth inning of Game Five proved too difficult for the Reds to overcome.

Series MVP: Brandon Crawford barely edged Sergio Romo for MVP honors with .041 ChampAdded. Taken as a whole, Crawford's NLDS was a poor showing. He went 2-for-11 with three walks and four strikeouts. What he lacked in overall value, though, he made up for with timeliness. His two hits came in Game Five of the series. His first hit drove in the first run of the game and he later scored.

Series Goat: Ryan Hanigan quietly put together a rough series. His three runs and three RBI belie a 3-for-15 performance with no extra base hits. A double play in the second inning of Game Five and a strikeout in the sixth contributed to the majority of his -.058 ChampAdded.

Big Play: Crawford's RBI triple opened up the scoring in the fifth inning of the pivotal game. The play alone was worth .051 ChampAdded and the Giants ultimately scored all six of their runs in that frame.

NL Division Series: St. Louis Cardinals vs. Washington Nationals

Having survived the Wild Card game, the Cardinals found themselves pitted against the 98-win Nationals.

The Nationals took Game One with the help of an eighth-inning, two-run rally. That 3-2 victory was a harbinger of things to come later in this series. First, though, the Cardinals struck back in the next two games by outscoring the Nationals 20-4.

That set the stage for a pair of dramatic finishes. Game Four was tightly contested. After three innings, the score was tied 1-1. That held up until the bottom of the ninth, when Jayson Werth launched a walk-off, solo home run.

With everything on the line, the Nats tidily won the first eight innings of Game Five, but then imploded in the ninth. Drew Storen's fourth appearance of the series was a disasterpiece. The four runs he allowed turned a 7-5 lead into a 9-7 deficit.

Somewhere, somebody is wondering if Stephen Strasburg could have saved the Nats.

Series MVP: Daniel Descalso had a strong series. The utility infielder drove in six runs and scored seven with the help of two home runs. All told, he compiled .115 ChampAdded, which is quite a total that early in the postseason. His .684 slugging percentage in the series was higher than his career OPS of .654

Series Goat: Storen parlayed a comfortable Game Five lead into offseason golf plans. The Nationals opened the top of the ninth inning up two runs and exited it down by two. Carlos Beltran led off with a double, but it was mostly a two-out rally capped by Kozma that did the damage. For the series, Storen received credit for a brutal -.179 ChampAdded.

Big Play: Kozma's two-run single with two outs in the ninth inning of that final game gave the Cardinals their first lead of the evening. The play was worth .103 ChampAdded.

AL Division Series: Oakland Athletics vs. Detroit Tigers

This may have been the most exciting series of the postseason. Four of the five games were nail-biters.

Coco Crisp started the series off on a good foot for the Athletics with a leadoff, solo home run against Justin Verlander. That was the last whimper for the Athletics in Game One. Verlander allowed only two more hits in seven innings of work. The Tigers took the game 3-1.

Game Two was a hard-fought match with the two teams trading leads multiple times. The Tigers entered the bottom of the eighth trailing 4-3. They managed to tie the game in the eighth and added the game-winning run in the ninth.

Just one win from the ALCS, the Tigers were blanked by Brett Anderson and friends in Game Three. In Game Four, Tigers closer Jose Valverde blew a 3-1 lead in the ninth inning.

The Athletics never got going in Game Five. Verlander provided the Tigers with a complete-game shutout in which he faced just 31 batters (four batters more than the minimum).

Series MVP: Verlander stifled the Athletics across 16 innings which included a complete game shutout in the pivotal Game Five. He allowed one run and struck out 22 while limiting A's batters to seven hits. The performance was good for .085 ChampAdded.

Series Goat: Valverde imploded in the ninth inning of Game Four, allowing three runs and taking the loss. His -.116 ChampAdded reflects the pain of blowing a series-clinching game.

This was just the opening bell of a terrible postseason for Valverde, although the Tigers limited the damage by using him sparingly.

Big Play: Coco Crisp delivered a walk-off single against Valverde in Game 4 of the series. Seth Smith scored on the play, which was worth .050 ChampAdded.

AL Division Series: Baltimore Orioles vs. New York Yankees

For the first time in the Wild Card era, two teams from the same division met in the Division Series round. Back in April, any self-respecting baseball fan would have scoffed at the suggestion that these two teams would meet in the first round of the postseason—including many Orioles fans. That is the beauty of baseball.

This was a fantastic series, with the teams trading wins back and forth. The Yankees struck first and so also struck last, but three one-run games—including two extra inning affairs—added plenty of excitement.

Raul Ibanez earned himself postseason notoriety, hitting both a game-tying and game-winning home run in the third game of the series. Remove that clutch performance and the Yankees lose in four games.

Series MVP: CC Sabathia quietly outshone Ibanez's heroics. He dominated the series in two starts, going 17.2 innings while allowing only three runs. The Orioles struggled to reach base against him with only 12 hits, three walks and 16 strikeouts. Altogether, Sabathia earned .130 ChampAdded.

Series Goat: J.J. Hardy had an unpleasant series, going just 3-for-22 with a ChampAdded of -.074. He made a few critical outs in the final game of the series that contributed to his total.

Big Play: The two biggest plays in the series came off the bat of Ibanez in Game Three. His game-tying, solo home run in the ninth was technically the biggest play, with a ChampAdded of .058, but his game-winning homer in the 12th might have been more memorable. That drive was worth .045 ChampAdded.

NL Championship Series: St. Louis Cardinals vs. San Francisco Giants

With the pressure of elimination finally relieved, the Giants got out to a slow start, losing three of the first four games to the Cardinals. As in the series against the Reds, the Giants dug one final trench and held their ground, defeating the Cardinals in three lopsided games.

While the series was interesting since it stretched the full seven games, none of the games were particularly stressful. The Cardinals won the first and third games by two runs, but the remaining five contests were decided by at least five runs. The crowning blow in the last was the weird double that scooted past Kozma after Pence's bat broke in the process of striking the ball three times.

Series MVP: After a disappointing NLDS, Marco Scutaro caught fire at the perfect time for the Giants. He swatted 14 hits in 28 at-bats to go along with six runs and four RBI. He played a pivotal role in Games Six and Seven, in which he contributed the bulk of his run production. All told, he had a series total of .149 ChampAdded.

Series Goat: The Cardinals began the series by winning three of the first four games. That accomplished, they had to win just one out of three games to advance to their second consecutive World Series. Instead, they found themselves in deep holes when their starting pitchers allowed crooked numbers early in the final three games. Per ChampAdded, the worst offender was Chris Carpenter, though his -.136 ChampAdded might overstate his poor performance, since Kozma contributed with a costly error.

Big Play: The biggest play of the NLCS came early in Game Seven. In the bottom of the first with Angel Pagan on first, Scutaro laced a single to left. Pagan advanced to third on the play. On the next play, Pagan scored the first run of the game. It also turned out to be the game-winning run. Scutaro's hit was worth .049 ChampAdded.

AL Championship Series: Detroit Tigers vs. New York Yankees

Somewhere there must be a book detailing all the rules of sports writing. And somewhere in this book, it states that anything that can be named, shall be named. Thus we have "Annihilation Series," the term used to describe the Tigers utter… annihilation of the Yankees. The Tigers never once trailed in the series and the Yankees rarely even threatened to take a lead.

Game One held that one vague threat. The Yankees trailed the Tigers 4-0 heading into the bottom of the ninth inning. Valverde contributed another meltdown, capped by a game-tying home run from Ibanez. The Tigers reclaimed the lead in the 12th inning and closed out the game. The remaining games were all Tigers from start to finish.

Series MVP: In a race that was almost a tie, Anibal Sanchez's strong pitching performance edged out Delmon Young's timely hitting. In Game Two of the series, Sanchez shut down the Yankees lineup over seven innings. He allowed just three hits along with four walks (one intentional) while striking out seven. That was good for .073 ChampAdded.

Young's two home runs and six RBIs in the series clocked in at .0729 ChampAdded. Good pitching and timely hitting contribute to postseason victories, and the Tigers got a generous helping of both in this series.

Series Goat: Despite throwing only two-thirds of an inning for a team that swept the series, Valverde still managed to lay claim to the Series Goat hardware. His -.081 ChampAdded was the result of his Game One failure. With a 4-0 lead in the bottom of the ninth, the Tigers brought on their closer and watched their lead evaporate after a walk, three hits, and two home runs. Phil Coke salvaged the inning and the Tigers ultimately won the game.

Valverde did not pitch again in the ALCS.

Big Play: The biggest play of the series had no effect on the outcome. Ibanez walked to the plate against Valverde in the bottom of the ninth of Game One.

Ichiro Suzuki had already delivered a two-run homer, but the Yankees still trailed by two runs with Mark Teixeira on base. Ibanez came through with the second two-run home run of the inning and tied the game. The play was worth .076 ChampAdded.

World Series: Detroit Tigers vs. San Francisco Giants

The Giants jumped out to a 1-0 series lead with an 8-3 victory in Game One. The Tigers then forgot how to score. They lost the next two games 2-0.

The final game might have been interesting had the series not already been 3-0. The Giants opened the scoring at 1-0 with a RBI triple from Brandon Belt. Miguel Cabrera answered with an opposite-field, two-run home run. In the sixth, Buster Posey briefly gave the Giants a 3-2 lead with a two-run home run of his own before Young tied the game with a solo shot in the bottom of the inning. The game remained 3-3 through regulation. In the top of the 10th, playoff hero Scutaro delivered the final run of the postseason, sealing a 4-3 Giants victory and a series sweep.

Series MVP: Pablo Sandoval won the World Series MVP award and it's hard to deny him the honor since he put together some gaudy statistics. He went 8-for-16 in the series with three home runs in Game One. That translates to a triple slash line of .500/.529/1.125. ChampAdded credits him with a total of .059.

However, as wonderful as Sandoval's performance was, Madison Bumgarner's strong Game Two performance took home the gold in the eyes of ChampAdded. Bumgarner stifled the Tigers' offense over seven innings, allowing only two hits, two walks, and one hit batsman. He also struck out eight. His ChampAdded of .126 more than doubled Sandoval's total.

Series Goat: The Tigers received disappointing contributions from two of their three best players. Prince Fielder earned Series Goat "honors" by going just 1-for-14 with a pair of double plays. All told, he came to the plate 15 times and was responsible for 15 outs. That utter dearth of production resulted in -.101 ChampAdded.

Fielder's poor play lets Justin Verlander off the hook for his Game One performance. The Tigers had to feel good about opening the series with Verlander facing Barry Zito. Prior to the World Series, Verlander had been masterful in 24.1 innings with only two runs and 10 hits allowed. Against the Giants, he allowed six hits in four innings, including two home runs to Sandoval. Verlander's clunker was worth -.089 ChampAdded.

Big Play: Scutaro didn't put forth as superhuman an effort in the World Series as he did in the NLCS, but he did deliver the series-clinching run in the 10th inning of Game Four. With two outs and Ryan Theriot at second, Scutaro delivered a single up the middle that brought Theriot in. The play was worth .045 ChampAdded.

Overall Playoffs

Player	Team	ChampAdded
Marco Scutaro	SFG	0.196
Raul Ibanez	NYY	0.171
Ryan Vogelsong	SFG	0.165
CC Sabathia	NYY	0.146
Doug Fister	DET	0.135
Darren O'Day	BAL	0.132
Sergio Romo	SFG	0.107
Pablo Sandoval	SFG	0.100
Anibal Sanchez	DET	0.091
Barry Zito	SFG	0.087

Playoff MVP: At the July trade deadline, the Giants traded Charlie Culberson to the Colorado Rockies for a journeyman utility infielder by the name of Marco Scutaro. The return on that investment was huge.

In the regular season, Scutaro gave the Giants a healthy .362/.385/.473 line in 268 plate appearances. He continued his hitting ways in the postseason with a .328/.377/.391 line that included several timely hits and 11 runs scored.

Player	Team	ChampAdded
Jose Valverde	DET	-0.192
Drew Storen	WSN	-0.179
Prince Fielder	DET	-0.140
Nick Swisher	NYY	-0.116
Alex Rodriguez	NYY	-0.114
Robinson Cano	NYY	-0.105
Kyle Lohse	STL	-0.102
Lance Lynn	STL	-0.096
Jhonny Peralta	DET	-0.095
Chris Carpenter	STL	-0.089

Playoff Goat: Traditional and advanced statistics agree that Jose Valverde was Chief Goat. In 2.2 innings, he faced 22 batters and allowed 11 hits, one walk, and nine runs. Do the math and you come away with a 30.38 ERA and -.192 ChampAdded. He blew a two-run lead in the ALDS and a four-run lead in the ALCS, and allowed two more runs in the World Series while recording just one out.

The Nationals' closer, Drew Storen, came close to beating Valverde despite ending his postseason in the NLDS. Storen's first three outings were uneventful. He allowed one walk in three innings while earning a win and a save. Those outings totaled a healthy .034 ChampAdded.

Unfortunately, giving up four runs in the ninth inning of a winner-take-all contest will undo quite a bit of good will. The outing alone was worth -.213 ChampAdded. To put that in perspective, the next worst performance in the entire playoffs was Kyle Lohse's poor outing in Game Seven of the NLCS. That one scored -.125.

Commentary

The Year in Frivolity

by Craig Calcaterra

This book is chock full of information about the 2012 baseball season. If you read even a portion of it and don't know who won, who lost, and why this past year, there's no helping you.

But you can be forgiven if you forgot the year's ephemeral, trivial, embarrassing and pathetic events. That stuff doesn't stick in a fan's mind, like who won the Most Valuable Player Award. That's why I'm here. So, without further ado, I give you an overview of all things funny, sad, stupid and ignominious from the 2012 baseball season!

Spring Training

The Cardinals and White Sox begin spring training with rookie managers at the helm, both of whom have absolutely no managerial experience whatsoever. There are legitimate questions about whether Mike Matheny and Robin Ventura will be able to grasp the subtleties and nuances of a big league managerial job like an experienced skipper can. You know, guys like the Red Sox' new manager, Bobby Valentine.

In late March, Chipper Jones announces he will retire at the conclusion of the season. He says there is no one specific reason why he wants to call it a career now, but notes that it will be nice to spend more time with his knees, which retired back in 2004.

The Mets begin the season with new dimensions at Citi Field that are designed to make the place more hitter-friendly. Opposing hitters thank the Mets for their generosity, as they plan to take far greater advantage of the new dimensions than the Mets hitters are capable of doing.

Despite his promise and obvious skill, the Angels decide to break camp without Mike Trout, who is sent to Triple-A. This is of no consequence, however, given that the Angels and their new high-profile free agent signings clearly will have no need for Trout's services as they cruise to the division title.

In a late spring training game, Indians starter Ubaldo Jimenez intentionally plunks Rockies shortstop Troy Tulowitzki in retaliation for critical comments Tulowitzki made about Jimenez when they were teammates the previous year. After the incident, Jimenez claims he did not mean to hit Tulowitzki. While that seems implausible given the circumstances, anyone who has seen him pitch since 2010 will agree that hitting an intended target is not exactly Jimenez's strong suit.

Jayson Werth, when asked about his poor 2011 season and his future prospects in Washington, voices confidence about the new year and says, "I'll look back, and 2011 will be a fart in the wind." Werth is immediately awarded the Pulitzer Prize for poetry and the Nobel Prize for physics, on account of being the first person ever to actually look back and see a fart.

April

Marlins Park opens in Miami, representing the most conspicuous change for the new-look Marlins. The most notable feature of the park: a gigantic home run sculpture featuring garish colors, sounds, and motions every time a Marlins player hits a home run. It is expected that this monstrosity will cause a distraction for fans and players alike as many as a dozen times this season.

New Marlins manager Ozzie Guillen creates a controversy in Miami when he gives an interview in which he notes his "respect" for Fidel Castro. After an uproar, the Marlins—with the full support of Major League Baseball—suspends Guillen five games for his insensitivity in arguably lending some kind of legitimacy and support to the hated Cuban dictator. When asked how Guillen could be suspended for an off-the-cuff opinion about Castro when, back in 1999, the Orioles went down to Havana, met with Castro in an official capacity and played the Cuban national team in an exhibition, Bud Selig placed a finger in each ear and said "nanananana, I can't hear you," over and over again.

Following a game in New York, Tigers outfielder Delmon Young is arrested for public intoxication and for allegedly shouting anti-Semitic epithets at passers-by. He is subsequently suspended by MLB. In a statement, Selig says that Major League Baseball has no tolerance for its players walking down a sidewalk drunk and hurling hurtful words at people. MLB continues, however, to have a hands-off approach to players driving down a road drunk and hurling 4,000-pound vehicles at people.

On April 21, journeyman swingman Philip Humber throws a perfect game for the White Sox. A rare feat indeed! Wow!

Valentine and Curt Schilling get into a public spat, with Schilling saying that Valentine was the wrong man to take over the Red Sox, and Valentine saying that Schilling doesn't know what he's talking about. Boys, boys, can't we just agree that you're both right and stop this bickering?

Jones makes his final visit to Houston to play the Astros. In a touching development that becomes standard in each city in which Jones plays his final game, the Astros present him with a gift. It's a rice cooker, which the Astros' brother-in-law gave them last Christmas, but it is very nice, and no one is the wiser.

May

On May 2, Jered Weaver throws a no-hitter for the Angels. A somewhat less rare feat than usual given Humber's perfecto 11 days previously, but pretty cool all the same!

Mariano Rivera tears his anterior cruciate ligament (ACL) in his right knee while shagging fly balls in the outfield before a game, ending his season. Before doing so, he predicts that if he is struck down he shall become more powerful than opposing hitters can possibly imagine. Throughout the season his ghostly visage appears whenever Rafael Soriano needs his guidance and support.

Jones plays his last game in Cincinnati, where he is presented with a trophy of the actual third base bag from Great American Ballpark. Every other team yet to bid Jones farewell mutters angrily under its breath about how the Reds took the lowest hanging fruit possible, and about how they actually have to put some thought into their gift now.

A game at Marlins Park is delayed for nearly 25 minutes when a group of teenagers wander onto the field, believing that they were on the 16th hole of the miniature golf course on which they had been playing. "I mean, really," one of them says, "There's a pool, a fish tank, a revolving sculpture with an aquatic theme and bright neon colors everywhere. How were we supposed to know this was a ballpark?"

Former Red Sox pitcher Dennis "Oil Can" Boyd reveals in interviews that he used crack cocaine before every game of the 1986 season, including a start in Oakland where he claims he kept a vial of crack stuffed in his ball cap during the game. Looking back at the box scores reveals his only start in Oakland that year to be on May 11. His line: 7 IP, 4 H, 4 ER, 2 BB, 2 K, with three homers allowed. One of the homers was hit by Jose Canseco, making it the most drugged up homer in the history of baseball. At least until April 21, 1990, anyway, when Boyd gave up a home run to Darryl Strawberry.

Roger Clemens is on trial in Washington arising out of his 2008 testimony before Congress in which he stated that he never took performance-enhancing drugs. The prosecution's star witness is Andy Pettitte, who is expected to establish that Clemens admitted to taking PEDs. On the stand, however, Pettitte says Clemens never told him that. This brings Pettitte's career record to 240 wins, 138 losses and one save.

June

On June 1, Johan Santana throws a no-hitter for the Mets. Um, how nice. I suppose this is becoming a monthly thing now, but no-hitters are still feats that do not happen too terribly often, so we should offer kudos and accolades.

On June 8, Kevin Millwood, Brandon League, Tom Wilhelmsen, Charlie Furbush, Stephen Pryor and Lucas Luetge combine to throw a no-hitter for the Mariners. Oh, for Pete's sake, this is getting tiresome. Good job, boys. I guess.

Jones and the Braves play an interleague game against the Red Sox in Boston. Given that it's an interleague matchup, Jones has not played many games at Fenway, and thus, his history there is nowhere near as notable as it is with National League teams, so the Red Sox are at a bit of a loss as to what to give him for a retirement gift. They settle on a $15 gift card from Dunkin' Donuts, and an awkward man-hug with a pat on the back and considerable distance between their torsos.

On June 13, Matt Cain throws a perfect game for the Giants. What are you waiting for, Cain? A pat on the head? Get out of here, this is old hat now.

Following a months-long trial and concluding a years-long prosecution, Clemens is acquitted of perjury charges. On the courthouse steps, Clemens claims vindication and notes that, apart from the world finding out about abscesses on his buttocks, his wife's drug use and his adultery with a drug-and-alcohol addled underage country singer—and apart from the entire thing costing him millions in legal fees—his decision to deny his obvious PED use was totally worth it.

First the Rockies and then the Orioles release 49-year-old pitcher Jamie Moyer. The Blue Jays then release Vladimir Guerrero who, while still in his 30s, moves as though he was 49. And had sustained multiple leg fractures. Their baseball careers seemingly over, Moyer and Guerrero embark on a string of financially successful but critically panned buddy movies with Moyer as the Jack Lemmon character and Guerrero in the Walter Matthau role.

R.A. Dickey pitches a controversial one-hitter against the Rays. The source of the controversy: the game's lone hit, a first inning single by B.J. Upton, easily could have been ruled an error. The Mets appeal the ruling, arguing that David Wright should have been charged with an E-5. The appeal is unsuccessful, but most agree it's for the best inasmuch as, if it had prevailed, it would have rendered the no-hitter "cheap." And that's something the Mets simply can not ever be accused of.

July

After a series of controversial calls in the season's first half, commissioner Selig holds a press conference in which he denies the need to expand instant replay. Selig says, "People in our sport don't want any more. Given our attendance and everything we're doing, we're in the right place with instant replay." He later said that he had no reason to visit the doctor given how large his bank account is and how much his wife loves him.

In the same press conference, after noting that part of his reason for opposing more replay is that he does not like tinkering with tradition and messing with fans' expectations, Selig says that he and Joe Torre are seriously considering having interleague games in NL parks feature the designated hitter and interleague games in American League parks feature pitchers batting. Because if there is any tradition that NL fans love more than the designated hitter and AL fans love more than pitchers batting, it's news to him.

As is the case every July, the teams who are out of it and have a rebuilding plan start shopping their useful but marketable players to contenders as the trade deadline approaches. None of this describes a single aspect of the Astros trading Carlos Lee to the Marlins, but the deal goes down anyway.

David Ortiz says in an interview that he was "humiliated" by the way he was treated by the Boston Red Sox in the course of contract negotiations during the previous offseason. "As a member of the Boston Red Sox, I much prefer to be humiliated during the regular season," Ortiz later added.

Tony La Russa comes out of retirement to manage the NL in the All-Star Game. While most managers would think leaving the game victorious in the seventh game of the World Series could not be topped, La Russa tells the media that he could think of no better ending to his career than to manage a game in which he can make ten pitching changes in nine innings and have no one question him about it afterward.

Because of an early ejection in the second-to-last game before the All-Star break, a start the next day in the first half's final game and then four days off before the second half begins, Zack Greinke starts three games in a row for the Brewers. The ghosts of Cy Young, Pud Galvin and Old Hoss Radbourn laugh and mock that anyone considers this to be a notable accomplishment.

A war of words breaks out between Yankees first baseman Mark Teixeira and Red Sox pitcher Vicente Padilla. Teixeira says that Padilla "does not have many friends in the game." Padilla fires back, questioning Teixeira's masculinity and saying that he should "play a women's sport." The next day, the Yankees sign Serena Williams, Gina Carano, Misty May-Treanor, Stephanie Rice, Lolo Jones and the entire U.S. women's gymnastics team, who go 15-for-19 against Padilla with six homers before he is chased to the showers.

The video board operator at Fenway Park runs a replay of a controversial call on a putout at first base in a Yankees-Red Sox game, causing the crowd to boo furiously upon viewing it. The next day, a Major League Baseball official calls the Red Sox, reminding them of a rule in place that prohibits teams from showing replays of such calls for fear of inciting the crowd. The official also reminds the Red Sox that war is peace, freedom is slavery, ignorance is strength and that Oceania has always been at war with Eastasia.

It is revealed that Red Sox players attended a team meeting with the team's owners in which they blasted manager Valentine and said that they could no longer play for him. At particular issue was the players' dissatisfaction with Valentine's harsh treatment of them during the Sox' recent breadfruit gathering expedition to the south seas, and their attraction to the idyllic life on the Pacific island of Tahiti, to which they wished to return.

August

A nasty rumor begins flying around that Giants outfielder Melky Cabrera has tested positive for performance-enhancing drugs. Reporter Andrew Baggarly of CSNBayArea.com asks Cabrera about it, and Cabrera denies it. Baggarly then writes a public apology to Cabrera for his poor judgment, which is the only appropriate thing to do given such an egregious lapse in professional judgment.

Reggie Jackson gives an interview in which he says that he hates "showboating" players, players who are "arrogant" and players who focus too much on their personal style. Meanwhile, the real Reggie Jackson remains trapped in an alien pod someplace trying to figure out how to escape his kidnappers.

Nationals pitching coach Steve McCatty gives an interview in which he says "strikeouts are bulls**t," and talks about how he'd rather have guys get groundball outs. McCatty is then sued for copyright infringement by the writer of the movie, *Bull Durham*, and sued for slander by Nationals starters Stephen Strasburg and Gio Gonzalez, who are currently No. 1 and No. 3 in the league in strikeouts per nine innings pitched. McCatty is unaware of the lawsuits, however, because of his general obliviousness.

Speaking of Mr. Strasburg, a months-long controversy begins to build as it is revealed that the Nationals intend to shut down their ace pitcher when he reaches 160 innings pitched, and to not reactive him even if they make the playoffs. Nationals general manager Mike Rizzo faces heavy criticism over the decision but dismisses it, noting that it's highly improbable that one decent pitching performance in a short playoff series could be the difference between the Nats advancing or going home.

On August 15, Felix Hernandez throws a perfect game for the Mariners. We've reached the point where it's more newsworthy to report when pitchers do not throw perfect games.

Jones plays his last game in San Francisco. As a retirement gift, the Giants present him with a proclamation that, henceforth, he shall be entitled to one pig every month, as well, as "two comely lasses of virtue true."

In a blockbuster deal, Adrian Gonzalez, Carl Crawford, Josh Beckett and Nick Punto are traded to the Los Angeles Dodgers in exchange for James Loney, Rubby De La Rosa, Allen Webster, Jerry Sands and Ivan De Jesus Jr. Meanwhile Dustin Pedroia, Clay Buchholz and the other mutineers against Valentine settle on Pitcairn Island with their Tahitian consorts.

Giants outfielder Melky Cabrera is suspended for 50 games after testing positive for performance-enhancing drugs. Baggarly sorta wishes he hadn't offered that apology earlier in the month.

A's pitcher Bartolo Colon is suspended for 50 games after testing positive for performance-enhancing drugs. In his case, Major League Baseball feels obligated to note that "PEDs" does not stand for Pastries: Eclairs and Danishes.

The back-to-back suspensions of Cabrera and Colon lead many baseball scribes to call for a change in the way Major League Baseball tests for performance-enhancing drugs. Because apparently a system that never catches anyone is better than one that does.

September

Clemens, fresh off his acquittal for perjury, mounts a comeback to baseball by signing a contract with the Sugarland Skeeters of the independent Atlantic League.

Many see the stint in the indies as a prelude to a dramatic comeback to Major League Baseball. Others disagree, thinking that it may just result in a couple of starts for the Houston Astros.

The baseball world waits all summer for the Orioles to fall back to Earth, but they continue their winning ways. The credit goes mostly to the bullpen, some to Buck Showalter and a lot to a temporarily team-friendly contract with The Dark Angel Lucifer, the Father of All Lies.

Following through on their plans, the Washington Nationals shut down Strasburg, banking on a playoff rotation of Gio Gonzalez, Jordan Zimmermann, Edwin Jackson and Ross Detwiler. In related developments, students stop studying for tests figuring they know the material cold, drivers stop wearing seat belts figuring they won't get into accidents, and the army stops issuing Kevlar vests assuming that the enemy can't shoot straight.

Great dissatisfaction among the chattering classes begins as it becomes apparent that Melky Cabrera, despite his suspension for PEDs, is likely to be the 2012 NL batting champion. As a result, Major League Baseball announces that the rules that determine a player's batting average in the event that he falls short of 502 plate appearances will be suspended in Cabrera's case, rendering him ineligible for the batting crown. Later that day, Adam Dunn and Miguel Cabrera ask for the rules determining who leads the league in strikeouts and grounding into doubles plays be suspended, respectively.

Jones' retirement tour continues, as he plays his last game in New York against the team he has tormented most of all, the Mets. His gift: a paternity test, so that Mets fans might, once and for all, accept that Jones is their daddy.

As the season winds to a close, a great debate rages over who should win the AL Most Valuable Player Award, with one faction supporting the player with good numbers in some random statistical categories and the other faction imploring its opponents to get their heads out of the stat sheets and actually watch their guy play a baseball game once in a while to see just how damn good an all-around player he is. Of course, those stat nerds in the Baseball Writers Association of America will never leave their mom's basements long enough to realize that they're wrong about supporting Miguel Cabrera over Trout.

On September 28, Homer Bailey throws a no-hitter for the Reds. Given the new standards of excellence for starting pitchers in 2012, Bailey is roundly criticized in the media for not throwing a perfect game. Reds GM Walt Jocketty looks into releasing Bailey and signing Humber.

October

The regular season ends with the Athletics as AL West champions, the Orioles as a 93-win wild card team that fought the Yankees for the division title until the last week and the Phillies and Red Sox with depressing losing records. Despite this, everyone will do preseason predictions this coming spring as if we all aren't just making this stuff up as we go along.

Valentine is fired by the Red Sox. Following his dismissal, he and his loyal lieutenants are placed in a small launch and make a seemingly impossible 3,618 nautical-mile voyage to Timor, where at press time they await transport back to Boston, where they hope to obtain the use of a ship with which they can pursue the mutineers and bring them to justice.

The Nationals lose the NL Division Series in five games to the St. Louis Cardinals. In the course of the series, the Nationals get one quality start out of their rotation and surrender 32 runs. A defiant Rizzo says that having Strasburg on the roster would have made no difference. Rizzo then goes on to say that black is white, walks out of his office and is tragically killed at the next zebra crossing.

The Giants announce that even though would-be batting champion Melky Cabrera is eligible to come off his drug suspension in time for the NL Championship Series, they will not add him to the postseason roster. When reached for comment, Giants general manager Brian Sabean says that he was inspired by the example of Rizzo and the Nationals. In keeping with baseball's finest follow-the-leader tradition, the Cardinals announce the preemptive deactivation of Carlos Beltran, the Tigers put Justin Verlander in a box and ship him to China, and the Yankees arrange to have Derek Jeter's ankle broken.

Sorry. Too soon?

Oakland Okey Dokes AL West

by Dan Lependorf

Upon the beginning of the 2012 season, Baseball Prospectus launched their daily postseason odds calculation. They arrive at this number by simulating the season over and over and over again, keeping track of the playoff qualifiers each time. The Oakland Athletics were near the bottom of the list with a three percent probability of making the postseason, ahead of only Seattle, Kansas City, and Minnesota in the American League.

But honestly, who in their right mind would have picked the A's? They had just finished a difficult 74-win season in 2011, and the franchise had failed to post a winning record for the fifth straight year. During the offseason, general manager Billy Beane completely tore down the roster, trading away four starting pitchers and their closer, who had combined for four career All-Star selections.

Things looked dim. But things don't always turn out as expected. The A's ended up making the postseason and adding 20 victories to their win total.

The 2012 A's are the best story of the year, but to tell it properly, it has to start all the way back with *Moneyball*.

Everyone knows the tale. In 2002, reeling after losing former MVP Jason Giambi to a $120 million contract from the New York Yankees, Beane and the A's had to scramble to patch the hole. The outcome inspired a book that sat on the *New York Times* bestseller list, which inspired a movie that garnered six Academy Award nominations, all of which had an incalculable effect on the public acceptance of data analysis in baseball.

But while the 2002 Athletics were being lauded for ingenious decision-making in the wake of the book and the film, the team had started to fade into mediocrity. What happened after *Moneyball*? How did the A's torpedo themselves in the latter half of the decade, only to rise up in 2012 and secure one of the most improbable division titles in baseball history?

It's really a story of three demolitions.

In 2004, Beane knew he needed to make a move. The A's had failed to qualify for the postseason after four consecutive years of playoff appearances, and his talent core was rapidly getting too expensive for the small-market club. And while the 2002 team was able to compensate for the loss of 2000 MVP Giambi with some nifty patchwork, doing the same with their trio of fan favorite All-Star pitchers would take some extra work and a little head start.

October 2, 2004

Barry Zito had thrown seven fantastic innings, and he left the game with a two-run lead. What else could you ask of a starting pitcher?

The A's were in a do-or-die situation, needing to win two of the three games in the final regular season series to clinch a postseason berth over the Angels. They dropped the first game, letting Anaheim score early and often on the way to a 10-0 blowout. But as Zito walked off the mound in the second game, the A's were six outs away from setting up a climactic final game for their fifth appearance in the playoffs in as many years. The A's needed just six outs.

They managed to get only one. The Angels' Darin Erstad doubled in the eighth inning, driving home Curtis Pride and Chone Figgins. A's reliever Ricardo Rincon walked the ever-dangerous Vladimir Guerrero, and then Erstad crossed the plate on a Troy Glaus single. The A's wouldn't record another hit on the day, and they were left to watch the Angels celebrate in the Athletics' own stadium. The A's had lost four AL Division Series Game Fives in a row. This year, they wouldn't even get the chance.

In December, months after falling just shy of the division title, Beane made his moves:

- 12/16/04: RHP Tim Hudson traded to Atlanta for LHP Dan Meyer, RHP Juan Cruz, and OF Charles Thomas.
- 12/18/04: LHP Mark Mulder traded to St. Louis for RHP Dan Haren, RHP Kiko Calero, and C Daric Barton.

Prospect valuation can be a difficult game at times. The minor leagues serve as a winnowing process, the levels of competition act like a progressively narrowing filter. Prospects who succeed get promoted to higher and higher levels of competition, while those who fail get left behind. A tantalizing prospect in Triple-A with a league-leading batting line is worth a lot more than an identical prospect with an identical batting line in Single-A, simply because the Triple-A prospect has passed through a few more layers of the filter.

Beane had to make a calculated decision, and he chose to target upper-level prospects and major league rookies. This is the same general manager who famously preferred college players in the *Moneyball* draft over high school athletes for the same reason. A large amount of the young boom-or-bust talent with sky-high potential is plucked from high school before college, so college players on the whole tend to be a little more polished and a little less risky, with the tradeoff being lower upside. For a guy popularly known as a radical iconoclast, willing to trade away anyone and everyone, Beane has quietly been rather conservative with his team-building.

Of course, other general managers have similar thought processes on prospect valuation. So if Beane wanted to get low-risk players in return for his two star pitchers, he would have to either sacrifice quantity or quality. Beane did both. For Mulder and Hudson, the A's received four players with significant major league time, a Triple-A pitcher, and a Low-A catcher.

It made sense at the time. The A's had a talented squad, and while replacing pitchers of such a high caliber is never easy, Beane figured that the A's would be able to continue their success if they paused just a bit to reload. He kept Zito, but traded Mulder and Hudson a year before free agency to grab an infusion of talent and some spending money. A pitcher here, a free-agent hitter there, and the A's would be right back where they started.

The problem? Beane didn't receive very much for his low-risk investment. It's immediately obvious, purely by name recognition alone, that it didn't work out. The three players Oakland received for Hudson totaled -1.1 WAR in an A's uniform. Meyer was waived after a handful of seasons marred by injuries and poor performance, while Cruz and Thomas were quickly traded away after a couple of years for players of limited value. The Mulder trade turned out stronger, with an All-Star in Haren, but with the disappointing Hudson return, it was simply too little, too late.

The post-trade 2005 A's finished at 88 wins, seven games behind the division-leading Angels. The 2006 A's were forced to compensate for their poor trade returns by cashing in a few valuable minor league assets and making a few key free-agent signings. It worked. The A's again qualified for the playoffs, this time advancing to the AL Championship Series, but Beane smartly recognized in the offseason that he was holding a quickly decaying hand.

October 14, 2006

The A's were tied, 3-3, but the air was heavy with trepidation. They had finally, finally, advanced through the first round of the playoffs, and in emphatic fashion, too, sweeping the Twins just a week earlier. But in flew the Detroit Tigers, and the A's quickly found themselves down three games to none, grasping at their rapidly deteriorating chances at a World Series trophy. It was Game 4, and the score was tied.

Closer Huston Street jogged out to the mound once again in the bottom of the ninth, already having recorded a crucial game-saving double play in the bottom of the seventh. He had pitched a perfect eighth, as well, but Oakland's bullpen was quickly getting thin. Manager Ken Macha had to make a difficult decision and decided to use his closer for one more inning. Street had only been used for more than two innings twice in his career to date, but he was fairly well-rested, and he was the best pitcher left on the staff.

Street recorded the first two outs without incident, but Craig Monroe punched a belt-high slider into center field to keep the inning alive. On the very next pitch, Placido Polanco, who already had an incredible showing with eight hits on the series, smacked another belt-high slider into right field. Up came Magglio Ordonez.

Street turned and threw. A fastball, this time belt-high but inside. Ball one. Street stood atop the mound, watching Ordonez crouch in his stance, his bat twirling in little circles. Street fired again. Ordonez swung. The ball flew.

Ordonez watched it fly. He took a few slow, walking steps towards first base, keeping his eye on the ball the whole way. His teammates already had started sprinting out of the dugout. As it flew over the bullpen into the fifth, sixth, maybe the seventh row, Ordonez raised one, then two, fists into the air and broke into a victory lap around the bases. Polanco, forever goofy in his cold-weather balaclava, hopped all the way home. Ivan Rodriguez stood at the front of the exuberant crowd at home plate, bounding up and down.

Street's delivery took him a few steps off of the mound, and he spun around and trotted backwards a few steps as he watched the ball fly. As it cleared the wall, he turned around and hung his head, slowly walking back to the dugout. The A's had made it into the ALCS for the first time since 1992, but in four quick games, all of Oakland's hopes had extinguished into the cold Detroit night.

The second demolition happened in the aftermath of a disappointing 2007 campaign. After getting swept in the 2006 ALCS, the A's won only 76 games the following year. Zito was leaving in free agency, and the talent acquired in the Hudson and Mulder trades had failed to pan out. And so, Beane picked up the phone:

- 12/14/07: RHP Haren and RHP Connor Robertson traded to Arizona for LHP Brett Anderson, LHP Dana Eveland, LHP Greg Smith, 1B Chris Carter, OF Aaron Cunningham and OF Carlos Gonzalez.
- 1/3/08: OF Nick Swisher traded to Chicago White Sox for LHP Gio Gonzalez, RHP Fautino de los Santos and OF Ryan Sweeney.

Whether by design or by necessity, the return from these two trades showed a clear change in strategy. Burned by seeking out a small quantity of upper-level talent just three years earlier, Beane turned around and acquired the opposite. The A's received a large collection of raw talent—three players in Triple-A, two players in Double-A, three players in Single-A, and only a single player who had exhausted his rookie eligibility.

In total, Beane received three future cornerstones and a handful of valuable role players. By acquiring high-upside raw players in the lower levels of the minors, he had spent less and gained more. And just like the *Moneyball* A's earlier in the decade,

Oakland had a trio of quality starting pitchers at its disposal: Trevor Cahill, Anderson and Gonzalez.

And yet, it wasn't enough.

From the beginning of Beane's tenure as general manager until 2007, the A's scored an average of 817 runs per season. From 2008-2011, that mark fell to 678. With this second group of trades, Beane had managed to preserve Oakland's quality pitching, but the bats fell short. Beane compounded the problem by attempting his 2006 strategy in 2009. He traded future Rockies star Gonzalez, along with Street and Smith, for Matt Holliday, a big bat to put the A's back on top. Even with their new star hitter, the A's offense faltered, and Beane ended the Holliday experiment after 93 games.

For the first time since Beane's first year on the job, the A's were on track to lose more games than they won. And four years later, after continuously attempting and failing to find some offense to support the young pitching, Beane shrewdly planned one more demolition.

The 2011 A's were like many of the other A's teams in the second half of the 2000s. The pitching was solid, yet unspectacular, and the offense was poor across the board. The 2011 A's scored fewer runs than any Oakland team since the 54-108 A's in 1979, and the pitching wasn't good enough to make up the difference. The A's had a bright spot in their collection of young starting pitchers, but it simply wasn't enough. With a depleted farm system not able to contribute much in the way of reinforcements, Beane finally had to do something he had never done before.

The previous two demolitions were attempts to bolster the talent the A's already had. Beane had traded away Hudson and Mulder not to tear things down and rebuild, but to allow the franchise to keep its competitive window open. The 2002 A's replaced Giambi to continue winning with players like Zito, Mulder, Hudson, Eric Chavez and Miguel Tejada. The 2005 A's suffered after losing Mulder and Hudson, but the franchise came back the very next year on the strength of a similar cast of batters, joined by the young players acquired from the trade. The 2008 A's attempted to pull off a similar trick, but fell short.

Finally, with a franchise running on empty in 2011, Beane was forced to gut the roster for benefit in the long-term, while preparing for the worst in the short-term:

- 12/9/11: RHP Trevor Cahill and LHP Craig Breslow traded to Arizona for RHP Ryan Cook, OF Collin Cowgill and RHP Jarrod Parker.
- 12/23/11: LHP Gonzalez and RHP Robert Gilliam traded to Washington for RHP A.J. Cole, LHP Tommy Milone, C Derek Norris and RHP Brad Peacock.
- 12/28/11: RHP Andrew Bailey and OF Ryan Sweeney traded to Boston for 1B Miles Head, RHP Raul Alcantara and OF Josh Reddick.

Even though Beane had a reputation for shocking trades of beloved players, he had never attempted a complete roster overhaul like this. Five starting pitchers who started nearly 70 percent of Oakland's games were sent packing. In their place came a bevy of untested rookies and freely available cheap pickups.

In total, the A's gave two full-time rotation spots to rookies from day one. When two veteran starters had to bow out later in the year, the A's gave the available spots to two more players called up from Triple-A. By the end of the season, the A's had the most atypical roster in the league. They had a rotation consisting of five rookies, a first baseman who had been released twice in the two previous years, a third baseman who tore his ACL in February and was replaced by a catcher, a left fielder whom the A's signed out of Cuba with no professional experience whatsoever, and a setup man who was a minor league first baseman just one year ago. It made for an incredible collection of individual stories.

Those five rookies in the rotation—Parker, Milone, A.J. Griffin, Dan Straily, and Travis Blackley—combined for a 3.59 ERA over 595.2 innings. The A's received 114 starts from their rookies in 2012, and somehow, Oakland managed to allow fewer runs than any Oakland team since 1990, a team that had an AL Cy Young Award winner in Bob Welch, as well as the third- and fifth-place finishers in Dave Stewart and Dennis Eckersley. Brandon Moss, a first baseman who was a freely available pickup for any team who wanted him, hit an absolutely ridiculous .291/.358/.596 in 296 plate appearances. He was released by the Red Sox in 2010, and the Phillies in 2011, but by the end of 2012, he had earned a regular job in the cleanup spot of a division-winning team.

The catcher-turned-third baseman, Josh Donaldson, struggled early on. But after being sent down to Triple-A, he, too, started hitting up a storm and proceeded to bat .290/.356/.489 for the A's in the second half.

Yoenis Cespedes, the enormously hyped Cuban import with the enormously weird scouting video, managed to exceed every rational expectation by hitting .292/.356/.505 in his first year in the United States.

Sean Doolittle was a first baseman in the Athletics minor league system who hadn't appeared in a game since 2009. While the former first-round pick was attempting to return from several injuries in late 2011, he asked the A's if he could try pitching, as he had at the University of Virginia. The A's started him off at Single-A, and he was so dominant that he was promoted up through Double-A and Triple-A and out into Oakland after only 16 games. He struck out more than half of the batters he faced in his miniscule minor league pitching career, and he went on to put up a 3.04 ERA in the majors.

We follow baseball for stories like these. Players who rise from ashes, incredible talents who take the league by storm, and inexperience coolly morphing into confident excellence. But while all of these stories are amazing on their own, the best of them all is about the guy who orchestrated everything—Beane. After two attempts at reloading a roster while keeping some momentum intact, Beane finally decided to slam that competitive window shut and tear the whole thing down to the ground. He ended up with the opposite.

October 3, 2012

Grant Balfour was tired. It was his fifth straight day on the mound, but he insisted—no, demanded—that he was ready to go. The A's certainly didn't need him. They were leading the Texas Rangers, 12-5 in the ninth inning. But Balfour had come too far to watch this final inning from the bench.

Down 13 games at the end of June and four out just one week earlier, Oakland had surged, pulling into a tie with Texas with one game left to play. It would be one of the largest division race comebacks in baseball history, but Oakland needed three more outs, and Balfour wanted to be the one to get them.

The A's had needed just one win in these final three games against Texas to secure a trip to the postseason, but they wanted the sweep and the division crown. Balfour had finished the first game as amped up as he had ever been, striking out the side on 11 blistering pitches. He wasn't quite as incendiary this time out, but he didn't need to be. The score was 12-5, and Balfour wasn't on the mound out of necessity, but out of desire.

Balfour watched as Michael Young strode up to the plate, determined not to make the final out. Balfour launched a fastball down the middle around the knees, which Young took for a strike. Balfour threw a second identical pitch, this time a little higher and on the inner half of the plate. Young fouled it off. With the count 0-2, and 36,067 fans on their feet in anticipation, Balfour threw a third fastball, this time at shoulder level. Young swung anyway.

And just like that, with Coco Crisp sprinting in from center field with the lucky baseball in his glove, the A's mobbed each other. The most incredible season in decades had come to a close. And the A's had won.

The Red Sox's Rudderless Ship

by Evan Brunell

It all started with Jonathan Papelbon.

The greatest closer in Red Sox lore trudged off the mound in Camden Yards, his stoic gaze cast downward as the Orioles engineered a stunning comeback to win Game 162 of the 2011 season, sealing one of the most historic collapses in baseball history. Improbably, the Sox had blown a nine-game lead, missing out on the post-season when Dan Johnson clinched the wild card for Tampa Bay in walk-off fashion. At that moment, everything changed.

I grew up a Red Sox fan. Throughout my still-young life, I've been a die-hard fan, a Red Sox blogger and a professional baseball journalist. That's afforded me a unique perspective on the Red Sox, and I've seen the team go through three distinct eras—and now we're entering a fourth—during my time as an active follower.

Back in the mid-1990s, the Red Sox simply weren't that good, but they played hard and tried to get the most out of their talent. Names like Darren Bragg, Jeff Frye and Troy O'Leary will always stick in my head. In those days, Fenway Park was a crumbling yard, standing proud on tradition as the team battled to make it to October. It wasn't until Pedro Martinez and Manny Ramirez arrived that the club started transforming into a burgeoning powerhouse.

Suddenly, the ballpark was alive and electric, especially on the nights Pedro stood on the mound, tall and majestic with a legion of fans hanging on his every pitch. Pedro changed baseball in Boston in a distinct way for the first time since 1986, and before that, 1967.

This powerhouse was built on a foundation of hard work and perseverance, and it served them well when they hoisted the World Series trophy in 2004, and again in 2007. Boy wonder general manager Theo Epstein had taken the pieces assembled by Dan Duquette and surrounded them with savvy acquisitions, many of them under the radar—and the occasional star. But then the culture of winning took over.

Players felt entitled, fans loaded the bandwagon and demanded a winner, and meanwhile, ownership fell under the influence of star power. Epstein did nothing but advance this mindset, proving all too willing to just throw a blank check at the perceived best player on the market and call it a day.

Slowly, but surely, the team turned into a club even Red Sox fans thought was unwatchable. Big-ticket items like Adrian Gonzalez and Carl Crawford did nothing but drive up payroll and paint Boston as the town where you went to get paid, not to produce. At this point, I was a professional journalist, and watching it all unfold in real time made me realize how far my childhood team had deviated.

How did the Red Sox go from being America's darlings to a team spoken about in the same breath as the Yankees? Boston has never been defined as a team with a blank check. The Red Sox franchise is a blue-collar, dirt-dog team, currently personified by Dustin Pedroia and before him, Trot Nixon. The Sox had completely gotten away from their identity, not just in appearances but in philosophy, and had morphed into a team I was having trouble getting behind, even as they were razing the opposition leading up to September, 2011.

By the time Papelbon walked off the field, it was apparent there had to be significant changes in how things were done in Boston. The pitching completely collapsed down the stretch, both in true performance and in luck. The pitching wasn't just bad, it was historically bad, and the offense couldn't keep up. But it wasn't just the pitching. The team just never jelled together—the "25 players for 25 cabs" Red Sox were back. The greatest impetus to change is shame, and the Red Sox had been through plenty of shame that September of 2011. They had no idea, however, that things were going to get much worse.

Fried chicken and beer ruled the entire offseason, as the two biggest architects of the most successful run in Red Sox history fled. Epstein, himself having grown up a Red Sox fan, decided he would be better off trying to make himself into a living legend with the Cubs. Epstein would later mention that he felt the organization had gotten away from its values and relied too much on free agency, a departure that he oversaw. In addition, Bill James' influence on the front office waned, calling into question just how insular upper management had become. To replace Epstein, the team graduated Ben Cherington to the GM seat. It's too early to fully judge Cherington, but the early returns are good, as he recognizes the Red Sox got away from what had allowed them to become a powerhouse. But before he could worry about the team, he had to find a new manager.

Terry Francona, the best manager in the history of the franchise, also parted ways with Boston that offseason, doing so with a stained reputation thanks to a Boston Globe exposé with anonymous sources. Perhaps the biggest accusation levied was that Francona had become addicted to prescription pills. There's no question that Francona had lost the clubhouse, partly due to his own managerial style, but there was no call to make such an accusation without accountability. Amid the Francona controversy roiling Boston, the Sox embarked on a search for a new skipper, and Cherington settled on Dale Sveum, a former Red Sox third-base coach who was unpopular in that role. However, president Larry Lucchino swatted away the recommendation and forced his own man into the role in the misguided belief that Red Sox fans cared more about name value than making proper decisions, citing a strange emphasis on prior managerial experience. That's how Bobby Valentine became manager of the Red Sox.

Thanks in part to the managerial search dragging out—Valentine was hired at the end of November—the Red Sox roster barely saw any overturn, with 18 of 25 players on the 2012 Opening Day roster having seen time with Boston in 2011. That in and of itself is not necessarily a bad thing, but only two of the new faces—Cody Ross and Andrew Bailey—were expected to play a substantial role on a team that needed more help than it got. A major constricting point in roster construction was the payroll, which had bloated to the point of being unnavigable, given the commitments Epstein had locked the team into. There was lack of pitching depth and precious few arms brought in despite a solid free-agent class. The Red Sox team that congregated in Ft. Myers, Fla., was essentially the same team that had left Baltimore etched in Boston lore as a cautionary tale.

Valentine entered spring training having to shepherd a team that already had collapsed once before, and do so with a style that was a virtual 180-degree turn from Francona. Valentine simply wasn't the right man for the job, and he was put in an impossible position. To be sure, he exacerbated situations due to his managerial tendencies and personality, but no manager could have prevented the historic slew of injuries that overtook the club, nor could a different skipper have prevented an entitled bunch of veterans from chafing under someone who didn't mirror Francona's laissez-faire tendencies. A whopping 26 players hit the disabled list (some more than once), the most since 1987. Is that Valentine's fault? Or is it the fault of the trainers, infrastructure, player commitment (already called into question during the 2011 season) and dumb luck?

Back in April, Valentine began the season without Crawford and, in a nasty bit of timing, lost new closer Bailey just before the year started. Valentine wasn't able to adjust to Bailey's loss quickly enough, and the bullpen yanked away some early would-be victories. By the time the pen stabilized, Boston was already several games below .500.

Pitching was the main issue the entire year, as it was in September, 2011. The Red Sox had a top-five offense for much of 2012 until the end, finishing eighth in runs scored. For comparison, the National League Central division champion Cincinnati Reds came in 21st; but the Reds posted a 3.80 xFIP that was the seventh-lowest in baseball. The Red Sox? They had a 4.16 xFIP, good for 22nd in the league. Daisuke Matsuzaka made 11 starts with a 4.84 xFIP, while Daniel Bard finished the season with a 5.95 xFIP over 10 starts and seven relief appearances. Among big-league pitchers with at least 50 innings pitched, only Jonathan Sanchez's xFIP was worse than Bard's. Jon Lester went from a perennial Cy Young candidate to a No. 4 starter.

Clay Buchholz also struggled, looking at one point like he was going to be demoted to Triple-A. Through the first 10 starts of the year, he had a 7.09 ERA. However, things changed once he returned from a DL stint for inflammation of the esophagus. First, Lady Luck veered back to Buchholz. In April and May, Buchholz had a .344 BABIP, 19 percent home run-per-fly ball rate, and a left-on-base percentage well below the expected average of the mid-70s. However, starting in June and stretching into late August, Buchholz's fortunes completely reversed themselves, seeing his BABIP drop to .229, his HR/FB spiral to 8.9 percent and runners being stranded above and beyond the league average.

Buchholz also started throwing more overhand, an arm angle that better hides the ball from the batter, and also boosts accuracy at the cost of movement. In addition, he started throwing a split-fingered fastball, taught to him by Josh Beckett. This gave Buchholz a second off-speed pitch to go with his changeup, which was getting hammered after being his bread-and-butter offering in 2011. Whether due to the new release point, the split-finger or some combination of both, Buchholz rediscovered his changeup and rode it all the way to a sterling 2.80 ERA over his next 17 starts before two forgettable outings to close out the season.

It wasn't just injuries and pitching that complicated the Red Sox's season. All year long, all you heard about was controversy in the clubhouse, inevitably all circling back to Valentine. Here's where the motivational differences between Francona and Valentine were on display for everyone to see. Francona believed in keeping absolutely everything outside of the public eye. There's certainly reason to believe in that model, but at the same time, it can create a culture with a lack of accountability to the team and fans. Valentine, on the other hand, preferred to do more of his motivating in public, using the press as a conduit.

Really, the approaches of Francona and Valentine were so starkly different that some displeasure was inevitable. From a first-person perspective, Valentine's candor was at times refreshing, necessary and more tame than has been perceived. However, the perception of Valentine, the coddling of players under Francona and the harsh spotlight of the Boston media were just too much. It's one thing to hire a manager with a different personality and traits than the former manager—a popular strategy employed by many—but this was a veteran-laden team without any capacity for change that was being asked to adjust to a completely different style. Part of that is on the players for tuning out Francona and allowing the culture to settle in that way, but part of that is on the front office for not realizing that such a significant shift in the manager's seat would be ill-suited.

There were three spats in particular that really crystallized Valentine's tenure in Boston. The most widely publicized were his ill-advised comments that Kevin Youkilis wasn't as "physically or emotionally" into the game as in the past, creating a firestorm that alienated Youkilis from Valentine and saw Pedroia publicly flagellate Valentine. This was an event that shaped the rest of the season. Valentine has said repeatedly he did not intend the comment to be taken the way it was, but it is difficult to parse those words into anything less (In fairness, Youkilis never made any effort to repair the situation and had strained relationships with other teammates. Beckett accused Youkilis of being the "snitch" in the fried chicken-and-beer scandal, allegations Youkilis has not firmly denied.).

But there were warning signs in spring training, too, that all was not well between Valentine and his players. A popular story that circulated after Valentine's firing but was largely glossed over at the time had Valentine berating shortstop Mike Aviles for not being in the correct cut-off position during drills. Valentine wanted to change how relay plays were made, and arrived to drills seeing Aviles at the previously expected position under Francona. Valentine publicly upbraided Aviles, but unbeknownst to Valentine, Aviles had not been informed of the change yet. Afterward, Valentine attempted to sweep the issue under the rug rather than apologize and clean the slate, despite several veterans later voicing concern to Valentine.

The third spat happened over a two-week span in late August and early September. A little context first: when Bailey went down at the last minute back in March, Valentine had to scramble to find a new closer. He anointed Alfredo Aceves as the stopper, which came as a surprise to many. There had been speculation that Mark Melancon, who had closed for the Astros the previous year, or even Bard, could assume the role, but Valentine placed his faith in Aceves. And for most of the year, Aceves held his own. The bloom had come off the rose by the time Aug. 24 rolled around, though, and his job security was tenuous. He blew a save the night before against the Angels, throwing 37 pitches, then watched as Bailey—having just recently returned to the roster—was called on for a four-out save the next day against Kansas City. Aceves blew up, storming into Valentine's office after the game and having an animated conversation before slamming the door to Valentine's office forcefully. For that, Aceves received a three-game suspension and lost the closer's job for good.

But it wasn't over. On Sept. 12, Aceves was pitching the sixth inning of a tight game against the Yankees. After giving up a two-run home run, he was removed from the game. As Valentine was walking out to the mound, Aceves opted to hand the baseball to catcher Jarrod Saltalamacchia, stand on the other side of the mound from Valentine, then take a circuitous route to the dugout, all to pointedly avoid Valentine. None of this, at least on the surface, was Valentine's fault, as Aceves has a reputation for incidents like this, but it only added to the perception that the entire clubhouse hated Valentine, and it didn't do him any favors as he tried to manage his way to returning for another season.

It wasn't just Valentine that suffered a stained reputation. One of the more bizarre occurrences of the 2012 season was hearing Pedroia get booed. This occurred after all but four Red Sox players skipped franchise great Johnny Pesky's funeral. The lack of respect accorded here was so vile to Red Sox fans that Pedroia, who was one of the players not to attend and had his own controversies throughout the year, received no mercy when the fans let the players know exactly how they felt. This is when the fans finally turned on the team and may have also been the turning point for the front office. There was no saving the team; players had to go. The team later honored Pesky with a memorial at Fenway Park that was (surprise!) attended by the team, but the damage was done—only David Ortiz, Vicente Padilla, Buchholz and Saltalamacchia thought it a good idea to attend Pesky's funeral to honor one of Boston's best ambassadors of the game, a man who had been part of Major League Baseball since debuting as a player in 1942.

There were plenty more team-wide incidents that happened than could be discussed here. There was Valentine's lineup mistakes, the obvious schism between Valentine and his coaches (with some relationships being reduced to teenage-style silent treatment), Pedroia's undermining of Valentine, a heated discussion between Aceves and Pedroia, and of course, the mid-summer meeting between ownership and players to talk about Valentine after a text from Gonzalez's phone that had Pedroia's fingerprints on it, as well. And those are just the controversies that we know about.

Boston has a reputation for skewering players and managers on their way out the door, as is what happened with Francona. Others deserved some of the blame for their skewering—Johnny Damon and Manny Ramirez come to mind—and Beckett absolutely shares the blame for becoming persona non grata in Boston. You would have thought it was the Fourth of July, not August 25, when stunning news broke of the biggest Red Sox trade since Babe Ruth left town. Beckett, Gonzalez and Crawford were shipped off to Los Angeles (with Nick Punto) in a deal that transformed the face of the Sox and gave fans a reason to watch down the stretch even if the post-trade club was among the most miserable in team history.

Beckett's downfall was his pride, and his attitude that had been on display for years. This was a cocky Texan who had two World Series rings on his hand, who made his living and earned millions of dollars with his unrepentant, fiery attitude, who backed down from no one. But once his fastball slowed down from a 2011 average of 93.1 mph to 91.4 mph and he hid from the public eye all offseason, ignoring the necessity of confronting the fried chicken-and-beer scandal, things changed. Suddenly, Beckett's attitude was a cancer, and he was a negative influence in the clubhouse, unhappy about the new sense of accountability surrounding him after years of doing what he wanted under Francona.

Beckett and accountability do not go well together, perhaps best evidenced by the scandal early in the season when Beckett was caught golfing on an off-day despite skipping his start the night before due to a sore shoulder. After dodging the media, he finally had to answer for his actions after failing to make it out of the third inning in his return to the rotation. Beckett ignored the controversy, steadfastly maintaining that he would do whatever he wanted on his off-day, and nuts to anyone who felt differently. Before that event, while many fans might not have been pleased with Beckett's performance and increasingly surly attitude, he was still a Red Sox. Afterward, he was marked for doom.

What happened to Beckett? It's easy to point to his fastball velocity as the reason his career in Boston fell apart. He could no longer use his fastball and cutter to get strikeouts, and the loss in fastball velocity created less separation from his change-up. His curveball tailed off in velocity, as well, which impacted how tightly the pitch spun toward the ground. A year after serving as a strikeout pitch, it served as a pitch to be hit all over the yard. He started using his fastball less and tried to get batters to chase the change-up, but that didn't work at all. He got significantly worse as the year went on, too, with his walks and home runs spiking to levels where a pitcher with less stature would have been removed from the rotation.

Beckett wasn't the only under-performer sent to Los Angeles. Another was first baseman Gonzalez, who developed a reputation as a five-star slugger in San Diego, only to see his plate discipline vanish once he joined the Red Sox. It wasn't a problem in 2011 because A-Gon masked the regression with a .338 batting average, but in 2012, his lack of patience really showed through. Gonzo's 2012 walk percentage of 6.1 percent was the lowest since his debut season of 2004, when he had 16 plate appearances. A-Gon also set a career high in swing rate, swinging at just over half of all pitches to make their way to the plate.

In 2011, pitchers tried to stay low and away from Gonzalez, but that changed in 2012. Pitchers came inside on him at a higher clip, daring the first baseman to beat the pitch, while distributing the ball all over the strike zone more frequently, forcing Gonzalez to adjust to different planes of the ball. While he was still able to turn on inside pitches, that was about it for his power production, and pitchers got even more aggressive as the year went on, challenging Gonzalez in and around the strike zone. By the end of the year, it was obvious: pitchers were no longer afraid of Gonzalez.

The team took advantage of new ownership in Los Angeles, who were desperate to make an impact, and completely rewrote the future of the Red Sox in one day. Instead of Sox fans having to steel themselves through a few years of overpaid, underperforming and unengaged players, suddenly, Boston had a blank slate, saving roughly a quarter-billion dollars.

Just one problem: the team that was left in the wake of the trade was stupefyingly bad, nigh unwatchable until the very end of September, when the kids got to play. The Sox used a club-record 56 players during the 2012 season, which was glaringly apparent down the stretch in September, especially on October 1, when CC Sabathia carved up a lineup that had just two players with a wRC+ over 100 in Ross and Daniel Nava, the latter of whom does not belong in a starting lineup. Ortiz had a superlative season before an Achilles heel injury in late July knocked him out for the year and turned the Sox offense into a pumpkin. Ortiz was one of Valentine's lone public defenders, but that didn't stop Valentine from unfairly ripping Ortiz's dedication to returning from injury in late October.

During the 2011 collapse, the Red Sox went 7-20 down the stretch. By the time September, 2012 rolled around, the Red Sox had been so gutted that they outpaced that mark, finishing the season with a 7-22 mark to ensure their first 90-plus loss season since 1996 and the most losses since the 1922 Sox also had 93. At this point, nothing Valentine said or did seemed to work, and the team was doomed to play out the string. Valentine admitted to reporters that Boston's September roster was one of the weakest ever—and had to scramble to correct himself once controversy flared up once more. This time, though, the controversy was ridiculous. Anyone and everyone could see how terrible the roster was. Heck, once Triple-A Pawtucket's season finally ended by winning the International League championship, the club recalled Danny Valencia to man third base down the stretch. Valencia had been dumped by the 96-loss Twins earlier in the year and finished the season with a 23 wRC+.

Fittingly, the season ended in New York as the Yankees prepared for another dose of postseason play. The Red Sox could have played spoiler by dropping the Yankees into a tie for first or even into second place. If they had come away with two of three, New York would have been forced to play a Wild Card playoff game, which could have changed the entire complexion of the postseason. After losing the first game, it looked like Boston might at least be able to force a tie for first place, leading New York 3-1 in the ninth inning of the second game. Alas, Bailey gave up a two-run home run to Raul Ibanez, and Boston rolled over, getting swept in one last bout of humiliation. How could the 2012 season otherwise have ended? A Yankees sweep was the taunting cherry on top of the dessert of nightmares.

Valentine was fired 14 hours after the last pitch of the season.

Case Study: Kris Medlen

After throwing just 2.1 innings in 2011 after Tommy John surgery in late 2010, Kris Medlen's role to start the season was up in the air. The Braves liked the way Medlen performed as a starting pitcher in 2010 before his injury—they had won 13 of his 14 starts while he posted a solid 3.86 ERA. But at the start of spring training, Atlanta had one of the deepest rotations in the league, so the bullpen seemed like a likely destination for Medlen. It made a great deal of sense, considering his success in the bullpen, the team's lack of right-handed middle relief options, and the fact that wear and tear on the team's top three relievers in late 2011 had helped cause the worst collapse in franchise history.

The Braves stretched him out a bit as a starter in spring training, then moved Medlen to the bullpen to start the year, with the idea that if they needed him in the rotation later in the season, they could still keep his overall innings total down. Medlen pitched well in his 54.1 innings of relief work, often throwing multiple innings per outing. He recorded a 2.48 ERA over 38 appearances. His performance was vital to the Braves' early success, since Jonny Venters and Eric O'Flaherty—the team's top set-up men over the past two seasons—struggled to start the year.

The bullpen arms eventually straightened themselves out, but the starting staff began to thin due to injury and poor performance. Medlen was asked to get stretched out in the minors and be ready to start. He came back up in the bullpen as Mike Minor and Randall Delgado performed well, but Medlen was eventually put in the rotation, which kick-started his tremendous season.

He started 12 games, recording a miniscule 0.97 ERA in 83.2 innings. He walked just 10 batters in those 12 starts, striking out just over a batter per inning. That level of performance, combined with his body of work as a reliever, made Medlen a candidate for the National League Cy Young Award. So what did he do that made him so dominant? Why was his season such a surprise?

The simple answer: Medlen is one of the better athletes in the Braves organization. At Santa Ana Junior College, Medlen primarily played shortstop while also pitching out of the bullpen. Not only is he athletic enough to play shortstop, but he's a switch hitter. His athleticism has translated into success on the mound; his delivery is extremely consistent and he is able to locate all three of his pitches with relative ease. He works fast, fields his position very well, runs well, and can handle the bat. He is more than just a pitcher; he is a baseball player.

On the mound, Medlen understands the importance of throwing strikes. This season, he was in the top five in baseball (minimum 130 innings) in pitches in the strike zone, and in the top 15 in first-strike percentage. While he doesn't have a deep repertoire or overpowering stuff, throwing strikes, and more importantly throwing strikes on the corners and being deceptive while doing so, can enhance a player's repertoire. With a fastball that sits in the high 80s, his location and deception have been the main drivers of his success.

The pitch that drives Medlen's repertoire is his change-up, which he throws roughly 20 percent of the time. Since he does not have a power fastball, he relies heavily on his change-up—he ranked in the top-15 in change-up frequency among pitchers who threw 130 innings this season. While he does throw the pitch more frequently to lefties than righties, as is the norm, he does not completely abandon the pitch against right-handed batters, as many pitchers do. He throws about 13 percent change-ups to right-handers compared to 26 percent against left-handers, with his curveball being a bit more frequently used against righties than lefties.

Because he uses both breaking balls and change-ups in any situation, he causes a hitter to have more on his mind than just a fastball and the coinciding off-speed pitch. With such a high strike frequency, Medlen can do this and not suffer the consequences of hitters letting his breaking balls go by and waiting for his unimposing fastball. Without the high quality off-speed offerings, Medlen probably wouldn't be able to limit home runs and other extra base hits as well as he has. For the season, Medlen allowed just six home runs, while recording the lowest home run per fly ball ratio in baseball at 5.7 percent.

Medlen has said he uses his two-seam fastball more than the four-seamer because there is "more room for error" with the pitch, and that the movement on the pitch looks similar to his change-up. His swinging-strike rate with his two-seamer is slightly below average, at around three percent compared to the league average of five percent. However, since he relies on his two-seamer more than any other pitch, it seems likely that some of the success Medlen receives from his change-up is due to the fact that the pitch moves just like his primary two-seamer.

Again, Medlen thrives on his ability to both locate pitches and deceive hitters. So although the two-seamer is not comparable to the best in the league, it does help make his change-up one of the most dangerous in baseball.

General sabermetric thinking dictates that striking out many, while walking few and not allowing home runs is the optimal way to have continued success on the mound. That is exactly what Medlen did this season, which points to him being able to sustain success at a high level, even if the 2012 level was a slight aberration. In doing very well in these three facets as a starter, combined with success in the bullpen, Medlen recorded the second highest Win Probability Added (WPA) of all NL pitchers, behind only Johnny Cueto. WPA, as defined by FanGraphs, measures how individual players affect their team's win expectancy on a per-play basis. So Medlen affected the Braves' win expectancy at a level higher than any other starter in his league aside from Cueto. This, above all else, helps explain how important Medlen was to the Braves' march to the postseason.

While nobody expected Medlen to be this good, the Braves did know that they had a very useful player entering the season. Medlen was to the pitching staff as Martin Prado was for the position players: one who was undervalued because he didn't have a sole position or top-prospect status, but who provides the team with flexibility and high level performance across multiple facets of the game. Even though the Braves and their fans are less surprised by Medlen's season than the rest of baseball, nobody could have predicted the Braves would win a major league record 23 consecutive games started by Medlen.

With a change-up that baffles both left-handed and right-handed hitters, along with great sequencing and the ability to locate his two fastballs and curveball at an elite level, there is little reason to think this season was a fluke. Will he continue to have an ERA below 1.00 as a starting pitcher for the remainder of his career? No, but if he pitches to his capabilities, he can be the ace of the Braves staff for the foreseeable future.

- Ben Duronio

Leaderboard: Best Pitches of 2012

There probably are multiple ways to identify what the league's "best" pitches are, and, of course, the effectiveness of one offering in a pitcher's repertoire depends on the quality of all the others, too.

One way of evaluating the quality of a pitch, using a methodology developed by Dave Allen, is to see what it's been worth in terms of linear-weight runs. What follows are the top 10 pitches by linear-weight runs (relative to league average) for every 100 thrown—with a minimum of 250 thrown for each pitch. In the chart below, FA means four-seam fastball, FT means two-seam fastball, FC means cut fastball, SL means slider, CU means curveball and CH means changeup.

Name	Team	IP	Type	%	R/100
Fernando Rodney	Rays	74.2	CH	36.2%	5.05
Kris Medlen	Braves	138.0	CH	20.0%	4.49
Mitchell Boggs	Cardinals	73.1	SL	24.7%	3.63
Craig Kimbrel	Braves	62.2	SL	32.6%	3.20
Clayton Kershaw	Dodgers	227.2	CU	11.2%	3.10
Ernesto Frieri	- - -	66.0	FT	31.9%	2.97
Charlie Furbush	Mariners	46.1	CU	34.8%	2.97
Jered Weaver	Angels	188.2	FC	9.0%	2.93
Craig Kimbrel	Braves	62.2	FA	62.3%	2.92
Matt Cain	Giants	219.1	SL	21.0%	2.91

Notes

Fernando Rodney's changeup always has been his best pitch, having produced about 30 linear-weight runs above average (or, about 1.5 runs per every 100 thrown) from 2002 to 2011. However, he almost doubled that total in 2012. The reason for the improvement? A considerably higher swinging-strike rate (25.8 percent) on the offering than in previous seasons, when it typically sat in the 12-15 percent range. Notably, Rodney's changeup featured the least amount of armside run and most amount of sink in 2012 relative to any of the years for which we have PITCHf/x data (since 2007). This seems to have encouraged batters to offer at the pitch more frequently—and to miss while so doing.

While ranked ninth by *Baseball America* among Braves prospects in 2009 (his last season with rookie eligibility), Kris Medlen—likely owing to a lack both of fastball velocity and physicality—never was considered an elite prospect. Moreover, a Tommy John procedure that limited him to all of 2.1 innings in 2011 obscured the memory of the 170 above-average innings he threw in a swing role between 2009 and 2010. So it was that Medlen entered 2012 with little pomp and even less circumstance. After pitching well out of the bullpen (54.1 IP, 17.1% K, 6.2% BB, 51.6% GB, 3.70 xFIP), Medlen was added to the bullpen at the end of July and dominated (83.2 IP, 27.2% K, 3.2% BB, 54.7% GB, 2.50 xFIP). Medlen's changeup was worth 9.4 linear-weight runs above average from August on, the best such mark in the majors.

It likely won't surprise readers to find Craig Kimbrel's name on this leaderboard twice. The right-hander became the first pitcher in major-league history to record at least 30 innings and strike out half of the batters he faced. In fact, as FanGraphs' Eric Seidman noted at the beginning of October, Kimbrel also became the first pitcher to record more than 30 innings and strike out at least 45 percent of batters faced. Only three pitchers have even reached the 44 percent threshold: Eric Gagne (44.7 percent, 2003), Aroldis Chapman (44.4 percent, 2012), and Kenley Jansen (44.0 percent, 2011). While classified by PITCHf/x as a slider—likely owing to the velocity (85-87 mph) at which it's thrown—Kimbrel's breaking ball is actually thrown with more of a curveball-type grip.

- Carson Cistulli

Bryce Harper and Mike Trout Make History

by Jeff Moore

As sports fans, we live to see greatness. It's why we watch, root, and spend countless hours putting together fake teams, and then root against our real teams in deference to them. It's why we paint our faces and chests and who knows what else. It's why we read this book.

In the constant search for a greater greatness than we've yet seen, we have a tendency to fabricate things in our minds. Whether it's the sports fan in us or just the American need to always find what's next before it arrives, this desire plays tricks with our minds, often causing us to believe things that simply aren't true. We always feel that what we're seeing now is the greatest we've ever seen, mainly because it's what we want to see. In our hope to see greatness, we often conjure it up out of thin air.

We do this with the Hall of Fame, perhaps more than anywhere else in our sports fandom. Players who don't get inducted on their first, second, or even tenth time on the ballot ultimately end up enshrined with the best the game has ever seen. Did they get better in the 15 years since they hung up their cleats? Or did their supporters simply get better at describing their greatness, which in fact may have just been, for lack of a better term, goodness?

The overwhelming amount of sports coverage available today has made us numb to the adjectives that once were saved for only the best performances on the field, to the point when words like incredible and historic have virtually lost their meaning. The 2012 baseball season was no different, with the seasons put forth by Los Angeles Angels 20-year-old outfielder Mike Trout and Washington Nationals 19-year-old outfielder Bryce Harper receiving outstanding accolades. But in this case, extravagant descriptions of their accomplishments were not overstated. What the two young stars did in 2012 was, in fact, truly historic.

We don't know what the future has in store for Trout and Harper, but we know what history has offered us to this point, and it is difficult to find seasons that replicate what that pair did in 2012 at the age they did it.

Baseball isn't like other sports. In football, young players don't even get an opportunity to compete with the big boys, for their own protection. Even the best 19-year-olds would get hurt if they tried to line up against grown men nearly twice their age. But once they become professionals, they are thrust into the spotlight to sink or swim. As evidenced most recently by the emergence of Andrew Luck and Robert Griffin III this season, gone are the days of learning in the NFL after getting drafted. Our society's need for instant gratification has forced the hands of players and coaches alike, and the players have risen to the challenge in preparation and ability alike.

In the NBA, teenagers can compete with professionals, and in many cases, they are professionals themselves. The NBA allows for that integration much like baseball does, but the process seems much more seamless. The game of basketball, with its beautiful use of athleticism, allows for pure ability to overcome a lack of experience and refinement. A teenager may not be at his best yet, but he can compete and succeed right away based solely on his ability to run and jump.

That's not supposed to work in baseball. There's a reason baseball has the most intricate development process of any professional sport in the world, with six different levels of minor league baseball ranging from 16-year-olds who speak no English to veterans in their mid-30s trying to extend their livelihood.

The game of baseball doesn't care how athletic a player is or how much ability he has. A certain amount of hand-eye coordination can make up for some lack of experience, but eventually the league figures every player out.

Baseball is a game of adjustments. No matter how good a start a player has to his career, the league will adjust, and his career trajectory will be determined by how he adjusts back. The baseball landscape is littered with players blessed with early success who failed to adjust to the league's response to their abilities. Career trajectories that once appeared to be limitless ultimately found their limit.

Trout struggled in 2011. As a 19-year-old who had dominated the minor leagues, his much-anticipated promotion was a bit of a letdown to the highly-expectant Angels fans, when he hit just .220/.281/.390 in his first major league season. His plate discipline broke down, his power didn't respond to major league pitching, and he failed to make an impact.

He adjusted. The league has yet to respond.

Rarely, if ever, have we seen players make the adjustment as quickly or as successfully as Trout did in 2012, as he hit .326/.399/.564 in his first full season and became only the third player in major league history to hit 30 home runs and steal 49 bases. It was a season that bordered on historic when standing alone, but it becomes even rarer when we are reminded of his age.

In Washington, Harper struggled slightly more with the adjustment in the majors, not surprising considering he had 776 fewer minor league plate appearances than even the fast-moving Trout. For all of Harper's accomplishments, the league figured him out for a two-month stretch in July and August, when he hit .222 and .243, respectively. His aggressiveness was exploited, his extremely competitive nature got the best of him, and the league knew it. While no one doubted Harper's long-term potential, his ability to help the Nationals down the stretch came into question.

Before those questions became full-fledged doubts however, Harper adjusted to the league's adjustment in magnificent fashion—he hit .330 in September and re-affirmed the Nationals' faith in him as an intelligent player. He remained at the top of their lineup down the stretch and into their brief postseason run.

These types of adjustments by Trout and Harper are part of the historic nature of what they accomplished in 2012. Most players are making these adjustments at their age in the Carolina League, taking buses from town to town. These two did it in the majors, with the eyes of the sports world watching.

The Most Valuable Player Award may carry historical significance, but it can't always tell the true story of a major league season. When you tell your kids or grandkids about what you witnessed during the 2012 season, the stories will begin with Trout and Harper.

We heard all season about how historic what these two players were doing was, and at ages 19 and 20, respectively, everything we heard was true. But now that it's complete, just how historic was it?

The beauty of baseball, with its endless statistical evidence with which we can make arguments, is that there are endless ways to quantify what happened.

While Harper took over the storylines in spring training, Trout actually didn't make the Angels' Opening Day roster thanks to a March illness that cost him about 20 pounds and a crowded outfield in Anaheim full of bulky contracts and seemingly immovable veterans. To think that Trout was giving up playing time to Vernon Wells early in the season is unfathomable now, but Wells' massive contract and presence in left field played a role in Trout's month-long minor league exile. Once he was called up on April 28, however, he wasted little time before taking over the American League, rendering Wells the game's most expensive pinch-hitter.

Trout's 2012 season, in which he produced 10.7 Wins Above Replacement (all WAR here is courtesy of Baseball Reference), ranks as the 20th-highest single-season total of all time for a position player. Above Trout, there are only three seasons after 1975, and two of them came at the hands of the questionably enhanced Barry Bonds during his video game-esque stretch at the end of his career. Essentially, there has only been one season by a position player since 1975 that was better than Mike Trout's 2012 season that didn't have chemical help—Cal Ripken's 1991 MVP season.

Making the season even more impressive was the fact that Trout missed the first month. WAR is a stat aided by accumulation, and Trout only had 139 games in which he could accumulate value.

Among hitters who, for whatever reason, played in 139 games or fewer, Trout's season produced the highest WAR in major league history, beating out Roger Hornsby's 1925 season, in which he produced a WAR of 10.1. It is a list filled primarily with Hall of Famers.

Rk	Player	WAR	G	Year	Age
1	Mike Trout	10.7	139	2012	20
2	Rogers Hornsby	10.1	138	1925	29
3	Rickey Henderson	9.8	136	1990	31
4	Babe Ruth	9.7	130	1919	24
5	Ted Williams	9.5	132	1957	38
6	George Brett	9.3	117	1980	27
7	Arky Vaughan	9.1	137	1935	23
8	Honus Wagner	9.0	137	1909	35
9	Barry Bonds	8.9	130	2003	38
10	Lonnie Smith	8.7	134	1989	33

His performance alone makes what Trout did impressive, but not necessarily historic. A historic performance has to be something we haven't seen before, and as great as a 10-plus WAR season is, we have seen it before.

Just not from a 20-year-old.

Players who can't buy beer aren't supposed to be able to dominate the AL. Forget renting a car, Trout can barely rent a jet ski.

Trout's season has never been seen from the likes of anyone his age, and rarely has anyone encroached upon this territory.

Before 2012, the closest thing we had seen to what Trout did was Alex Rodriguez in 1996 when he won the batting title, but Trout distances himself from even that amazing season. There also have been clouds of doubt surrounding Rodriguez's physical cleanliness, even at that early point in his career.

Rk	Player	WAR	Year	Age
1	Mike Trout	10.7	2012	20
2	Alex Rodriguez	9.2	1996	20
3	Al Kaline	8.0	1955	20
4	Mel Ott	7.3	1929	20
5	Ted Williams	6.6	1939	20
6	Ty Cobb	6.6	1907	20
7	Jason Heyward	6.3	2010	20
8	Vada Pinson	6.3	1959	20
9	Mickey Mantle	6.3	1952	20
10	Frank Robinson	6.2	1956	20

In 2012, Trout put together the best season in baseball history by a 20-year-old player and did so without playing the first month of the season. That is something, we can safely say, is historic.

When discussing historical performance by age, Trout's accomplishments are great, but Harper's exploits are incredible.

Think about what you were doing at 19. Or better yet, don't. Whatever it was, it certainly wasn't done in the spotlight that Harper had to deal with in 2012.

Most fans, especially those in our nation's capital, would have been happy with a season from Harper in which he merely survived his first major league campaign without dragging the team into controversy or being overwhelmed by the game's best breaking pitches. Harper, having been in the spotlight since he was 16, is no stranger to publicity. The camera had followed him since his high school days and, often through no real fault of his own, the attention he received rarely portrayed him in a positive light.

The statistical expectations for Harper entering the season ranged from the absurd to the non-existent, with no one even sure when he would join Washington's major league roster. The Nationals were thought still to be a year away from competing, and with a 19-year-old at the center of their offensive production, fans were doing their best to limit their expectations despite the growing anticipation of a changing of the guard in the National League East.

In hindsight, it's hard to believe that Harper didn't make the Nationals roster last spring, even though it was likely the right decision at the time.

Despite his midseason struggles, Harper hit .270/.340/.477 on the year with 22 home runs and 18 stolen bases, a season that statistically was almost as good as his only full minor league season.

The production itself was good enough to be a starter on—and bat at the top of the order for—a pennant-winning team and also good enough to get him on an All-Star team, but without age as a context, it's hardly historic.

But when you remember that he's 19, the context renders it magnificent.

Regardless of his success, the fact that Harper got as much playing time as he did is an impressive feat in and of itself. Only four players have had more PAs during their 19-year-old seasons than Harper, who accumulated 597 in 2012, with only Robin Yount's 1975 season occurring within the last 72 years.

The playing time alone helped Harper's ability to rack up an impressive WAR, but it wasn't just handed to him. He had to hit to stay in the Nationals lineup, as Washington began to realize its window for competing in the NL was opening earlier than the team may have thought.

Harper posted a 5.0 WAR in 2012, over a full win higher than any other teenage hitter in baseball history.

Rk	Player	WAR	Year	Age
1	Bryce Harper	5.0	2012	19
2	Mel Ott	3.7	1928	19
3	Edgar Renteria	3.1	1996	19
4	Ken Griffey	2.9	1989	19
5	Ty Cobb	2.3	1906	19

That list of teenage seasons includes two Hall of Famers (Ott and Cobb), one impending inductee (Griffey), and a World Series MVP who had a very nice major league career in Renteria.

It's a historic start for Harper, and one that sets him on an impressive path.

Much was made this season of not only Trout and Harper, but also of what felt like a collectively historic rookie class. But as we discussed earlier, sometimes greatness is something we fabricate in our minds.

Trout and Harper stole the headlines, but the 2012 class of rookies also included Cuban defector Yoenis Cespedes and Japanese rookie Yu Darvish, even though they aren't traditional rookies. Manny Machado and Will Middlebrooks were also strong first-year players who should go on to productive major league careers.

But as a whole, the 2012 rookie class was not historic. It was top heavy, but it does not compare to some of the classes that have come before it. Since the inception of the Rookie of the Year Award in 1947, the following are the seasons that have included multiple Hall of Famers (or potential Hall of Famers):

Year	Hall of Famers	Other Notable Rookies	Notes
1951	Willie Mays, Mickey Mantle	Minnie Minoso	
1954	Hank Aaron, Ernie Banks, Al Kaline		None of the three won Rookie of the Year Award
1967	Tom Seaver, Rod Carew		One of two years where both ROYs became HOFers
1975	Jim Rice, Gary Carter	Fred Lynn	
1977	Andre Dawson, Eddie Murray		One of two years where both ROYs became HOFers
1978	Paul Molitor, Ozzie Smith	Lou Whitaker, Alan Trammell, Bob Horner	
1982	Cal Ripken Jr., Wade Boggs, Ryne Sandberg		
1984	Roger Clemens, Kirby Puckett	Dwight Gooden, Orel Hershiser	
1986	Barry Larkin	Jose Canseco, Barry Bonds	

Year	Hall of Famers	Other Notable Rookies	Notes
1993		Mike Piazza, Pedro Martinez	Two eventual HOFers
2001		Ichiro Suzuki, Albert Pujols, Jimmy Rollins, CC Sabathia	

There probably are not three Hall of Famers in the 2012 rookie class. We can legitimately say that Trout and Harper have a shot (as much as any player can have a shot after one season), but it's way too early to put Machado in that class.

Perhaps no class in baseball history will touch the ones seen in the 1950s, such as the 1951 class that featured two of the greatest outfielders of all time in Mickey Mantle and Willie Mays, and the 1954 class, which featured three no-doubt-about-it Hall of Famers in Hank Aaron, Ernie Banks and Al Kaline.

In more recent years, the 1982 rookie class featured a full Hall of Fame infield in Wade Boggs, Cal Ripken and Ryne Sandberg.

Can the 2012 class, with Trout, Harper, Machado and Darvish, join the class of these past years? Absolutely, but there are still some big hurdles to overcome. If talent was the only thing in question, then Dwight Gooden would be one column over to the left in the table above. But the talent and potential is there for a pair of Hall of Famers and some long careers.

Despite the historic relevance of what Trout and Harper accomplished at such a young age, the very good 2012 class of rookies, as a whole, doesn't qualify as historic.

What we saw from Trout and Harper in 2012 was a pair of impressive performances, each of which was historic in its own right, the likes of which we have not seen in decades, if ever. The fact that we got to see them take place in the same season borders on an absurdity of riches for baseball fans.

There has never been a season in major league history, all 141 years of it, that saw two hitters who were 20 or younger each produce a WAR over four. Ever. That alone makes what we saw in 2012 historic.

We don't know what will become of Trout and Harper. Baseball history is littered with careers that began with a blaze of glory only to fizzle early and fall back into the lore of what could have been. But it is also filled with great careers and historic performances, many of which began in much the same way that Harper and Trout began their journeys in 2012.

This Game Is Rigged: The Orioles' Amazing Bullpen

by Dave Studenmund

The Baltimore Orioles bullpen set a record this year. They posted a Win Probability Added (WPA) total of almost 14 (13.9, to be exact), the most in major league history by a good margin. What does that mean? It means that Baltimore, which finished 93-69—a 12-game advantage over a .500 record—owes that entire difference to its bullpen. Combined, the starting pitchers and batters were two games below .500. At least, that is what WPA says.

There are lots of problems with thinking about baseball this way, but hang in there with me for a few minutes, because I'd like to tell you the story of the Baltimore Bullpen. It's an amazing tale.

Let me start by asking you a question. Which game would you rather win, the first game of the World Series or the last one? The last one, I hope. If you win the first one, you still have to win three more games. If you win the last one, that's it, the trophy is yours.

Here's another one. Which out would you rather make, the first out of a game or the last one? The first one, I hope. If you make the last out of a game, your team probably has lost (exception: walk-off wins with at least one out).

Timing matters. When things unfold, they unfold in an order. Fortunes rise and fall based on that order, and so do our spirits and our attentions. Win Probability is just about the only statistic that reflects the unfolding of a game.

When a batter hits a home run in the first inning of a tie game, that's a good thing. When he hits a home run in the ninth inning of a tie game, that's a great thing. WPA—which calculates the change in win probability of an event based on the score, inning, outs and base situation—captures the difference between these two events. In essence, it puts a number to the story as the story unfolds.

Once a game is over, a run is a run. Once the season is over, a win is a win. It doesn't matter when you hit or won it. After-the-fact stats are the best way to judge a player's value or a team's performance. But when the competition is afoot, timing matters a great deal. Real-time contribution, instead of value, is the thing that captures the essence of timing. And measuring real-time contribution is the best way to understand what the Orioles accomplished this year.

The surprising O's were no one's idea of a contending team before the season began. However, they started out strong, in second place with a 14-9 tally at the end of April, scoring 96 runs and allowing 84. Few thought they could keep it going. By the end of May, however, they were in first place in the American League East with a 29-22 record. At this point, they had scored 230 runs and allowed 222. This means that, in May, the Orioles actually allowed more runs (222-84=138) than they scored (230-96=134), but still improved their record and climbed the standings into first place.

By the end of June, Baltimore still was three-and-a-half games ahead of a .500 pace (42-35), in second place. At this stage of the season, they had scored 327 runs and allowed 349—a negative run differential of 22. It's very difficult to be above .500 when you've allowed that many more runs than you've scored.

> *Sidebar: When a team is, say 12-10, you often hear people say that they are two games above .500. But that's not really true. They're just one game above .500, because if they were to lose one of their games instead of winning it, their record would be 11-11. It would take just one game to even their record. For this article, we would say that the team is two wins above .500, but one game above .500. The difference is critical when discussing WPA, because 0.5 WPA equals a win, but 1.0 WPA equals a game (changing a loss to a win).*

In 1984, the Mets finished 90-72, in second place in the NL East, despite allowing 24 more runs than they scored. That is the worst run differential for a team with a winning percentage above .550 in major league history. If Baltimore had maintained their 2012 pace, they would have shattered that record.

And they tried. By the end of July, the Orioles were 55-49, in second place, and they had a run differential of -51 runs. That's NEGATIVE 51 RUNS!

Here's a simple rule of thumb: for every ten-run difference in run differential, teams will average one game away from .500. So if you know that a team has a run differential of -51 runs after 104 games, you'd expect them to have a record around 47-57. The O's were 55-49 instead, a difference of eight games. The major league record for a run/win difference over a full season belongs to the 1905 Tigers, who were about 13 games better than expected. The Orioles were in another world, one in which runs take flight and records warp.

Full major league seasons have a way of bringing record-setting paces back to earth. By the end of August, the Orioles were 73-58, with a run differential of -39 (yes, that's still negative)—an 11.5 game difference. More importantly, however, they were playing better. Their winning pace hadn't slowed; their run differential had improved.

September and October finally brought some real normalcy back to Camden Yards. Baltimore maintained its winning ways, finishing 93-69, 12 games above .500 and qualifying for the postseason. They also posted a run differential of POSITIVE seven runs. They didn't break the Tigers' record, but they came close.

How did they do it? The simple answer is easy: they won close games. The Orioles were 29-9 in one-run games and 25-14 in two-run games. They were 39-46 in all other games. Said in the language of runs, Baltimore won when run differentials were narrow; they gave up games when run differentials were large.

Well, how did they do this? Timing and luck, but also the bullpen. Baltimore famously did not give up a lead after the seventh inning during the regular season (we won't talk about their postseason woes here). Although the Orioles' bullpen was fifth in overall major league ERA (3.00; the Reds were first at 2.65), they were first in pitching when it counted.

Let's look at some numbers. Here's a list of the top five team bullpens in WPA:

Baltimore	13.9
Texas	8.0
Atlanta	7.1
Tampa Bay	7.1
Oakland	6.6

As you can see, the Orioles blew the competition out of the water—nearly six games better than the No. 2 team, Texas. As I said in the intro, that WPA mark is the highest of any bullpen ever.

The leader of the pen was closer Jim Johnson. Johnson was drafted by the Orioles out of high school in 2001. A good starter throughout his minor league career, Johnson blossomed when moved to the bullpen in 2008, where he was able to take full advantage of his 95-mile-per-hour sinker. Johnson took over Baltimore's closer duties in the second half of 2011, and this year he led all major league pitchers in WPA:

Jim Johnson/BAL	5.4
Fernando Rodney/TB	4.8
Craig Kimbrel/ATL	4.2
Justin Verlander/DET	4.0
Chris Sale/CHW	3.7

As you can see, WPA favors relievers because they get more opportunities to pitch at the end of close games. We'll come back to that issue for starting pitchers later. In the meantime, the key takeaway here is that Johnson—despite a relatively pedestrian ERA of 2.49 (pedestrian when compared to ERAs like Fernando Rodney's 0.60 or Craig Kimbrel's 1.01)—led all relievers in contributing to wins. He did it by—pay attention, you're going to hear this a lot—pitching best when it counted most.

To measure critical situations, I like to use something called Leverage Index (LI). Leverage Index measures the criticality of each individual situation by calculating the potential range of win probability outcomes that arise from that situation. Early innings have less leverage because teams have time to attempt to come back and win. Late innings have much more leverage, because they are more likely to cement a win or loss.

The average LI is 1.0, and the maximum (which is reached only a few times a season) is around 10. The leaders in bullpen LI last year (with a minimum of 100 batters faced) were:

Jonathan Broxton/KC	2.64
Jim Johnson/BAL	2.07
Addison Reed/CHW	2.01
Rafael Betancourt/COL	2.00
Brett Myers/HOU	1.90

As you can see, only Jonathan Broxton, while pitching in Kansas City (he was traded to Cincinnati in midseason), pitched innings that were more critical than Johnson's innings. That's what happens when your team plays lots of close games.

By the way, Broxton's WPA total was only 1.00 despite pitching in a bunch of high-leverage innings. The difference was that Broxton didn't pitch well in the most critical situations.

I'm going to throw one more WPA-related creation at you: WPA/LI, which is sometimes called Situational Wins. The math is exactly how it looks: we take a pitcher's WPA and divide it by LI, each situation at a time, and then we add it up. The result is a stat that shows how well a pitcher (or batter) did without all that critical situation stuff. It's a performance metric that is influenced by the simple aspects of the situation.

Anyway, Broxton had one appearance in which the LI was above nine. His WPA/LI in that appearance was -0.012 (that's a negative sign). He actually didn't pitch badly—he got Coco Crisp to ground out with the bases loaded—but a run scored on the play because there were fewer than two outs.

Sidebar: *An average WPA/LI, in absolute terms, is 0.035 per play. That is, an average play swings 0.035 wins in either direction, depending on your point of view (batter vs. pitcher). That 0.035 wins is also the average swing in WPA, which is what you get when your average Leverage Index is one. Don't forget, however, that once you include negatives in the result, the overall average of WPA and WPA/LI is zero. Every step forward for one team is an equal step backward for another.*

Broxton wasn't really penalized too badly for giving up the run. After all, he got an out. On the other hand, Crisp did what he was supposed to do—he drove in the run by putting the ball in play. With no one on, that would have been a negative WPA/LI for Crisp, but with a runner on third it was a positive event. This is a good example of what WPA/LI captures and what normal counting stats don't.

Broxton faced six more situations with an LI between seven and eight and posted a positive WPA/LI only half the time. He gave up two singles and a walk, and netted two fly outs and one strikeout. Broxton definitely had a mixed record in critical situations.

Back in Baltimore, Johnson had one situation with an LI above ten (ground out; WPA/LI of 0.026) and 28 situations (plate appearances, mostly) with an LI between 4 and 10. In those 28 situations, he posted a positive WPA/LI 18 times and an overall average of 0.011. In all other less-leveraged situations, his WPA/LI was 0.007. In other words, the more critical the situation, the better he pitched.

Johnson was the star of the bullpen, but he wasn't the only superb reliever on the Orioles roster. Their next two best relievers were waiver pickups off the Rangers' roster: Pedro Strop and Darren O'Day.

Strop was the Orioles' setup man, and his LI was second on the team behind Johnson (1.68). He also finished with 1.23 WPA and 0.35 WPA/LI total. These aren't impressive totals for a pitcher with a devastating sinker, an ERA of 2.44, a 5-2 record and plentiful opportunities in the Baltimore bullpen. Strop didn't always pitch to the situation.

In his one very high-leverage situation, Strop walked Kyle Seagar with the bases loaded. In 21 situations with a Leverage Index between four and eight, he basically broke even (0.001 average WPA/LI). On the other hand, in 76 situations with the LI between two and four (typical high-profile setup situations), Strop was very good (average WPA/LI of 0.005). When the LI was below two, he once again broke even.

Strop contributed to the Orioles' remarkable record most when he played the standard, eighth-inning setup role. Manager Buck Showalter managed to find the right spots for Strop, bringing him in before the eighth inning only five times.

O'Day was a more versatile reliever and the overlooked key to the bullpen's success. The side-armer appeared in 69 games and posted a 2.28 ERA. Although his average Leverage Index was 1.12, he was fifth among all major league relievers with a 3.42 WPA.

No one was better than O'Day at rising to the occasion. In 51 situations with the LI between two and six, he posted a 0.010 WPA/LI, similar to Johnson's record. He also pitched in 27 low-LI situations (below two), but his WPA/LI was just 0.003.

No AL reliever came close to matching O'Day's ability to deliver the most when the game truly mattered. Although Showalter liked to use the side-armer against right-handed batters, O'Day held his own against lefties and sometimes stayed in the game for more than one inning. His versatility helped the Orioles a number of times, and O'Day was particularly impressive down the stretch, when he posted WPA game totals over 0.10 in four different outings.

Other relievers contributed to Baltimore's record-setting effort. Luis Ayala, a free agent pickup from the Yankees, appeared in 66 games with a 2.64 ERA. His WPA total was 1.23, and his average Leverage Index was 1.12. He is another pitcher who achieved better results when the situation was more critical, though not as extremely as O'Day did.

Left-hander Troy Patton, one of the pieces Baltimore acquired in the trade that sent Miguel Tejada to the Astros back in 2007, was in his second full major-league season. He has a strong sinker/slider combination that is particularly tough on lefties. Showalter liked to use him primarily against left-handed batters, but Patton handled right-handed batters too. His ERA was 2.43 in 54 games, and he had a 0.99 WPA and an average LI of 0.86.

Brian Matusz was dropped from the starting rotation and sent to the bullpen in the second half of the year, where he proved to be an effective reliever (0.017 average WPA/LI), as Showalter used him against left-handed batters frequently.

And no review of the Orioles' bullpen is complete without mentioning first baseman Chris Davis' appearance on the mound in the final two innings of a 17-inning, 9-6 win over Boston. Davis not only got the win, but he picked up 0.20 WPA wins.

This may be the easiest way to understand how the Orioles broke the major league record for bullpen WPA and won all those close games:

- Oriole relievers pitched more innings than the average team (their 545 innings was the fourth-highest total in the majors).
- They pitched well. Their WPA/LI was second-highest in the majors (5.5 vs. Tampa Bay's 6.0)
- Their Leverage Index was higher than average (1.09 vs. 1.03, though many teams were higher; Cincinnati's LI was 1.18, for example).
- Most importantly, they pitched to the situation. Check out the following table of bullpen situations:

LI	% of Situations		Average WPA/LI	
	League	BAL	League	BAL
4+	3.29%	3.61%	0.0009	0.0077
2-4	14.22%	16.82%	0.0018	0.0077
0-2	82.49%	79.56%	0.0013	0.0010

Here you can see that they pitched in relatively more high-leverage situations (16.8 percent vs. 14.2 percent of total situations had an LI between two and four) and, more importantly—thanks to the remarkable clutch performances of O'Day, Johnson and Ayala—they performed much better than the league average in those situations (0.0077 vs. 0.0018). They had an even more lopsided advantage in the most critical situations (LI higher than four).

Okay, let's move onto batting. You didn't hear much about him after the season was over, but it was Joey Votto who actually led the major leagues in batting WPA last year. His 6.32 WPA led second-place Mike Trout by a full game.

At 4.81, Votto's WPA/LI was lower than his WPA. This means he did a fine job of matching his performance to the situation, because you increase your overall WPA by posting a better WPA/LI in higher-leverage situations. For most batters (those with an average Leverage Index close to one), you can calculate their clutch performance by subtracting WPA/LI from their WPA. This is a quick and easy way to calculate the "O'Day effect" of performing better in more important situations.

Votto's figure wasn't the most clutch in the majors last year—that distinction belongs to Jimmy Rollins—but it was close. You can find this stat by looking up Clutch on FanGraphs.com, in the Win Probability section.

Would it surprise you to find out that the Orioles' bullpen was first in the majors in Clutch last year (7.19)? Would it surprise you to find out that this was also a new major league record?

Sorry, back to batting. The Orioles scored 712 runs last year, eight runs below the major league average. Their WPA was -0.81, almost exactly what you would expect, given their number of runs scored. Yet Orioles hitters contributed to Baltimore's amazing record, too. Their Clutch score was 1.77.

Baltimore's top WPA contributor with the bat was Adam Jones, who hit .287/.334/.505, and finished with a WPA of 3.03 and a Clutch score of 1.09. His biggest hit of the year was a single to left with two outs in the 11th inning of a July 13 game against the Tigers. The Leverage Index for that situation was 6.7.

Yes, Jones rose to the occasion, too. When the LI of a situation was between zero and two, his average WPA/LI was 0.002. When it was between two and four, his average WPA/LI was 0.008. And when the LI rose above four, his average WPA/LI was 0.010. No other Baltimore batter contributed quite the way Jones did.

WPA is unkind to starting pitching because starters don't often get to pitch in high-leverage situations. At least, not these days. That's why we prefer to rank starters by WPA/LI. It won't surprise you to find out that Justin Verlander led the majors in pitching WPA/LI, at 4.46. His Clutch score was negative, but that obviously wasn't a large issue for the big guy.

Jason Hammel led the Orioles' rotation in WPA/LI with a 1.43 mark, despite missing much of the second half. Baltimore starters weren't a dynamic bunch, but they were surprisingly solid. They don't enter into this story because they weren't really factors in the quirkiness of the Orioles' year, but don't count them out in future years.

Other WPA Stories in 2012

In the current implementation of WPA, each team starts out with a 50 percent chance of winning a game (other implementations could give the home team a 54 percent chance, or could factor in the quality of the starting pitchers, but Fangraphs and Baseball Reference don't do that). The winning team moves toward a 100 percent chance of winning by the end of the game; the losing team moves toward zero.

So the quickest, least competitive game would have only 0.5 WPA points in total. The winning team would take over right away and crush the opponent, effectively reaching nearly 100 percent very early in the game.

The least competitive game of 2012 was played between the Giants and Astros on June 13. The Giants, in their friendly home confines, rolled out to a 2-0 lead by the end of the first, a 5-0 lead by the end of the second and a 7-0 lead by the end of the third. They eventually won the game by a score of 10-0, and there was a total of only 0.62 WPA points accrued during the game.

Oh, and Matt Cain pitched a perfect game.

Since the game was a rout, Cain picked up only 0.12 WPA points on his perfect day. On the other hand, he did post a WPA/LI of 0.505. Not bad.

The most competitive game of 2012 was the May 17 affair between Colorado and Arizona in Denver. The Rockies had a 4-2 lead after six innings (77 percent probability of winning), but the Diamondbacks scored one in the seventh and four in the eighth to take a 7-4 lead (an 87 percent probability of victory for them). The Rockies scored three in the eighth to tie things up (all runs scored with two outs), but Arizona took the game in the top of the ninth on a Justin Upton home run (worth 0.4 WPA points itself).

Given all the ups and downs, this game totaled 9.45 WPA points before being settled, the largest total for a nine-inning game.

Felix Hernandez turned in the two best pitching performances of the year according to his WPA totals. On August 8, he pitched a complete-game, 1-0 victory over the Yankees in Yankee Stadium. Hernandez struck out six and gave up only two hits while making a lone second-inning run stand for the Mariners victory. His WPA total was 0.85.

Three weeks later, on August 27, he did the same thing against the Twins, this time making an eighth-inning run hold up for the Seattle victory. His 0.82 WPA total was the second-best single-game total in the majors.

On June 8, the Diamondbacks were playing an interleague game against the A's and were losing, 8-6, with two runners on and two outs in the bottom of the ninth.

Ryan Roberts hit a home run off Brian Fuentes to win it for Arizona, 9-8. In WPA terms, that was the biggest hit of the year, worth 0.90 WPA.

The biggest batting day of the year was Votto's May 13th. The Reds first baseman was 4-for-5 with three home runs and six RBI, which is, you know, pretty impressive. But the key thing is that his last home run was a grand slam in the bottom of the ninth, with two outs and the Reds losing, 6-5. That is how you win ballgames. Votto's WPA was 1.05 that day.

On July 13, San Diego second baseman Everth Cabrera was on third base with two outs in the top of the ninth and his team down by a run to the Dodgers. When Kenley Jansen got a little too focused on dirt in his shoe, Cabrera took off and stole home. Will Venable scored, too, because when Jansen threw home to try to nail Cabrera, he did so wildly. The Padres took the lead and, eventually, the game. That play, including the stolen base and error, was the biggest stolen-base play of the year, at 0.65 WPA.

> Sidebar: This play is a good illustration of the hazards of using play-by-play data on an automated basis to create stats like WPA. This play was a single event in the record books, but it's unclear how credit should be allocated between Cabrera and Venable. Dealing with fielding errors is also problematic.

Cabrera was the best basestealer in the majors last year, with his stolen bases accounting for 1.15 WPA points. That's what you get when you steal 44 bases and get caught only four times.

Raul Ibanez faced James Shields 17 times in 2012, and hit two doubles, one triple and two home runs. He was also walked four times. All of which added up to a 0.84 WPA total in that one batter/pitcher matchup, the most lopsided in the majors last year (minimum five plate appearances).

At the other end of the spreadsheet, the Twins' Glen Perkins was brought in seven times to face the Royals' left-handed batter Mike Moustakas, all in high-leverage situations. Perkins had Moustakas' number, as he struck him out four times and allowed only one hit. That was the most lopsided matchup for pitchers in 2012.

Finally, I want to return to Rollins' big year in the clutch. Overall, Rollins only hit .250/.316/.427. But in 188 plate appearances in which the Leverage Index was over 1.5, Rollins hit .368/.397/.585, a remarkable performance in the clutch. And this is where I remind you that clutch performances are almost entirely random and Rollins almost certainly won't approach this level of clutchiness again. Almost certainly...

Win Probability, the Math

Win Probability tables are nothing more than Run Expectancy tables built on top of each other. You know those Run Expectancy tables? The ones that say that with no one on and zero outs, the average team will score 0.55 runs in the inning? Or with a runner on second and one out, an average team will score 0.73 runs in the rest of the inning?

I highly recommend them, because they are the foundation of much of sabermetrics these days. You can find modeled Run Expectancy tables at Tangotiger's site. Try this URL:

http://www.insidethebook.com/ee/index.php/site/article/run_expectancy_by_run_environment/

You can also find a terrific piece of research highlighting year-by-year run expectancy changes at Retrosheet:

http://www.retrosheet.org/Research/RuaneT/valueadd_art.htm

As I said, Win Probability tables are simply Run Expectancy tables built on top of each other. You start with a potential game-ending situation—say a runner on first with two out in the bottom of the ninth—and you add the run expectancy table to see how probable it is the team will score enough runs to tie or win. And then you move backwards from there, to the beginning of the game.

Perhaps this sounds complicated, but it really isn't. I created the tables myself, in Excel, and you can download the Excel spreadsheet at the following website to see exactly how it's done:

ftp://ftp.baseballgraphs.com/wpa/

The results match closely with actual experience, which verifies the model. The reason you want to use the model instead of experience, by the way, is because you find some strange variations in specific situations in the real world. That's because there's not enough data to smooth things out. The model takes care of that.

As for Leverage Index, that is simply based on the range of possible win expectancy outcomes from the play in question. The larger the range of potential outcomes, the higher the leverage. It's been calculated by Tom Tango, but you can create a quick Leverage Index yourself simply by taking the difference between the current win expectancy and the win expectancy if the batter strikes out. This will work for all situations except when there's a runner on third with fewer than two outs.

One Last Point

I sometimes hear people say that Leverage Index doesn't work because getting outs in high leverage situations doesn't seem to correlate with winning. I found this hard to believe, so I decided to investigate it myself. In 2012...

- If a team got an out with an LI between 1.5 and 2, it won the game 60% of the time.
- If it got an out with leverage between 2 and 2.5, it won 62% of the time.
- If it got an out with leverage between 2.5 and 3, it won 68% of the time.
- If it got an out with leverage between 3 and 4, it won 69% of the time.
- If it got an out with leverage between 4 and 5, it won 71% of the time.
- If it got an out with leverage over 5, it won 76% of the time.

As you can see, when pitchers succeed in high-leverage situations, their teams are more likely to win the game. WPA isn't for everyone, but it does what it says it does.

Case Study: Edwin Encarnacion

Not many things went well for the Toronto Blue Jays in 2012. Jose Bautista got hurt. "Canadian hero" Brett Lawrie's power returned to earth and then some. Yunel Escobar not only hit poorly, but had an ugly incident with anti-gay slurs written onto his eye black in Spanish. Second baseman Kelly Johnson struggled badly at the plate, while the player the Jays traded for him, Aaron Hill, had a career year for Arizona. Adam Lind stunk it up. Pretty much every pitcher on the Opening Day starting rotation got hurt at some point, except for Rickey Romero, who was one of the worst pitchers in baseball in 2012.

Let's put it this way: When Jeff Mathis getting almost 300 plate appearances is not close to the worst thing that happened to a team, it was a rough year. It is sort of amazing that the Jays managed to win more than 70 games.

But one does not have to sift through the wreckage for long to find one thing that did go very well for the 2012 Blue Jays: Edwin Encarnacion, who broke out in a big way at age 29, hitting .280/.384/.557 (153 wRC+) with 42 homers for Toronto.

Encarnacion, nicknamed "E5" for his less-than-stellar glovework at third base (his former position), has had an interesting ride. Originally drafted out of his high school in Caguas, Puerto Rico in 2000 by the Rangers, Encarnacion was sent (along with Ruben Mateo) to the Cincinnati Reds in a trade for the forgettable Rob Bell.

Encarnacion showed some potential during his four-plus season with the Reds, especially in terms of power. In 2008, he hit 26 home runs. That would have been fine for a third baseman, except it was becoming increasingly apparent that Encarnacion was not much of a third baseman.

By the middle of 2009, the Reds had apparently seen enough, and sent Encarnacion to Toronto in a trade for Scott Rolen, mostly because the Blue Jays were trying to dump Rolen's salary. It may be hard to believe now, but Encarnacion was not the Jays' main target in the trade: They also received pitchers Josh Roenicke and Zach Stewart (neither of whom remains in the Toronto organization). The Reds did not want to pay Encarnacion's salary when they didn't have a place to play him, and the Jays needed someone to stand around third base.

It should have been obvious to everyone that 2010 was going to be a weird season for Encarnacion when he suffered facial burns from fireworks during the offseason. Strange stuff continued during and after the season. On the positive side, he managed 21 home runs in only 367 plate appearances. On the down side, Encarnacion's fielding was still poor. In addition, his walk rate dropped while his strikeouts went up. When he hit the ball, he hit tons of pop-ups, which kept his average down.

Encarnacion also suffered from injuries; he landed on the 15-day disabled list twice. In June, the Jays became so disenchanted with him that they outrighted him to Triple-A, although he was called back up a couple of weeks later. He ended the year with power and little else: .244/.305/.482, which equaled a 109 wRC+.

The strangeness continued after the season. Encarnacion was put on waivers and was claimed by Oakland in November. After less than a month "in" the As' organization, he was non-tendered. Two weeks later he returned to Toronto by signing a one-year contract for 2011 plus a club option for 2012.

Encarnacion had a good year in 2011 (batting .272/.334/.453) but he was a revelation in 2012. He played only one game at third base, and the defense he displayed in his 68 games at first was hardly dazzling. However, if a player can hit .280/.384/.557, he does not need a position. The Jays decided they did not want to wait for another team to bid on E5 ("EDH" doesn't really roll off of the tongue) in free agency, so they signed him to a three-year, $29 million extension for 2013 through 2015, with a $10 million club option for 2016. Some regression is to be expected, but Encarnacion does project to be worth the money.

What changed for Encarnacion at the plate in 2012? Obviously, he "hit better" and for "more power," but what is behind those facts? There seem to be two primary and related sources for his big year: improved plate discipline and hitting the ball harder.

While Encarnacion's on-base percentage had been middling-to-poor in prior seasons, that had less to do with a bad plate approach than with a poor average on balls in play (more on that in a minute). Encarnacion actually has mostly displayed good overall plate discipline. Although his walk rates were about average or below in 2010 and 2011, his strikeout rates were better than average in both years.

This has generally been the case for most of Encarnacion's major league career. Unlike some sluggers, he also has generally had average or slightly above-average contact rates. Even in 2011, one could find the roots of this improved approach: He had a career-best strikeout rate of only 14.5 percent. What we can take from this is that Encarnacion has always had a pretty good grasp on what pitches to swing at, even when he was not drawing a walk particularly often or getting hits.

In 2012, Encarnacion's plate discipline further improved. While his strikeout rate (14.6 percent) was basically the same as it was in 2011, his walk rate jumped from eight to 13 percent. This might be partly due to pitchers avoiding the strike zone against him after his increased power became evident. During this past season, 49.7 percent of the pitches Encarnacion saw were in the strike zone, as opposed to 52.3 in 2011. However, since his 2012 "Zone" percentage was essentially the same in 2010 as it was in 2012, this can't account for all of the improvement.

Encarnacion simply showed better selectivity all around. He had previously been a league average hitter as measured by the percentage of pitches at which he swung. In 2011, for example, the league average swing rate was 45.3 percent, while Encarnacion swung at 46.2 of pitches he saw. In 2012, he took it to a new level. While the league average swing rate at all pitches was again 45.3 percent, Encarnacion swung at only 40.4 percent of the pitches he saw.

He was more patient with pitches both inside and out of the zone. In 2011 he swung at 64.9 percent of pitches in the zone; in 2012 only 59.8 percent. In 2011, Encarnacion swung at 25.7 percent of pitches he saw outside the zone. That was better than league average, but not nearly as good as his 21.1 percent swing rate at non-strikes in 2012. All three figures for 2012—swings generally, swings at pitches in the zone, and swings at pitches outside the zone—were career lows for Encarnacion. He was simply more patient.

When he did choose to take the bat off of his shoulder, the ball tended to go a long, long way. According to ESPN Hit Tracker, in 2010 the average speed of a home run off of Encarnacion's bat was 104.9 mph, and the average standard distance ("standard distance" meaning adjusted for win, altitude, and other physical issues so that home runs from different parks and environments can be compared) was 402 feet. In 2011, the speed and distance of his home runs remained basically the same: slightly faster at 105.2 mph, but a bit shorter at (399.9 feet). In both years, Encarnacion's home run velocity and distance were comfortably above league average. This season, he took things to a new level. His home runs averaged 106.4 miles per hour off of the bat and 411.5 feet standard distance. So yes, when he hit home runs, he was simply hitting them harder.

If we look at his rates of home runs per batted ball compared to his rate of extra base hits on hits in play (triples and doubles—well, in E5's case the last three years, just doubles, as he has not hit a triple since 2009) during the last three seasons, we see a pattern. In 2012, he posted his highest rate of home runs on batted balls (9.2 percent), better than in 2010 (7.6 percent) and much better than in 2011 (4.1 percent). However, the ranking of seasons based on rate of extra-base hits on hits in play goes the opposite direction—the highest rate is in 2011 (31.6 percent of hits in play), the next highest in 2010 (26.7 percent), then 2012 (21.8 percent). What this likely means is that many of the balls that Encarnacion had been hitting for doubles in the previous two seasons left the yard in 2012.

Although I noted above that Encarnacion's increase in walks cannot be necessarily attributed simply to pitchers "fearing" his newfound home run power, there is certainly a general relation between home runs and walks (and plate discipline more generally). It is likely a circular relation, though. To a certain extent, pitchers probably did try to avoid the center of the plate more often in 2012 once Encarnacion made it clear he was destroying baseballs more frequently than in the past.

However, it is also probably the case that Encarnacion was able to do the damage he did because he was picking his spots more carefully. Not only did being more patient increase his walk rate, but it also made it more likely that he was going to get a pitch that he could knock over the fence. In particular, his increased willingness or ability to let a pitch outside of the strike zone pass by might indicate that he had a better idea of where pitches were in the zone in general, and where he could take those.

Indeed, in recent years we have seen that other hitters who seem to develop monster power seemingly overnight, such as Ben Zobrist in 2009 and Encarnacion's teammate Jose Bautista starting in 2010, develop good strike zone judgment first as a prerequisite for choosing the pitches that they can drive.

Right until the end of the season, it looked as though Encarnacion might deprive Miguel Cabrera of the Triple Crown. He did not, but the very fact that he is being mentioned in the same sentence as Cabrera gives a pretty good idea of the monster season Encarnacion had.

While Encarnacion's age, past history, and plain old regression to the mean make it likely that he will not repeat this level of performance again, he does have a good foundation for at least being very good at the plate: good strike zone judgment, plate patience, and simple brute power. Whatever else went wrong for the Toronto Blue Jays in 2012, they and their fans should be very happy with Encarnacion's emergence and his contract.

- Matt Klaassen

Ethics and Major League Baseball, 2012

by Jack Marshall

In our fast-paced world, traditions are established every 15 minutes, and fads burn out on the Internet before the majority of people even learn about them. In the process of jumping from one story, one controversy, one game, one tweet to the next, ethics often get lost. So it's good to take a step back at the end of the year and ruminate. As such, here are some of the year's most prominent ethics-twinged stories.

Cole Hamels Misses the Ethics Memo

When Phillies starter Cole Hamels plunked brash Nationals rookie Bryce Harper with a 92-mile-per-hour heater during a nationally televised game on May 6, nobody in the stands or watching at home knew that they were witnessing the beginning of an ethical adjustment in the culture of baseball. When Hamels admitted that he had thrown at Harper intentionally, however, the reaction from the public, the sports media and those within the game itself showed that something significant had changed.

"I was trying to hit him," Hamels told a reporter. "I'm not going to deny it. It's something I grew up watching ... I'm just trying to continue the old baseball. Some people get away from it. I remember when I was a rookie, the strike zone was really, really small and you didn't say anything. That's the way baseball is."

Not any more, it isn't. The backlash at Hamels was quick and furious. Washington Nationals general manager Mike Rizzo fumed, "I've never seen a more classless, gutless chicken s--- act in my 30 years in baseball!" NBC baseball blogger (and former Hardball Times "shyster") Craig Calcaterra agreed. "Spare me your 'it has always been thus' arguments," he wrote. "Just because something is a tradition doesn't make it right. People have had their careers ended by thrown baseballs before. ... We decry cheap shots and intentional efforts to harm opponents in every other sport. We should feel no differently about it in baseball."

Yet as reasoned and ethically sound as Calcaterra's sentiments were, the undeniable fact is that we did feel differently about it for a long time, and few gave it a second thought. The fastball in the ribs or the "close shave" was a rite of passage for hot-shot rookies like Harper for decades. The messages that these pitches were supposed to convey were many: "Welcome to the big leagues, rook!" "Respect your elders!" "You gotta earn the right to dig in on me, kid!" and "Let's see if you can take it!"

In *Field of Dreams*, the young "Moonlight Graham" goes to the plate knowing that the veteran (also dead) pitcher on the mound is likely to be throwing at his head. "Where do you think the next one's gonna be?" Shoeless Joe Jackson asks the kid. "Well, either low and away, or in my ear," the rookie replies. "He's not gonna wanna load the bases, so look low and away," Joe tells him. "But watch out for in your ear." This was not intoned as an admission of impending evil. This was how baseball was played, and the fans knew and accepted it. It wasn't brutality. It was fun.

The values of the game have changed, but some, like Hamels, didn't get the memo. Tony Conigliaro wasn't a rookie, but in August of 1967 he was a Boston outfielder just a few years older than Harper and the youngest player ever to reach 100 home runs. A Jack Hamilton pitch shattered his face, permanently damaged his vision, and robbed him of a potential Hall of Fame career. The handsome Conigliaro's swollen eye made the cover of national publications and gave fans nightmares, while his stuttering and ultimately failed comeback lasted several years and kept memories of the incident alive and ugly.

It was right at the end of Conigliaro's first abortive comeback (there would be another) that Major League Baseball made batting helmets mandatory. Two years later, the designated hitter arrived in the American League, and pitchers intentionally hitting batters, no matter what the message, tradition or provocation, seemed less sporting and more cowardly. No longer would the pitcher have his own moment of truth, standing at the plate with the ball in the hand of his previous target's teammate.

The seeds of cultural disapproval of the old tradition were sown. Gradually, umpires started enforcing a previously dead-letter rule, warning pitchers and throwing them and their managers out of games for intentionally hitting batters. Another star, Kirby Puckett, suffered a serious beaning in 1995, and by 2002, not merely helmets but helmets with Little League-style flaps were mandated.

The final shift in ethical perceptions might have occurred last year, when a hard slide into Giants catcher Buster Posey ended his season, endangered his career, and sparked a Rizzo-like condemnation of the play from Giants GM Brian Sabean. Though the incident involved a hard slide rather than a beanball, Posey—like Conigliaro and Harper—was (and still is) a young star, and this was a tipping point: No longer would baseball or, more importantly, the public tolerate sacrificing promising careers to tradition. A new ethics standard for baseball was in place.

The episode is an excellent example of how societal ethics affect ethical values in baseball. Sports are public rituals that both reflect and shape attitudes about what we like, don't like, tolerate and don't tolerate, as well as the conduct we want to encourage or eliminate. The result of all this is what we call culture: How a nation, a society or a sport defines its values and ideals.

The symbiotic relationship between baseball and the society that makes it popular and profitable means that neither half of the relationship can safely ignore shifts in values on the part of the other. The ethical choices of any profession—and MLB is no exception—are always based on a complex and eccentric relationship among three separate ethical systems.

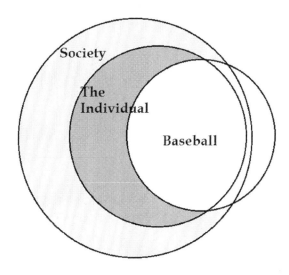

The diagram illustrates the components of the ethical mix. The big circle, light gray in the diagram, is by far the largest, heaviest and most influential—it is not drawn to scale, because it is too large. It is the Societal Circle, encompassing society's ethics and values, a huge and messy combination of religion, law, tradition, philosophy, history, family teaching, mythology, literature, popular culture and experience. As much of a dog's breakfast as this seems, our society, according to science and ethics writer Michael Shermer, reaches agreement on about 97 percent of what is right and wrong. We defy the Societal Circle at our peril, and it often exerts enough gravity through various means to force conformity from the other two circles.

The smallest circle, white in the diagram, is baseball, though it can be any separate profession or culture within society. It has its own alignment of values peculiar to its rules and traditions as a game, a sport, a business and "America's pastime." All such sub-cultures have that little bulge you see sticking outside society's big circle—it defines them. This is the segment of its ethics package where baseball approves of conduct that the public may think is unethical, for example, an outfielder trapping a fly ball the umpire mistakenly calls an out, and not flagging the umpire's mistake. In all professions and sub-cultures, this area tends to shrink as the gravitational pull of the Societal Circle forces conformity with societal values. The public is more influenced by society's ethics than baseball's ethics, and baseball is ultimately responsive to the public.

We are seeing this process in the area of video reviews of controversial umpire calls. Baseball's ethical standard for decades was that occasional bad calls were "part of the game," and what the umpire decided, accurate or not, was reality. I knew, and I assume MLB knew, that once this bedrock myth was exploded, the public would begin demanding a new standard, and that is what is taking place now.

When a series of important games in 2011 were adversely affected by umpires' home run calls that TV cameras showed were unequivocally wrong, the public outcry was so great that MLB surrendered, and installed a video review process that was supposedly going to be limited to questionable home runs and nothing else. That baseball bulge outside the big Societal Circle had been reduced a little more, however, and when the 2012 season started, the public and sports writers quickly showed that they no longer embraced the old "it's right, because it's part of the game" rationalization for blown calls.

In an April 16 game at Fenway Park, Boston outfielder Cody Ross had a chance to bat with the potential tying and winning runs on base. Ross had been hot, and since just one game between the Rays and Sox in the previous season had sent the Rays to the playoffs and the Red Sox to perdition, the moment had genuine tension.

But Ross never had a chance. Rays closer Fernando Rodney threw five pitches to Ross, and not one of them was even arguably over the plate. Still, home plate umpire Larry Vanover called Ross out on strikes without Ross ever taking the bat off his shoulder. After the game, several commentators posted the sequence in various graphic forms, confirming what the eye and the live video indicated. In a tight game, before a full park, at a critical point, with postseason significance given the competitors, Vanover blew three calls and cheated Ross, both teams, and the fans of a fairly decided contest.

While baseball held to its ethical standard that what the umps decided, even when wrong, was just an unalterable condition of the game, such instances were tolerable to the public: When you have no option, you have no problem. Baseball's capitulation on home run calls, however, constituted an admission that human error was a problem, not a feature, and that there were options.

No, nothing has changed yet, but another tipping point is nigh. All we need is a Ross-type sequence in a play-off game or two, and the bulge will grow smaller still.

Stephen Strasburg and the Individual Circle

Mediating between societal ethics and baseball ethics are the ethical decisions of bold or influential individuals, represented by the Individual Circle, who may side with either or chart new territory neither ever anticipated. Individuals often have to improvise around rules, laws and societal norms to solve peculiar problems, and if they do it successfully and convincingly, and if they have sufficient prestige and influence, the other two circles will notice and adjust accordingly.

Before the season began, the Washington Nationals had hopes of finally signaling their entry into the ranks of competitive teams for the foreseeable future. With that future firmly in mind, Nationals management pledged that Stephen Strasburg, the team's young fire-balling ace who seems destined for greatness, would be shut down for good once he approached the 160-180 inning barrier. Strasburg had already endured serious arm surgery once, and conventional baseball wisdom holds that throwing too many pitches before a pitcher has matured risks his arm, his effectiveness and his career.

Nobody blinked at the Nationals' pledge. The public had already seen the Yankees' "Joba Rules" in action (that worked out well!), and they, perhaps like Washington's brass, fully expected that by the time Strasburg's innings limit kicked in, the team would be basking in a season that would be a great step forward, but nowhere near good enough for a postseason appearance.

Wrong. As the limit approached, the Nationals were almost certain National League playoff qualifiers, and based on their record, a serious World Series contender. Did it make sense to battle the best teams in baseball in pursuit of a World Series title with their best pitcher completely healthy but in mothballs? Rizzo declared that it was. He would not yield: He had pledged to do what was in the pitcher's best long-term interests, and still believed that this was in the best interests of the team.

With this stance, Rizzo was bucking both the Societal Circle and Baseball Ethics from his own, personal sphere of values. The public believes that athletes, within reason, should give their all to win for their team, and that the team should encourage them to do so. Baseball has traditionally agreed. When it comes to winning the World Series, you play for today, not next year. This is why Curt Schilling pitched two games in the 2004 postseason with his ankle tendon crudely stitched to his skin, and was cheered for it.

In the *Washington Post*, baseball writer John Feinstein wrote a well-reasoned column on the controversy that ended with this:

"Pitching a healthy Strasburg in October is not a betrayal, it's simply recognizing that circumstances have changed. Not pitching him is a betrayal: to the pitcher, to the team, to the fans and to the city."

Feinstein's use of the word "betrayal" places the question squarely in the category of duty and obligation—the ethics strike zone. To whom does a baseball team owe its primary duty? The answer has always been, and still is, the sport, the city whose name is on its uniforms and the team's fans. The welfare of the players on the team's payroll is on the duty list for sure, but they finish fourth. When a championship is on the line, they are expected to take reasonable risks with their bodies, their health and their careers, and the team is obligated to let them do it. Taking such risks is "part of the game," and one of the good parts, as is playing hard, and harder when championships are on the line. It is essential to the integrity of baseball or any sport.

For the Nationals to have taken one of their top starting pitchers out of the rotation in an exercise of special caution—and in doing so sacrificing the strength of their team in the postseason—made neither logical nor ethical sense, based on prior standards, duties and priorities. From a purely business standpoint in today's free agent environment, there is no reason for the Nationals to care whether Strasburg's career is like Fernando Valenzuela's or Dwight Gooden's, a comet that peters out by the time he is 30, or like Roger Clemens', a pitcher who has early career arm surgery and then pitches into senility. Players are not reliably loyal, and Strasburg's agent is Scott Boras, who typically leads his stable to the biggest contracts possible, no matter how happy they were with their original teams. Why should the Nationals give up a possible World Series so the New York Yankees can have Strasburg winning 20 games a season for them? The team's duty is to maximize its own success, not to maximize Strasburg's career income.

The Nationals' leadership and some of Washington's sports journalists made noises about how the wisdom of the decision would be evident when the team was winning championships galore in future years. A cursory examination of baseball history shows that such an argument is either dishonest or ignorant.

There was also no consensus in the medical community that cutting off Strasburg's innings would preserve his arm, or that letting him pitch more than 180 innings would endanger it. In Chicago, the contending White Sox were continuing to pitch Chris Sale, their emerging young star who had never pitched 80 innings in a season.

For a decision that was supposed to be for Strasburg's benefit, this one seemed oddly cruel: It robbed Strasburg of the chance to help win a championship that his talents and efforts got his team in the position to seize, the opportunity to play and star in the national spotlight, and to burnish his career with World Series heroics. The argument that Strasburg is a young and budding superstar, and will have other chances, like the assumption of future success for the team, is belied by history. Great pitchers like Ferguson Jenkins, Gaylord Perry and Phil Neikro never played in a World Series. Nolan Ryan never started a game in the one in which he played. Juan Marichal got just one chance too, with a team, the 1962 Giants, that everyone thought would be back. It didn't turn out that way, and it might not for Strasburg.

The pledge to limit the young pitcher's innings made sense before the season when a postseason for the Nationals seemed like a distant dream. Once that dream became reality, Rizzo's ethical priorities were out of order. His duty was to the team, the city and the fans, not to keep an out-of-date promise.

Ironically, whether Rizzo's Individual Circle decision is remembered as a betrayal or influences the other ethical systems depends on factors having nothing to do with ethics, logic or the decision itself. The absence of the Nationals' star seems to have handicapped the team in the postseason, and if Strasburg's next World Series appearance is in another uniform, Rizzo's call will live in infamy, as it will if he is collecting Social Security when the Nats next reach the Fall Classic. If, in the alternative, the

Nationals win without Strasburg and he leads the team in subsequent championship campaigns, Rizzo's dubious ethics may even alter the game's traditional priorities.

If so, this would be a capitulation to consequentialism, the flawed theory that the rightness or wrongness of conduct should be assessed according to its ultimate results. Consequentialism is an invitation to extreme "ends justify the means" rationalizations. A decision is ethical or not based on the circumstances when it was made, and when the final decision was made to shelve Strasburg, it was an unethical one.

Individual Circle Corruption: Joe Maddon

Because the Individual Circle often serves as the mediator between the other two, any sub-culture, like baseball, requires responsible role models who use their influence properly and productively. When a perceived ethical figure in the culture fails this standard, the ethics of the culture are imperiled, or perhaps already corrupt.

A disturbing incident illustrating this occurred in June, when the Tampa Bay Rays were playing the Washington Nationals in an interleague game. Both teams were in the hunt for a playoff spot in their respective leagues. Rays manager Joe Maddon called in relief pitcher Joel Peralta to take the mound, and Nats manager Davey Johnson, apparently on more than a hunch, asked the umpires to check Peralta's glove for a "foreign substance" that might make his pitches do loop-de-loops on the way to the plate. Sure enough, Peralta had enough pine tar on his glove to have the baseball do the Macarena, and he was duly thrown out of the game.

Maddon has an established reputation as an ethical exemplar, a straight arrow who stands for playing the game "the right way." He's an educated man, a college grad, and a deep thinker, and—we are told—believes in integrity and honesty. He also was 2011's AL Manager of the Year, which means that he is one of the select group of baseball figures whose conduct and words have a real chance of influencing others in the game. So when his pitcher was caught cheating, I expected Maddon to be furious at a cheating player besmirching the honor of his Tampa Bay uniform. But no. Maddon was angry at Johnson.

He told reporters that Johnson's move was "cowardly," and found it objectionable that Johnson must have relied on "inside information." Maddon condemned the Nats manager for "ratting out" the Rays pitcher for cheating, and said that even players on Johnson's own team would be indignant at this breach of baseball ethics, as Maddon interpreted them. Maddon added that using pine tar to doctor pitches—like the spitball, only better—should be allowed, because so many pitchers do it.

In this one incident, Maddon revealed the dark side of baseball's ethics, and showed that he was not, as I assumed, one who would use the gravity of his own strong ethical values to bring the game into a sturdier ethical orbit. Maddon, a role model, endorsed three toxic ethical principles in this incident:

1. Loyalty to culture over ethical duty. Johnson's ethical obligation is to protect his team and win the game for his organization, not to uphold some misguided Mafia-like code of never blowing the whistle on cheating and misconduct.
2. "Ratting" is the pejorative word for self-policing, and every profession or organization must self-police to maintain its integrity.
3. Maddon's contention that doctoring the ball should be legal because it was so common is a classic articulation of the Golden Rationalization, "Everybody does it." It is the refrain of cheaters of all kinds in all pursuits, probably since the beginning of time.

We need look no further than these statements from one of the games' leaders who is respected for his ethical values to understand how baseball fell under the shadow of performance enhancing drugs for so long, and why the one who finally blew the whistle was not an ethics role model in the game, but Jose Canseco, an ex-player motivated by purely unethical motives, principally greed and vengeance.

The Individual Circle is probably the weakest component of baseball's ethical system.

PED's, Fairness, the Ethics Incompleteness Theorem and Melky Cabrera

One would think that ethics in baseball shouldn't be so complicated. There are rules and well-established traditions. The game is played out in the open air, and thoroughly covered in the press and the media. It's been around for about 150 years. But in baseball, as in every other endeavor, unique situations occur that the rules and traditions never anticipated and thus cannot handle neatly. Nothing demonstrates this better than the ongoing chaos surrounding performance-enhancing drug use in baseball.

The game thought it turned the page after the publication of the Mitchell Report and the establishment of tougher testing procedures, but as is always the case with any set of rules or laws, anomalies have arisen requiring new judgments about fairness and integrity. The 2012 baseball season was sandwiched between two such anomalies, neither of which had a completely satisfactory resolution.

Before the season began, it was revealed that Ryan Braun, the 2011 NL Most Valuable Player, tested positive for steroids during the postseason. The news sent a wave of nausea throughout baseball. He was supposed to be one of the game's rising young "post-steroid era" stars, and now the legitimacy of his MVP season was called into question. Braun vehemently denied the charges (as most positive-testing players have) and appealed them, a move that had been futile in every previous case. To the surprise of all, however, a three-member arbitration panel ruled 2-1 in Braun's favor. Braun prevailed because the MLB contractor responsible for sending Braun's urine samples to the testing facilities had to store them at his own house over a weekend because his local FedEx drop had closed before he could mail them to the lab. This created a sufficient break in the chain of custody, the deciding arbitrator ruled, to invalidate the results.

Though Braun immediately gave a public statement in which he claimed to be exonerated, and impugned the integrity of Dino Laurenzi, the contractor who collected the sample, there was and is no rational reason to believe that Laurenzi tampered with the specimens. The arbitration panel concluded that for the specimens to be in the possession of non-laboratory personnel for more than 24 hours undermined the integrity of the testing procedure, but while that invalidated Braun's results, it didn't make his positive test any less damning, unless someone can come up with a reason why Laurenzi or someone with access to his home would conspire to try to ruin Braun's career.

With something as career-staining as a positive drug test, and with the punishment so severe (Braun would have been suspended for 50 games to begin the 2012 season, costing him millions and seriously handicapping his team, the Milwaukee Brewers), it is right and just that testing procedures be unimpeachable. That is only a due process verdict, however. Whatever Braun did, he did in spite of that surprising arbitrator's vote. If he was guilty of cheating, the vote didn't make him innocent, and if he was innocent, he wouldn't have become guilty if the arbitrator had voted the other way. The results of the process don't change the facts, and the facts make it overwhelmingly likely that Braun was cheating with performance-enhancing drugs during the 2011 season.

Does that make his MVP award tainted? Of course it does. If these facts had been known before the voting, would Braun have still won? I doubt it. Did the ruling of the arbitration panel exonerate him? No; it simply registered the opinion, ultimately based on the decision of one arbitrator, that proper procedures weren't followed. Could MLB take any action against Braun (as, for example, Judge Landis took against Shoeless Joe Jackson, banning him from baseball based on his testimony at a trial that acquitted him), like taking away his MVP Award? Not with a players union to contend with, it couldn't, and such action would re-open the uncomfortable issue of other MVP Awards won by players widely assumed to have been steroid users.

In the absence of applicable rules or established ethical standards, therefore, an ethical result may be impossible. Is it fair to those Braun defeated for the MVP Award that he won it with the assistance of banned substances, if that is the case? No. Is it fair to Braun for him to be permanently sullied by the suspicion that he cheated, if he did not use PEDs? No. Does the failure of baseball's procedures require future fans, baseball historians and Hall of Fame voters to ignore Braun's positive test? No.

Sometimes an ethical result is made impossible by a bad recipe of unexpected events and imperfect rules or procedures.

Another messy PED situation arose in August, when Giants outfielder Melky Cabrera was suspended for the rest of the season for testing positive for performance-enhancing substances. The suspension froze his average, which was leading the NL. Because he had already amassed sufficient at-bats to qualify for the title, this meant that (1) he would benefit from what was supposed to be a punishment and (2) one of the most prestigious of all baseball season statistical titles would be won by a proven cheater. Again, baseball was caught without a rule or procedure that covered a situation affecting the integrity of the game. There were the predictable calls from fans and sportswriters to simply ignore due process—that is, not follow the existing rules—and declare Cabrera ineligible for the batting crown.

Ex post facto rules, however, are inherently unethical; this is why such laws are banned in the Constitution. Being fair means that even cheaters have rights, and one of them is to be able to know what their risks and penalties are if they cheat. Cabrera knew that he risked suspension, a loss of millions in income, and permanent harm to his reputation and career. He did not know that he risked forfeiting a batting championship if he qualified for it. It makes sense that a player suspended after testing positive for performance-enhancing drug use should be disqualified from winning honors in that season, but because MLB didn't think of it when it was making the rules, it would be unethical for Cabrera, like Braun, to be subjected to such a penalty.

In Cabrera's case, however, baseball created the ethics equivalent of Frankenstein's Monster, stitching together dubious components to arrive at what seemed like a desirable result. Cabrera himself wrote to the MLB Players Association and requested that it work with MLB to allow him to withdraw himself from consideration in the NL batting race. This the union did, with the result being that MLB added a "one time amendment" to Rule 10.22(a), which describes how a league determines its batting champion. This was a textbook erroneous response to what I call the ethics incompleteness dilemma.

With any rule or ethical principle, there will be anomalies that occur in which a strict application of the rule or principle leads to an undesirable or bizarre result. This is the incompleteness dilemma.

When faced with the consequences of ethics incompleteness, you have three choices:

1. Apply the rule anyway, and live with the results. This is the conservative approach, and if the anomalies are rare enough, it is often the best one. When following the rule is going to be unequivocally disastrous, however, as when an anti-torture absolutist knows that the last available way to get a madman to confess where he placed a world-ending nuclear bomb is to start pulling out his fingernails, stubbornly sticking to principle may be unwise.

2. Re-conceive the rule to include a reasonable solution to the dilemma created by the anomaly. There are dual problems with this approach. When it is done while the anomaly is still pending, that violates due process. When it involves an amendment after the fact, the amendment often makes the rule or principle less valid, less enforceable and subject to more anomalies. This is the liberal approach to ethics incompleteness.

3. Treat the anomaly as if there were no rule at all, making the most sensible decision, but not amending the rule or principle going forward. This is the favored approach of anarchists and supporters of ethical relativism. It is often the best and fairest response to an individual dilemma, but it is undisciplined and addictive, and rapidly turns into a bad habit that risks leaving all principles and rules vulnerable.

As you can see, any of the solutions may be appropriate in specific instances, or disastrous in others. In the Cabrera situation, MLB and the players union opted for a cross between No. 2 and No. 3: It amended the rule, but just for Cabrera, and nobody else. I think this was wrong. The ethical approach in this case was No. 2, an amendment to the rule going forward only, that would make players suspended for positive drug tests in the future ineligible for individual championships and awards for that season. Taking Cabrera out of the race using a "one time amendment" didn't really limit such an improvised solution to this single instance. It created several bad precedents:

1. The precedent of "one time amendments" any time a baseball rule has an undesirable result. That means that no baseball rule can be relied upon, ever.

2. The precedent of allowing a player to reject an achievement or record he has reached under the rules. Cabrera's request was self-serving; he knew that winning a batting championship in such a disreputable way would cause him to be resented by players and fans alike, and add to his humiliation. My reaction: good.

3. The precedent of allowing the offender in a disciplinary situation to have input into the terms of his own punishment.

So Cabrera ducks his tainted batting championship, while Braun proudly keeps his tainted MVP Award. What's the standard? Darned if I know. In baseball, as in life, ethics isn't easy.

Q&A: Optimizing the Batting Order

by David Laurila

The traditional baseball lineup includes several tenets. The leadoff hitter is fast and can steal bases. The guy in the two-hole is a good bunter and can execute the hit-and-run. Your biggest home run threat bats in the cleanup position. The ninth-place hitter is your worst hitter.

Even with the advancement of statistical analysis, some managers follow these old, familiar scripts. For every team that pays attention to run-probability charts and computer models, there is a Dusty Baker or a Bobby Valentine who will hit a poor on-base percentage guy at the top of his order because he runs well. Many still employ a bat-control artist in the two hole, even if that artistry doesn't include an ability to reach base consistently.

Strategy has its own traditions. The sacrifice bunt has been utilized for over 100 years and is still employed on a regular basis. Mike Scioscia, skippering a power-laden lineup, gave up a league-leading 47 outs via the sacrifice this past year.

Are these methods outdated or inherently wrong? That is partly in the eye of the beholder, as not all lineups are created equal, nor are the decision-makers and players. Throughout the course of the 2012 season, nine of them offered their perspectives—some of which have been previously published at FanGraphs.com—on lineup construction, the concept of both protection in the lineup and a second leadoff hitter, and the sacrifice bunt. Weighing in were [all job descriptions as of October, 2012]:

- Manny Acta, former Cleveland Indians and Washington Nationals manager
- Daniel Bard, Boston Red Sox pitcher
- Tim Bogar, Boston Red Sox bench coach
- Sam Fuld, Tampa Bay Rays outfielder
- Joe Maddon, Tampa Bay Rays manager
- Dave Martinez, Tampa Bay Rays bench coach
- Jarrod Saltalamacchia, Boston Red Sox catcher
- Buck Showalter, Baltimore Orioles manager
- Ned Yost, Kansas City Royals manager

The Top of the Order and Optimizing At-Bats for your Best Hitters

Joe Maddon:

"You want your best hitters up as often as you can. The thing with us—and you could make the argument about the third and fourth spots—is that I like Longo [Evan Longoria] in the four hole, because I truly like Jennings and Upton one-two. They work so well together. Part of it is that B.J.—for whatever the intangible reasons are—does a great job in the two-hole. He feels comfortable there.

"Zobrist in the three-hole is what really matters. If those two guys don't get on for Longo, I feel pretty confident that Zo will. That's as opposed to hitting Zobrist behind him, or moving one of those two guys down in the batting order. That's the part of it I really want to remain static: Jennings and Upton—speed, speed, power—Zobrist's high ability to get on base, and then Longo's ability to clean it up. After that, I fill the spots based on performance and matchups."

Buck Showalter:

"We haven't had a conventional leadoff hitter. We had Nick Markakis leading off. We also look at the nine hole differently. You're only assured of a guy leading off one time the whole game. The computer will tell you that if you look at all factors, you should take your best hitter and hit him first. Take your second-best hitter and hit him second, and your third-best hitter and hit him third. The whole idea is to get them to the plate as many times as possible. That's one thing with Nick. When I talked to him about leading off, I said, 'Nick, you're going to get an extra 50 at-bats on the year.' That put him over the edge."

Ned Yost:

"When I construct my lineup, I want a high-on-base-percentage guy leading off. I'm looking for a guy that gets on base. Alex Gordon fit that bill for us tremendously well over the course of the year. I think that Alex, though, changes his approach in the one spot and focuses more on on-base percentage. Alex is a run producer. He's a guy who has the capacity to hit 30 home runs a year. Ideally, I would like him in the middle of our lineup somewhere.

"We don't have a prototypical leadoff hitter. [Jarrod] Dyson has a lot of speed, so if he gets on, he can steal second, he can steal third. And he can steal the tough base. But as far as on-base percentage, he doesn't walk enough, and he hits too many balls in the air to utilize his speed."

Manny Acta:

"Speed at the top is important, but it doesn't do you any good if you can't get on base. It's been proven over the years. Guys like Wade Boggs had no speed, but if you have a high on-base guy, you have a better chance of scoring runs than if you have a guy leading off who can't steal first base. The guy who hits first obviously has to be an on-base-percentage guy. Then you go from there. The main thing is scoring runs, so you need to stack up your best hitters up front."

Tim Bogar:

"It's always important to get your best hitters up there as much as possible with an opportunity to give your team an advantage. But I think you also have to consider how they're going to get up there. I don't want them to get up there four times with no one on. I don't want to put somebody who might be my best hitter in the leadoff position and have him up with no one on base. That's not going to do us much good.

"You have to be able to find out who your best hitters are—which is usually quite obvious—and complement them. Not all nine at-bats are individual. They're connected."

Dave Martinez:

"It really depends on what your lineup is based on. Whether it is guys getting on base with walks, and power, or more of a speed lineup, you base your lineup accordingly. A perfect example would be when the St. Louis Cardinals were so good. They had nothing but speed. They had one guy who could really hit the ball out of the ballpark—that was Jack Clark—so they based everything on having guys who could run at the top of their lineup. There are other teams who base their lineup purely on on-base percentage.

"We had Carlos Pena leading off for us quite a bit. We did that because he was taking his walks and getting on base quite a bit. He had an over-.400 on-base percentage at one time. That's the type of thing we look at.

"You want your best hitters hitting third and fourth, and you also want those guys getting up as many times as possible with guys on base. That's what you're hoping for. We have Longo hitting fourth and when he gets up there, we want at least one guy on base. To me, your three, four and five are your key RBI guys."

Jarrod Saltalamacchia:

"You want to pack your lineup with guys that get on base. If I could pick a guy from our lineup, I would like [Dustin] Pedroia to be at the top. I want a guy up there who is a tough out. He's going to grind at-bats and be a set-the-tone type of guy. That would be a number-one priority, a guy who sets a tone from the beginning. You build around that with guys who can drive him in, particularly in the three-four area.

"I love Ells [Jacoby Ellsbury] being the number-two guy. It has to be a guy who can produce something, whether it's a hit-and-run or a bunt. If I'm going to have Pedey at the top of my lineup, I need a guy who is going to be able to get him in scoring position for my three-four guys. It can be an on-base guy or a guy who plays the game like a [Pedro] Ciriaco."

Sam Fuld:

"Generally speaking, you want your best hitters to get the most at-bats. I believe in the data that shows that, but each player is different, so it's also hard to make blanket statements. But I do like good hitters at the top. Given that the significance of the bunt has dwindled, I think it's important to have a high-OBP guy in the two-hole as well as leadoff."

Bat Control in the Two-Hole

Acta:

"I'm not a big believer in the second hitter being a guy who can just put the bat on the ball. I think that spot is one of the most important parts of your lineup. Forget about trying to put a guy in the second spot just because he can hit-and-run and bunt."

Bogar:

"I think a guy in the two-hole who is capable of handling the bat is pretty important. Personally, I think the bunt is coming back. At least, I don't think it's going to go away completely. I think there are times to use it. I know the statistics—a runner on first with none out, and a runner on second with one out, and all that—but in certain situations, it needs to be done. I'd prefer a guy in the two-hole who can do those things."

Maddon:

"I haven't thought that way in a long time. That, to me, hasn't been pertinent since the DH came on board and the American League became a home run league. Or baseball in general. In the 1990s [with the Anaheim Angels], we hit Jimmy Edmonds second. I loved Jimmy in the two hole.

"If you have productive eight and nine hitters, that two guy is sitting in a spot to see a lot of good pitches. He's sitting in the sweet spot between one and three, so if you get him fed into with a good eight-nine combination, that could be the garden spot to hit in."

Martinez:

"The two-hole guy pretty much knows how to use the bat. He knows how to use the field and knows the situation of the game. He hits behind runners and can bunt. He can do all of the little things to advance the runner, but he should also be able to drive the runner in himself, and get on base. I think on-base percentage in the two hole is underrated.

"Here, we tend to run. It's a big part of our game, so putting the ball in play is something we kind of like. Right now, we have B.J. Upton hitting second, because we feel that he'll get pitched to better there; he'll see more fastballs. Another guy we have is Jeff Keppinger. He can hit in the two hole, because he can handle the bat really well."

Daniel Bard:

"On-base percentage has to be a priority. It's a simple stat, but it tells a lot. In my mind, I think it's important in the two-hole as well as leadoff. And it doesn't matter how you're doing it, whether it's hits or walks. If you're setting the table for your RBI guys at three, four and five, you're doing your job. You're finding a way to get on base, and to me that's the most important thing.

"As a pitcher, I think it's tougher to have a more legit hitter in the second spot [as opposed to a bat-control specialist]. When you get to a Miguel Cabrera or an Albert Pujols, you want to face them with nobody on. That way you can make them hit your pitch, and if you walk them, you walk them. They're not going to hurt you. But if you're facing them with runners on first and second, or first and third, that changes the whole complexity of the at-bat. I'd put a higher priority on getting on base than I would on bunting and speed. If you get guys on base, good things can happen."

Yost:

"[Alcides] Escobar is a perfect two-type hitter. He's walking more, but what I like about him in the two hole is that he's very situational. He can bunt, he's our best hit-and-run guy, we can do a bunch of things with him. Plus, he's hitting close to .300. When he starts evolving into the next level, and phase, of his game as a hitter—and his approach has already refined to the point where he's been more productive– he'll learn to take more walks, and his on-base percentage will rise.

"Ideally, I want my number-two to get on base a lot. I kind of like my number-two hitter taking away some of the emphasis on the leadoff guy's on-base [percentage]."

The Nine-Hole as a Second Leadoff Hitter

Bogar:

"You're coming back to the top of the order, where your one-two-three-four guys are your best hitters, so I'd rather have better hitters at the bottom of the lineup. It makes for a more continuous flow. If you put your worst hitter ninth, you're almost guaranteeing that your best hitters will be coming up with no one on base.

"I think speed is important in the nine-hole. I've seen it here this year, where we've had [Jacoby] Ellsbury, [Pedro] Ciriaco and Scotty Podsednik. We've put those guys either eight-nine-one, or nine-one-two, and that makes it tough on the defense, because on a base hit we can usually go first to third and have speed at both corners. That makes it more difficult for the other team to defend you."

Saltalamacchia:

"You want some speed at the end of the lineup, so when they get on, they can score. If you look at some lineups, like the Yankees, one through nine, they have guys who can hit a home run at any time. They're not necessarily speed or on-base guys, and it works for them. But I kind of like a nine-hole guy who has speed and can get on base, as well."

Showalter:

"If you have somebody like that. Look at yesterday's game with [Ryan] Flaherty. He had a good game for us. But if you don't have one, you don't have one. We're looking for one leadoff hitter right now, not two. You have to play with what you have."

Martinez:

"Personally, I like a guy having a guy who can turn the lineup over in the nine hole. In a perfect world, that's the kind of guy you look for. We don't have a pitcher hitting here in the American League, so that makes it more conducive to having a guy who can get on base in front of the top of the lineup."

Acta:

"The bottom of your order should be the bottom. I've never been a big believer in the idea of having a second leadoff hitter. I don't like putting a guy in the nine hole who should be hitting in the seven or eight hole. To me, you have to maximize at-bats. Your better hitters should have a shot at getting that extra at-bat."

Yost:

"I view the nine-hole guy as a second leadoff hitter. I'd like a guy with a higher on-base percentage. I think we've maybe had more production out of the nine hole this year than anybody in baseball, because of that mind set. I like to get something going at the bottom order if I can.

"I want to create an offensive sequence. In Milwaukee, for years, our top six hitters were okay, but then we'd get to seven, eight, nine, and any offensive sequence that we had would end. We'd always have to restart our sequence back at the top of the order. My weakest hitter won't necessarily be in the nine hole. He might be eight or even seven."

Sam Fuld:

"I'm not a huge believer in that. I think you want your worst hitter in the nine hole. I don't think the significance of having a base stealer is enough to outweigh the cons of hitting your worst hitter seventh or eighth. Because of the change in leadoff hitters [from speed to on-base percentage], the role of the nine-hole hitter has changed, as well."

Power and Protection

Bogar:

"Your number-four hitter doesn't have to be your best power hitter. I think he has to be somebody that is going to put the ball in play consistently. He's going to be able to drive in runs, but he doesn't have to be a power guy. There are teams around the league that don't have that much power there. The Rays' best power hitter doesn't hit fourth. I don't believe you need to have that in that spot."

Yost:

"The four spot is generally my best power hitter, and the fifth spot is my best RBI guy. Billy Butler is the four spot now, not only because of his power going up, but because he is a phenomenal on-base guy. He'll take a walk, he can hit the ball to all fields, and he's got power to all fields. And he's a bona fide .300 hitter.

"That guy in the fifth spot is kind of your last line of defense in terms of driving in runs. Generally, he's a higher-on-base-percentage guy who can put the ball in play. I'm not saying that I value on-base over power in the five spot. I'd rather have power and the ability to put the ball in play."

Acta:

"Your cleanup hitter has to hit for extra bases. That's a big part of his job. I don't think I'd be going out on a limb to tell you that I don't want to put a singles hitter there just because he can drive in some runs with ground balls. He has to carry some fear with him when he comes to the plate, so that my best hitter sees some pitches."

Showalter:

"I like the protection thing in the batting order. And with Jonesy [Adam Jones] hitting third, that allows Matt [Wieters] to have some people in front of him who run pretty well. We haven't had a team of egos as far as where they hit in the batting order. That's been big. I've known a lot of guys who have been, 'I can't hit fifth, but I can hit fourth.' Really? You should just be glad your name is in the lineup."

The Sacrifice Bunt

Fuld:

"If I was a manager, I wouldn't bunt much. There are instances where you need to play for one run; they're just few and far between. I don't think you need to until you get to at least the eighth inning, or most likely the ninth inning. But it also depends on the hitter. A run-probability table doesn't show you who's hitting."

Bogar:

"We can do all the statistical analysis about the bunt, and take it completely out of the game, and say you're going to score more runs, but when you're out there facing a pitcher in a certain situation in a game, and a certain situation in the season, and on top of the stress of everything that's going on, you have to make players make plays. There are situations where a bunt gives your team the best opportunity to score.

"If we're saying that every time we have a runner at second base, and I have the bottom of my order coming up, and I shouldn't move him along, we're hoping for a hit from the worst hitters on the team."

Bard:

"As a pitcher, I like when that happens. If they're giving me an out, I'm always going to take it, even if it means a guy moving to second or third. When I'm at my best, I'm able to get a decent amount of strikeouts. I can rely on that, so if they want to give me an out, I'll take it every time."

Saltalamacchia:

"Bunting is part of the game. I don't think a bunt is an automatic out, and now you've got a guy in scoring position. They're usually sacrificing with no outs, and you want to keep the other team out of scoring position."

Acta:

"I'm not big on bunting guys from first to second. I don't think it's a secret, because the facts are out there. It's been proven that a guy has a better chance of scoring from first with no outs than from second with one out. I have to have way too much of an advantage late in the game, bullpen-wise and great hitters lined up, to do that. At first and second with no outs, I usually only do it with the bottom of the order, or maybe the top guy in the order, depending on how he's swinging the bat. It guarantees me a runner on third with less than two out and another runner in scoring position. But I probably won't if we need multiple runs. If it's the heart of my order, it won't happen."

Maddon:

"The situation is part of it. If you're moving a runner up, why are you giving up an out with two guys who really aren't good in that moment? Furthermore, look at who's pitching. You might not have a chance. So why not do something like a hit-and-run, and maybe end up with runners on first and third? There are a bunch of things you can do. You can steal, and then maybe bunt to get him to third base with one out. That might not be as bad of a play. But just to give up an out to move a guy to second ... I don't always agree with that.

"I'm not into the bunt, frankly. It's probably more of a National League play, when you have a pitcher hitting and you want to gain an advantage by moving the runner up. Then you can utilize your one and two hitters. I only like to bunt when it's advantageous based on the next two guys coming up. If your six-hole guys gets on, and you bunt seven, here come eight and nine. If you don't have a lot of confidence in them against that pitcher, why even do it? I don't like to give up outs just because it's been done for the last 100 years."

Leaderboard: Team Ball-in-Play Runs Saved

Owing, in particular, to the ubiquity of the shift in 2012, judging a team's defensive production based solely on its cumulative Ultimate Zone Rating or Defensive Runs Saved totals is a problematic endeavor. Now more than ever, defense—already difficult to measure—is more than just the sum of its parts.

At the heart of the matter, really, we're interested in measuring a team's ability to convert batted balls into outs. It was partially with that thought in mind—and also with a view to rewarding pitchers who seem capable of influencing batted balls—that this season FanGraphs introduced a measurement of runs saved on batted balls (by team and by pitcher) relative to league average.

There is still some bias extant in these figures: as noted, there appear to be pitchers who are capable of suppressing batting average on balls in play (BABIP). That said, there are clearly teams which, as a whole, are better at converting balls in play into outs. This is the most essential part of good fielding.

The Balls In Play (BIP) figures below are measured in wins (where 10 runs equals roughly one win) and are both park- and league-adjusted. The higher the Team BIP Wins Saved figure, the more proficiently a team (in conjunction with its pitchers) converted batted balls into outs relative to the rest of the league.

Team	BABIP	BIP Wins
Angels	.277	5.1
Rays	.277	5.0
Nationals	.282	4.6
Dodgers	.283	4.6
Athletics	.279	4.4
Braves	.284	4.3
Padres	.284	4.1
Pirates	.286	3.6
Mariners	.282	3.3
Reds	.288	2.4
Giants	.289	2.4
Orioles	.285	2.3
Mets	.290	1.8
Cubs	.291	1.5
White Sox	.288	1.2
Blue Jays	.291	0.2
Rangers	.292	-0.1
Twins	.294	-0.6

Team	BABIP	BIP Wins
Cardinals	.298	-0.9
Phillies	.298	-1.0
Yankees	.296	-1.3
Marlins	.300	-1.6
Red Sox	.296	-1.6
D-backs	.301	-2.0
Indians	.300	-3.1
Astros	.306	-4.0
Tigers	.307	-5.1
Brewers	.313	-6.1
Royals	.311	-6.6
Rockies	.325	-9.4

- Carson Cistulli

The Stanford Swing
by Eno Sarris

The Stanford Swing exists. There's no doubt that Stanford University has its own philosophy when it comes to hitting, complete with points of emphasis, peculiarities, drills, and, perhaps, flaws. Any organization in organized baseball has a hitting approach it believes in on some level, so this isn't a surprise.

The main point of contention when it comes to the Stanford Swing, though, is whether or not it has a detrimental effect on a player's professional future. That part of the picture is much harder to suss out, and the implications of such a search reach from the role of college baseball to the socio-economic status of the average amateur baseball player.

Every baseball organization has its own ideas about hitting. Dave Hudgens was hired by the Mets prior to the 2011 season because he preached patience while in the Indians system. He's kept his job because the team has become more patient under his watch, which pleases general manager Sandy Alderson. That follows the pattern in the pros—the overall approach is usually set by the GM and then implemented on a more incremental level by the hitting coaches and instructors. In college, it's much the same, but the main players are the coach and his hitting coach.

There's nothing really special about any of this—even when it comes to Stanford—other than perhaps longevity. Stanford's head coach Mark Marquess and stats-friendly associate head coach Dean Stotz have been coaching together for 35 years. It makes sense that they have a guiding philosophy that everyone knows. There's no other tandem in college baseball that's been preaching to its hitters with a consistent voice for as long as that Cardinal duo.

And, therefore, it's fairly easy to describe the Stanford Swing. You can say, as ESPN prospects guru Keith Law puts it, that the swing is "robotic." That's a commonly-held belief in draft rooms around the nation, if you've heard the off-record nods and references to "swings that lack rhythm." Or you can laud the swing's strengths and say it's a middle-of-the-field, contact-driven approach that's well suited to the college game. Both might be right.

But break the Swing down into the component beliefs, and it begins to sound more reasonable. "They don't like shoulder-y swings," one college coach says. Sure. Who does? "We like to hit the inside part of the ball so that you hit it straight as a string," Stotz says. Yeah, that sounds fine. The team likes to use the middle of the field, he adds. Sounds like something Hudgens once told me about his general philosophy.

So far, there still isn't much that would separate the Stanford Swing from your average well-run baseball team's swing.

Then you get to the feet.

"Coach Marquess believes in getting the foot down," says Oakland outfield prospect and Stanford baseball alum Michael Taylor, who also notes that Marquess stresses having two hands on the bat all the way through the swing. Tampa Bay outfielder Sam Fuld, who also played at Stanford, says that the school was "big on getting the front foot down early." Ask around, and the single most defining aspect of the Stanford Swing is that the school asks its players to make sure the foot is down before the batter swings. "You can't hit the ball until your feet are on the ground," Stotz agrees.

Here's the problem: hitting is about weight transfer. And if you put your foot down too early, you risk transferring your weight too early. "Stanford hitters often have their weight out in front," Law says. Being out on your front foot can sap your power even as the emphasis on being ready helps you make more contact.

It's what makes former Padres amateur scout Noah Jackson say that Stanford "overvalues contact, good or bad." Law, who worked in the Toronto Blue Jays organization before joining ESPN, says that there's a "fear of missing" at Stanford. Get the foot down, keep the top hand on, go the other way—now you're getting the picture of a swing that might be tailored to a league with mediocre defense (like college), but might not be suited for the pros.

Except Stotz doesn't see it that way.

"That interpretation is flawed," Stotz says. "When a golfer starts his swing toward the ball, his weight is back, but the very first thing he does is put the weight on his front side to release his back side. Bad golfers stay back and spin off the back foot. You want some inertia. Too far on the front foot is bad, but a slight transfer of back to front helps you thrust the ball towards center field. Look at Alex Rodriguez. Look at his back foot."

This difference in interpretation continues down to the level of daily drills. There's a drill that Stanford does called "live infield." During it, the team's hitters take batting practice with an infield on the field. The hitters are asked to hit the ball to the infielders. On the ground. They're asked to ground out to the second baseman.

"Sounds brutal," Law says. "What are you going to gain from that practice?" A major league scout agrees that that is probably a bad idea. "I can see where it might cultivate the wrong swing for an outfielder or catcher who is supposed to hit homers," the scout says. The well-traveled Fuld, who has played for eight different teams across two major league organizations in his eight years since leaving Stanford, says he has never encountered the drill in pro ball.

"That's a defensive drill," Stotz says, who notes that only certain hitters take part. The entire drill takes 20-30 minutes and rotates through 10-plus hitters. There's hardly enough time to develop bad muscle memory, and it helps Stanford defenders see difficult balls in the infield, as the fungo bat can do only so much.

Do other teams do similar drills or have similar philosophies? Well, the only places that scouts had ever seen the live infield drill before were places where Marquess disciples were running the show. So that one is a particular quirk that the Stanford legend has bred, and he just doesn't think it's a big deal.

As for other programs sharing Stanford's feelings about feet, that's more complicated. Gino DiMare, the hitting coach for the University of Miami, agrees with Stotz that feet are important. He even agrees that you normally want two feet on the ground to hit. Where they differ is in regards to the specifics of the hitter's footwork. "We don't want that front foot down so early that it will stop the rhythm," DiMare says. "We don't want them to stop and start again." Rhythm is important in Miami. "We don't want our kids to have the front foot down, waiting, waiting, waiting for that ball to come," he says.

Rather than stress getting the foot down, Miami hitters are instructed to stand tall and be quiet in their approach at the plate. When it's time to swing, DiMare says that players are taught to "load up and get as much power and leverage as you can." Even if he agrees that the best hitters in baseball hit to all fields, this sounds like a fundamentally different philosophy. Stotz didn't once talk about "getting loud and explosive in a controlled way," for example, as DiMare did. And they certainly don't feel the same way about the hitter's feet.

There's an idea that floats above all the drills and points of emphasis and the Stanford Swing, the idea that Stanford players are succeeding despite their instruction in college and not because of it. The problem with testing this idea is that not all of the players that go through Stanford find their swing altered.

Joe Borchard, Sean Ratliff, Ryan Garko and Carlos Quentin were great college sluggers, all four. They all have different-looking swings. Apparently, none of them had his swing altered at Stanford. "Ratliff looked like Sadaharu Oh, and we never touched him," Stotz says. This is an idea that was echoed by the scouts and coaches I talked to. If you hit, you're fine. If you don't, it's time to work with Stotz in the box. Chris Carter, who is currently playing in Japan, might see it differently—he played well in limited time at Stanford but resisted the Swing and never saw more playing time because of it, he felt (see references). But most, Fuld included, agreed that the swing wasn't coached into place until they encountered a little bit of failure.

Is that wrong? Should young players be given more time to show their true talent before changing their swings? DiMare mentioned that the school doesn't overhaul players' swings at Miami. Is it possible Stanford is alone in this?

College teams are expected to win—by their fans, their alumni, and their administration. "[Minor league teams] can live with losing," Stotz says. "I can't live with being unemployed." They aren't actually feeder programs for the minor leagues, Stotz points out. Law has a view more in line with the scouting community: "If they don't pay their players, then they shouldn't run them into the ground, and they should be about developing them."

But this isn't something that only happens in college. "College isn't a place for development, and they've never pretended to be," Jackson says. But the scout thinks that this idea, that those that hit well don't get touched, extends to the minor leagues. "Everyone has the fear that they don't want to be the one to mess you up," says Jackson, adding that leaving a guy alone when he's succeeding is pervasive in the minor leagues, too. Even if he thinks "your swing path is your swing path and can rarely be changed," Jackson also says hitting coaches are the ones who can help refine a player's game, and have a plan at the plate. Leaving successful guys alone isn't something unique to Stanford, even if it seems like a negative. It's a negative throughout organized baseball.

We may not be able to solve this. The scouting community has its beliefs, represented perhaps by Law's characterization that, at its worst, the Stanford Swing looks like "playing pepper with the second baseman." And the University would say that they hit 47 home runs in 2012, good for the top ten percent in NCAA baseball, and might also talk about its success in producing major leaguers, if you point too hard at their front-foot philosophy.

There is a difference, however, between producing major leaguers and productive major leaguers. The main focus of this debate is whether or not Stanford has a problem turning out productive major league position players.

Not really, no.

If you take all of the final top-25 NCAA rankings since 2000 and compile and sort them, you will find Florida State, South Carolina, Texas, Rice and Arizona State comfortably at the top. They are the heavy hitters, the elite tier of college baseball in the 2000s.

The next group is where you'll find Stanford, nestled between Miami and Clemson ahead, and North Carolina and Florida behind. Here are your "school comps" for Stanford, or programs that generally could be expected to turn out as many professional hitters as each other, all things being equal. Now it's as easy as finding all the position players that have been drafted out of the schools and comparing them—with the caveats to follow:

	University of Miami	Stanford University	University of Florida	U of North Carolina	Clemson University
WAR	55	22	0	18	16
500+ PAs	7	8	2	4	3
MLB	12	14	3	7	3
Drafted	48	46	39	31	34

You don't have to take these results and award Stanford the best results in its weight class when it comes to producing major leaguers. It's obvious from the numbers that

Miami has produced more wins above replacement, anyway. But it's difficult to take these results and claim that Stanford has a problem. In 12 years, the Cardinal has produced 14 major leaguers. That doesn't sound like an issue. They've produced eight major league regulars over that same time frame, and that's the most in this tier.

What about the big names? It's Ryan Braun (and his 32.9 WAR) that drives Miami's total so far past Stanford's. Stanford's superlative player of the aughts, Carlos Quentin, comes up just shy of 10 WAR so far in his career, and there's most of your difference. Should Stanford be penalized for not producing someone like Braun in the last 12 years? Or ever? That seems like a stretch, because Braun is doing things that nobody since Barry Bonds has done. And one miss—Stotz dejectedly admits that he missed on Braun during the recruitment process—does not a trend make.

These days, Braun might not even go to college. With the increased acceptance that young players are better investments, teams are picking high schoolers higher in every draft. And the higher they go, the fewer of them go to college.

"Approximately 90 percent of high schoolers drafted in the first ten rounds sign with a major league team," Stotz says. "And yet the big leagues are made up of, basically, 50 percent college, 25 percent high schoolers, and 25 percent international free agents."

"We get to pick from the smaller pool of talent two ways," Stotz says. Not only are the best high schoolers cherry-picked away from college—a truth that remains even if the exact numbers contain some selection bias stemming from the fact that signable high school stars are drafted higher—but Stanford also has higher educational standards and fewer scholarships to give out. Given these caveats, the Stanford record seems more impressive.

"Stanford has not lost a significant recruit in over a decade," Law says in response. But again, are they picking from the same pool? Baseball has slowly become a game for the affluent, with yearly fees for a young player with big aspirations pushing five thousand dollars a year. In a homogenous group of well-educated, well-heeled baseball players, Stanford might be on equal footing.

But there are still poor, young baseball players—Jackson founded First Base Foundation, an organization that helps those less fortunate get on the same travel teams and get the same exposure to great college coaches as their more fortunate teammates. The mere existence of FBF and like foundations suggests that there still are players out there who would have a hard time affording Stanford even on a half-scholarship, which in turn suggests that Stanford may get whom they want, but they can't want everybody.

Even if Stanford does turn out high draft picks, those who are selected are viewed more as "players with tools that teams think they can work with," Law says. Here's the idea, again, that picking a Stanford player comes rife with risk, and that you're looking past the Stanford instruction with your selection. Once again, the scouting community provides a different, if probably untestable, spin on the situation.

And so we're left with two poles on the topic. In one corner, you have a mindset that this "robotic" insistence on getting the front foot down, spraying to all fields, and going the other way is suited to the mediocre defenses of the college game but is a detriment to the players' long-term development for the professional game. In the other corner, you have a successful college program that has paired strong offense with its pitching year after year and sees the approach as a salve for struggling hitters.

"Fifty-seven players in the big leagues, 37 years at Stanford, or almost two major league players per draft class, and I have to defend this?" Stotz asks. He makes a good point. And yet you might look at the 6-foot-6, 250-pound John Mayberry Jr., and think that a few more strikeouts and a lot more power might make him a better professional player. And you might wonder what former first-round draft pick Kenny Diekroeger's swing might look like today if he had signed with the Rays out of high school instead of playing at Stanford before transitioning to the pros. After he hit just .208 in his pro debut in the Royals system last summer, many in the scouting community certainly do.

The Stanford Swing exists. Whether or not it's a detriment—and even whether or not Stanford should care if it is a problem—is a much harder question to answer.

References

- Http://diamondbacks.scout.com/2/466403.html

GM in a Box: Kenny Williams

by Chris Cwik

Record and Background

Age: 48

Previous organizations: None

Years of service with the Chicago White Sox: 20—12 years as general manager; recently promoted to team president.

Cumulative record: 1,014-931, .521 winning percentage

Playing career: Williams was drafted by the White Sox in the third round of the 1982 amateur draft. He played six years in the majors, predominantly as an outfielder, finishing his career with a .218/.269/.229 slash line. A year after his retirement, Williams joined the White Sox as a scout.

Personnel and Philosophy

Notable changes from the previous regime?

Ron Schueler was the longest-tenured American League general manger when he stepped down and allowed Williams to take over in October 2000. Schueler remained with the organization through 2002, acting as an advisor to Williams. Schueler was nowhere near as aggressive as Williams, but had a very successful run as general manager. The White Sox finished with the fourth-highest record in the majors under Schueler's reign—finishing behind the Braves, Yankees and Indians.

Schueler was responsible for building up the club's farm system. In 2000, the White Sox were named "Organization of the Year" by *Baseball America*. They were led by minor league "Player of the Year" Jon Rauch, who ranked as the fourth-best prospect in baseball the following season.

Schueler didn't have a ton of success in the first round of the draft. The best player he drafted in the first round was Kip Wells, whom the team traded to Pittsburgh following the 2001 season. In the same draft, Schueler picked up outfielder Aaron Rowand and pitcher Mark Buehrle, both of whom had a significant impact on the team after he stepped down. He also had success in the international market, signing both Carlos Lee and Magglio Ordonez, two of Chicago's most effective players throughout the 2000s.

While he was largely responsible for rebuilding the White Sox farm system, Schueler also managed to keep the team competitive while he was in charge. When he took over in 1991, Schueler inherited a team that had won 94 games the previous season. Schueler tried to push the team over the edge, acquiring veterans Tim Raines, Steve Sax, George Bell and Bo Jackson. After the team finished first in 1993, Schueler bolstered the roster by adding veterans Julio Franco and Darrin Jackson. It nearly worked, as the White Sox were considered strong favorites to play in the World Series before the players strike.

Schueler made a last-ditch effort to contend in 1997, signing slugger Albert Belle. Instead of bolstering the team that July though, Schueler dealt away Wilson Alvarez, Roberto Hernandez and Danny Darwin for a bevy of prospects, including Keith Foulke and Bobby Howry. While the deal—which became known as the "White Flag Trade"—became a PR nightmare, every player the White Sox dealt was set to become a free agent at the end of the season. The White Sox were also able to get considerable mileage out of Foulke and Howry. Shortstop Mike Caruso, also acquired in the deal, looked like a promising player after hitting .306/.331/.390 as a 21-year-old rookie, but he completely collapsed the following season.

Schueler's biggest move as the White Sox general manager may have come in 1998, when he traded away outfielder Mike Cameron for Paul Konerko. Konerko helped lead the team to a World Series victory in 2005, and still remains an integral part of the White Sox offense.

What characterizes his relationship with ownership? What type of people does he hire? Is he more collaborative or authoritative?

Williams has a strong relationship with chairman Jerry Reinsdorf. That relationship was tested during the 2011 season, when Reinsdorf fired manager Ozzie Guillen and kept Williams. Guillen and Williams had been at odds all season, and it was clear that they could no longer co-exist in the organization.

Reinsdorf is always hesitant to increase the White Sox payroll, citing poor attendance at the park. He's been willing to push the team's payroll over $100 million in recent years, but always threatens to stop spending if the fans don't show up. Still, when Williams has been in a position to make a move that will increase payroll, and help the White Sox win, he's been able to convince Reinsdorf to spend more money. This allowed the White Sox to sign Adam Dunn, and re-sign Konerko and A.J. Pierzynski during the 2011 offseason.

In an August interview with ESPN.com, Williams admitted that he has more freedom than some general managers, but always has to get Reinsdorf's approval when he's going to increase payroll.

Williams tends to hire people with whom he is familiar. Most of Williams' front office staff members have been with the White Sox organization for a number of years. Williams spent his entire post-baseball career with one organization and that likely influences his front office decisions. The biggest name to come over to the White Sox in recent seasons was former manager Buddy Bell. Before becoming a manager, Bell had worked as a minor league instructor with the White Sox from 1991 to 1993. Both the organization and Williams were familiar with his work, and decided he would be a good fit for the organization. Much of the White Sox commitment to hiring from within is influenced by Reinsdorf, who is extremely loyal to the people around him.

Assistant GM Hahn is an integral part of the club's front office. He's been involved in contract negotiations with some of the key players on the team, including John Danks, Gavin Floyd and Konerko. He is also credited with signing Esteban Loaiza, claiming Bobby Jenks and trading for Carlos Quentin. While Williams is more known for scouting, Hahn is known for being stat-friendly.

In 2011, Hahn was ranked as the top general manager candidate in baseball according to SI.com. He also topped a similar list by *Baseball America* in 2010. Despite that, the White Sox have managed to retain both him and Williams.

Former general manager Roland Hemond also played a major role in the team's front office. Hemond was the club's general manager from 1971-1985, and returned as an executive advisor during Williams' tenure. He left the White Sox for the Diamondbacks following the 2007 season. Hemond is extremely well-respected in baseball circles. He has 60 years of baseball experience, and was the second person to be awarded the Buck O'Neil Lifetime Achievement Award. That award goes to an individual who has broadened the game's appeal while showing integrity and dignity.

The team's front office was shaken up in 2008, when it was revealed that David Wilder, a team executive, and two scouts, Jorge Oquendo Rivera and Victor Mateo, were stealing bonus money from Latin American and Dominican prospects. Wilder's departure was significant. As the director of player development, he received a lot of credit for the White Sox World Series victory. Following the 2005 season, Wilder was a candidate to replace Theo Epstein as Boston's general manager.

What kinds of managers does he hire? How closely does he work with them?

Though Guillen managed the team for eight seasons of Williams' tenure as general manager, it's clear Williams prefers less animated managers. Jerry Manuel was the manager when Williams took over, and the two worked together for three seasons. Manuel was calm, almost serene, and rarely feuded with players or the media.

Williams took the opposite direction with Guillen. While the partnership lasted for quite some time, things did not end well. During their final season working together, numerous reports said they argued numerous times. One of the more publicized altercations dealt with personnel. Williams no longer wanted Juan Pierre to start. Guillen refused to bench the outfielder.

Toward the end of the season, Guillen began openly complaining about his contract, further exacerbating the issue. Before that season, Guillen was allowed input in roster decisions. Williams generally listened to his advice, which was widely believed to be the reason the White Sox traded Lee to the Brewers before the 2005 season. During the previous season, Lee hadn't given full effort in a rivalry game against the Twins. Guillen wanted to change the clubhouse culture, and that offseason, Lee was traded. Williams recounted this story at a White Sox fan festival before the 2005 season. And while he wouldn't name the player involved, it was widely believed to be Lee.

Guillen also had a poor relationship with Nick Swisher, which likely led to Swisher being dealt after just one season with the team. Swisher struggled in his only season with the White Sox, leading to reduced playing time down the stretch. Guillen reportedly did not like the way Swisher responded to the lack of at-bats, and no longer wanted him to be a part of the team.

After things imploded in 2011, Williams hired Robin Ventura. He was a major question mark at the time, but his impact was felt this season. Many players said Ventura's calm persona had a relaxing effect on the White Sox clubhouse. Even though he had no prior managerial experience, Williams had seen how Ventura carried himself when he was a part of the organization, and wasn't concerned about his lack of experience.

Player Development

How does he approach the amateur draft? Does he prefer major league-ready players or projects? Tools or performance? High schools or college? Pitchers or hitters?

Williams' philosophy in the draft has changed drastically since he first became a general manager. In Williams' first draft as general manager, the team took a chance with local high school pitcher Kris Honel, who pitched fairly well in his first couple of years before injuries ruined his career.

After Honel, the White Sox adopted a policy of drafting high-floor, low-upside college players. That approach failed to produce many viable major league prospects.

Williams finally changed his approach after the White Sox drafted college pitcher Lance Broadway in 2005 and Kyle McCulloch in 2006. Williams was quite vocal about the organization going away from low-upside players and focusing on players who had much higher ceilings. That approach has had mixed results. Aaron Poreda and Jared Mitchell were viewed as major projects when they were selected, but neither has panned out. Poreda was traded in the Jake Peavy deal, while Mitchell—despite an encouraging start to the 2012 season—remains extremely raw.

To offset project players, the White Sox have recently looked to draft players who are capable of contributing immediately. Gordon Beckham received only 259 minor league plate appearances before the team promoted him to the majors. Chris Sale debuted just months after he was drafted.

Due to poor drafts early on, and aggressive promotions in recent years, the White Sox farm system has consistently ranked fairly low among prospect gurus.

Does he rush players to the majors or is he patient?

Williams has let his major league roster dictate whether he's aggressive with promotions. When there's a clear need on the team, and a minor leaguer is performing well, Williams won't hesitate to aggressively promote him. Beckham and Sale are obvious examples. But Williams has shown a willingness to let players like Mitchell develop at their own rate. He seems to have a good grasp on when prospects are ready to make an impact in the majors.

Roster Construction

Is he especially fond of certain types of players? Does he like proven players or youngsters? Offensive players or glove men? Power pitchers or finesse guys?

In trades, Williams likes to target young, talented players who have fallen out of favor with their organization. Examples include Quentin, Danks, Floyd and Matt Thornton. Each of those players was either considered a strong prospect at one point or was a former first-round draft pick.

He also tends to stick with players he knows. The team has worked hard to keep Konerko and Pierzynski on the team following the 2005 World Series. Williams has also shown a fondness for bringing players back to the White Sox. Carl Everett, Freddy Garcia, Sandy Alomar Jr. and Bartolo Colon are a small sampling of players Williams has either traded for or signed numerous times in their careers.

The White Sox have mainly been built around power hitters during Williams' tenure, a strategy that may be partially due to the fact that the club's ballpark, U.S. Cellular Field, is a launching pad. The team had success with Frank Thomas, Lee, Ordonez and Konerko through a good portion of Williams' reign. He also traded for Jim Thome after 2005, and signed Dunn in 2011. While the team doesn't typically target defensive players, the Sox have signed Orlando Hudson and Omar Vizquel in recent years. Vizquel is credited for working closely with Alexei Ramirez to improve his defense.

Does he allocate resources primarily on impact players or role players? How does he flesh out his bullpen and bench? Does he often work the waiver wire, sign minor-league free agents, or make Rule 5 picks?

The White Sox tend to lock up their impact players, and typically don't add major pieces through free agency. Outside of Dunn, whom the team signed in 2011, the last big White Sox free agent signing was outfielder Jermaine Dye before the 2005 season. Williams prefers to acquire big players through trades, but doesn't typically hand out huge contracts. Peavy had the highest salary on the team last season, but he was already signed before the White Sox acquired him.

Most of the team's recent signings have been used to fortify the bullpen, where Williams isn't shy about handing out multiple-year contracts. Williams has extended Thornton for both three and two years. He also gave Jesse Crain a three-year deal, and famously signed Scott Linebrink to a four-year deal in 2007. Williams also signed Sergio Santos to a three-year extension before trading him to the Blue Jays last offseason.

Williams is always looking for available talent, and has used the waiver wire in a few different scenarios. The team added reliever Jenks in 2005, and he ended up closing out the World Series that year. Williams also acquired outfielder Alex Rios on a straight waiver claim in 2009. Not all of Williams' August gambles have worked out. The team took a chance on slugger Manny Ramirez in 2010. He had a tough time staying healthy and received only 88 plate appearances with the team.

The White Sox are rarely active in the Rule 5 draft. The last time the team made a selection was in 2007, claiming pitcher Santo Luis in the Triple-A phase of the draft. The team hasn't selected a player in the major league phase of the draft since 2003, when the Sox selected pitcher Jason Grilli from the Marlins.

Williams has signed minor league free agents, but they don't often make a major impact on the major league roster. He's had some success recently, however, as the team signed pitcher Philip Humber on a minor league deal in 2010. They also managed to snag pitcher Jose Quintana on a minor league contract before the 2012 season. Humber racked up 3.5 WAR in 2011, and threw a perfect game in '12. Quintana was surprisingly effective in the rotation while filling in for injured starters.

When will he release players? On whom has he given up? To whom has he given a shot? Does he cut bait early or late?

The biggest mistake Williams has made in recent memory is trading Swisher following the 2008 season. Swisher hit just .219/.332/.410 that season, but managed to rebound to his career numbers the following season. He's been a huge steal for the Yankees since. There were rumors that Swisher clashed with manager Guillen, which may have contributed to Williams giving up on Swisher after just one season.

Williams will always take shots on talented players, even when it's clear they are no longer effective. Williams coveted Hudson and Ken Griffey Jr. for quite some time. But once he was able to acquire them, they were clearly past their prime. The same thing happened with Manny Ramirez. Williams took a shot on his talent even though his skills were clearly in decline. Williams even took a chance on a 36-year-old Jose Canseco in 2001. If a player has shown talent in the past, Williams will give him a chance to rebound.

That said, Williams tends to have a good grasp on players on his team. He's handed out extensions to aging players like Konerko and Pierzynski, and both have rewarded him with tremendous seasons in spite of their age. He's traded away Rowand to make room for prospect Brian Anderson, which proved to be a mistake. But he was able to acquire Thome in the deal.

Williams has also cut bait with injury-riddled players, such as Ordonez and Thomas, a few seasons before they were finished. Thomas hadn't been healthy for two straight seasons, and was 37, so it was tough to argue that he should have been re-signed. Ordonez had suffered a catastrophic left knee injury heading into free agency, and still received a five-year, $85 million contract from the Tigers. Though Ordonez remained effective in Detroit when healthy, the deal was a massive overpay.

Is he passive or active? An optimist or a problem solver? Does he want to win now or wait out the success cycle?

Williams is one of the most active general managers in the game. He continually finds ways to fill Chicago's biggest needs, regardless of the cost. Williams acquired Peavy despite the fact that Peavy was on the disabled list at the time. He also acquired third baseman Kevin Youkilis this past season, filling the team's biggest weakness without giving up any significant talent.

If the White Sox are in contention, Williams is almost certainly going to make an acquisition at the trade deadline. The last couple of seasons, Williams has acquired Francisco Liriano, Edwin Jackson and Peavy at the deadline. But he's also been incredibly active on the waiver wire.

Williams made headlines leading into the 2012 season when he said the White Sox would try to rebuild. He then promptly extended pitcher Danks, causing confusion among the fan base and the media. Williams may say that he's willing to rebuild, but there's nothing in his history as a general manager that suggests he would ever follow through. Williams will try to do whatever it takes to put his team in contention.

Trades and Free Agents

Does he favor players acquired via trade, development, or free agency? Is he an active trader? Does he tend to move talent or hoard it? With whom does he trade and when? Will he make deals with other teams during the season? How does he approach the trade deadline?

Few of the team's current players came up through the organization. Outside of Sale, Beckham, Brent Morel and Addison Reed, the team has mainly been acquired through trades, waiver acquisitions and free agency.

Since trading for Jose Contreras in 2004, Chicago established itself as a popular destination for Cuban free agents. That relationship has allowed them to sign both Alexei Ramirez and Dayan Viciedo. Outside of Dunn, though, the team doesn't typically get involved on premier free agents. The Sox originally signed Pierzynski after the 2004 season, but his value was driven down after a forgettable season with the Giants. Most of the other players on the roster have been acquired through trades.

Williams rarely hoards talent, preferring to trade off assets once he finds a replacement. Once Viciedo was ready to play, the team traded away Quentin to open up a spot. Williams is also willing to deal away his prospects. He traded Brandon McCarthy to get Danks, Aaron Poreda to get Peavy and Chris Young for Javier Vazquez throughout his tenure.

Williams is an active trader at all points of the year. If the White Sox are close to contention, it's nearly guaranteed that he'll do something at the deadline. But Williams also strikes any time there's talent available. It doesn't matter if it's May, August or December. While Williams has been extremely active during the season in recent years, he's shown a willingness to make big deals in the offseason as well. In December 2008, Williams dealt pitchers Vazquez and Boone Logan to the Braves for prospects Tyler Flowers and Brent Lillibridge. If Williams feels he can trade for a talented player, he'll pull the trigger.

Are there teams or general managers with whom he trades frequently?

Williams has been around for such a long time, and is such an aggressive trader, that he's interacted with many general managers. While Williams doesn't necessarily favor certain teams, he's made a fair number of deals with Oakland general manager Billy Beane. That could be a result of both men being employed for a long time. Williams has also completed many trades with Josh Byrnes. They began their relationship when Byrnes was in Arizona, and it has continued since Byrnes joined the Padres. While Jim Bowden is no longer a general manager, Williams often made trades with his teams.

Contracts

Does he prefer long-term deals or short? Does he often backload his contracts? Does he lock up his players early in their careers or is he more likely to practice brinksmanship? Does he like to avoid arbitration?

Williams doesn't typically hand out excessive long-term deals. He's shown a willingness to give out multi-year contracts to relievers, but doesn't hand out deals in excess of four years to position players.

In recent years, Williams has shown some creativity with his contracts. He backloaded contracts to Pierzynski and Konerko to ensure the team would be able to manage its payroll this season. Williams also made sure that some of Konerko's $13.5 million salary in 2013 is deferred, giving him more flexibility that season.

Williams has shown a willingness to offer extensions to his key players before they hit free agency. Danks, Floyd and Alexei Ramirez were all handed extension before they could hit free agency. Williams also locked up closer Santos before dealing him to the Blue Jays.

Anything unique about his negotiating tactics? Is he vocal? Does he prefer to work behind the scenes or through the media?

Williams will always make it known that he's actively looking for deals, but rarely gets into specifics with the media. His deals rarely leak to the public before they happen. Many analysts assumed that the White Sox would have interest in Youkilis this past season, but no one was quite sure he was going to Chicago until the trade was actually completed.

Bonus

What is his strongest point as GM?

Williams' aggressiveness sets him apart as a general manager. If a talented player who will help his team hits the trade market, Williams will do whatever he can to make a deal. Last season, the White Sox had no business being in the Zack Greinke race, but they were often mentioned in trade rumors because Williams wanted Greinke so badly.

He's shown a willingness to take shots on players who have fallen out of favor with their original organizations, players who have come off injuries and talented players who are long past their primes. If there's a talented player on the market at a slight discount, Williams will target him.

What would he be doing if he weren't in baseball?

Williams was a two-sport athlete in college, playing both football and baseball at Stanford University. If he had not started a front office career after he retired, he would likely still be involved in the game in some capacity, perhaps as a high school or college coach. Williams has also said that he has more of a football mindset, and may have looked for a similar job in football.

Leaderboard: 2012 Reckless Power (RECK)

While patience and power are two different skills or tools, it's also generally the case that batters who hit for power are likely to draw more walks, simply because pitchers are afraid of conceding the home run. Among qualified batters in 2012, for example, Marco Scutaro received more pitches in the zone (55.6 percent of them) than any other, while Josh Hamilton (37.6 percent) received the fewest. Scutaro has averaged 9.1 home runs for every 600 plate appearances over his 11-year career; Hamilton, 30.7.

Certain players, however, seem to have little interest in taking the walks their power has earned for them. Reckless power is what we might say they have. RECK is a toy metric designed to identify the players who displayed the most reckless power. It's calculated by dividing Isolated Power by Isolated Patience, or, stated differently, (SLG − AVG) / (OBP − AVG). The results appear to approximate the Richter Scale, such that less than 2.0 is barely felt, 5.0 is considerable, and 9.0 and up happens less than every 10 years and is totally destructive.

Name	Team	PA	AVG	OBP	SLG	RECK
Alex Rios	White Sox	640	.304	.334	.516	7.1
Adrian Beltre	Rangers	654	.321	.359	.561	6.3
Garrett Jones	Pirates	515	.274	.317	.516	5.6
Omar Infante	- - -	588	.274	.300	.419	5.6
Ian Desmond	Nationals	547	.292	.335	.511	5.1
Delmon Young	Tigers	608	.267	.296	.411	5.0
A.J. Pierzynski	White Sox	520	.278	.326	.501	4.6
Adam Jones	Orioles	697	.287	.334	.505	4.6
Allen Craig	Cardinals	514	.307	.354	.522	4.6
Mark Trumbo	Angels	586	.268	.317	.491	4.6

Notes

Rangers third baseman Adrian Beltre, first overall on this leaderboard from 2011 with a 7.6 RECK (itself the largest figure since Bengie Molina's 8.9 RECK in 2009), drops to second on this year's edition of the list. In Beltre's case, it's likely less a case of improved discipline and more the case of a slight decline in his power numbers. Beltre's slugging percentage was precisely the same in 2011 as in this most recent season (.561 in both cases), but his batting average was also 25 points higher in 2012 (.321 vs. .296), forcing his Isolated Power figure down.

It's important that we recognize the achievement that is Garrett Jones's 2012 RECK score. Even while finishing the season having seen the 14th-lowest rate of strikes (among 143 qualified batters), the Pirates outfielder/first baseman still managed to swing and swing and swing his way to just a 6.4 percent walk rate and .043 Isolated Patience. Curiously, Jones's 34.7 percent O-Swing rate (that is, the percentage of pitches outside of the zone offered at by a batter) was not particularly miserable. Coupled, however, with a rather high swing rate within the zone—plus 27 home runs—it led to this very hard-fought honor for Jones.

Free agent (as of press time) Delmon Young appears on the Reckless Power leaderboard less because of the "power" part of it and more because of the "reckless" part of it. While generally credited with having excellent raw power, Young managed just 18 home runs in 608 plate appearances, making it the fourth time in five qualified seasons that Young has failed to reach the 20-home run threshold. Detroit teammate and middle infielder Omar Infante managed a higher Isolated Power figure. Meanwhile, Young offered at a league-worst (among qualified batters) 42.7 percent of pitches outside the zone, and has never finished below 40 percent by that measure, according to PITCHf/x.

- Carson Cistulli

History

Farmer Horace and His Bumper Crops

by Steve Treder

In early 1936, 33-year-old Horace Stoneham inherited ownership of the New York Giants. The franchise coming into his possession had long been an elite brand: the fabled Giants of McGraw and Mathewson. Stoneham's father, Charles, had purchased the team in 1919, and while the Babe Ruth-and-Lou-Gehrig-led New York Yankees had since surpassed the Giants as baseball's biggest winner and top draw, the franchise under Charles Stoneham had hardly struggled. Winning four pennants in the 1920s and another in 1933, the Giants remained a strong contender with a huge and loyal fanbase.

And certainly, the ball club Horace Stoneham inherited remained the top New York attraction within the National League. The Brooklyn Dodgers, the cross-town NL rival, hadn't won a pennant since 1920 and rarely contended for anything higher than fifth place. While the Giants' image was a legacy of high standards and sustained excellence, the Dodgers were instead a laughingstock, the "Daffiness Boys," "Dem Bums," a ragged band of amusing losers, nothing to be taken seriously. When Stoneham's team immediately graced the youthful owner with back-to-back pennants in 1936-37, the Dodgers languished deep in the second division, and the Giants' top-dog status seemed secure.

But change was afoot in Brooklyn. In 1938, the Dodgers hired Larry MacPhail as general manager. Fresh off a widely-admired rebuilding job in Cincinnati, the boldly innovative MacPhail immediately sparked a Flatbush transformation. He installed lights in Ebbetts Field (as he had done in groundbreaking fashion at Cincinnati's Crosley Field), and the cutting-edge product of night baseball was suddenly available to Dodgers fans—but not Giants fans. MacPhail persuaded a Reds employee named Red Barber to follow him to Brooklyn, and the Dodgers soon saturated the greater New York area with sharply modern access to radio baseball—something the Giants had hesitated to do.

MacPhail quickly improved his team on the field, as well. By 1939, he'd put brassy, talented, and media-savvy Leo Durocher in place as manager, and the Dodgers surpassed the Giants in the standings and at the box office—an unthinkable development just a few years before. Stoneham's ownership honeymoon had been grand, but brief, and it clearly was over. Reacting, the Giants' boss proved unafraid to make bold moves of his own: he hired shy, quiet Mel Ott as manager (which, as one writer put it, "surprised everybody, especially Ott"), he executed a bombshell deal to acquire slugger Johnny Mize from St. Louis, and finally and most shockingly, in 1948 he hired the hated Durocher away from the Dodgers to replace Ott.

But nothing worked. Through the decade of the 1940s, the Giants never finished higher than third, and only once ahead of the Dodgers, who spent the same period capturing three pennants. Moreover, all the while Ebbetts Field was better attended than was the Polo Grounds. Horace Stoneham's stewardship of his venerated franchise, which seemingly had everything going for it, was in real danger of turning out to be an exercise in forgettable mediocrity.

And to add to the challenge Stoneham faced: when in 1943 MacPhail left the helm of the Brooklyn organization to join the United States Army, his replacement was none other than Branch Rickey. The already-iconic longtime GM of the St. Louis Cardinals was, among so many other things, the sport's leading expert regarding the farm system (just ask him). After all, Rickey had invented it.

The Profundity of Farming

By the late 1940s, it was abundantly clear that Rickey's invention hadn't just "caught on," it was well into the process of transforming the sport. Between them, the Cardinals and the Dodgers dominated the NL through the '40s, and they did so simply and obviously because of their massive and highly productive farm systems. The same explained the Yankees' ongoing American League dynasty. Any team serious about consistently contending now had no choice but to undertake a comparable farming operation.

And so Horace Stoneham put on his overalls and got to work.

The Giants organization Stoneham inherited in the mid-1930s wasn't without a farm system. Under Stoneham's father, they had—like most teams in that era—put together the rudiments. But the Giants' five-team system was nothing like the vast network created by Rickey in St. Louis, with 24 affiliates active in 1936.

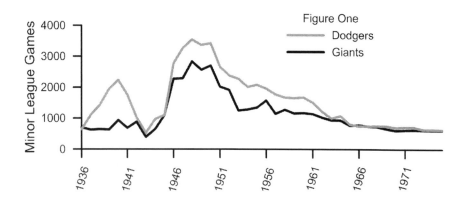

Even before MacPhail's arrival in Brooklyn, the Dodgers began investing in the creation of a serious farm system, and under MacPhail (and of course under Rickey) they expanded it further. Stoneham was late to respond to this challenge—and then inhibited by the restrictions imposed by World War II—but even before the war was over, the Giants began to create an extensive system of their own (see Figure One).

In the 1943-44 offseason, immediately following his retirement as a player, long-time Giants star pitcher Carl Hubbell was hired by Stoneham to fill the newly-created position of "general manager of farm system and scouting department," a position he would hold until the late 1970s, even after Stoneham sold the franchise in early 1976.

The Dodgers' pre-war head start was quickly mitigated by wartime conditions, but immediately following V-J Day, the race was on again in earnest. Both teams quickly amassed far larger systems than they'd ever overseen before. But the Dodgers' system still exceeded the Giants' in size; indeed the Dodgers' system, at its peak from 1948-50, was the biggest of any in baseball history.

As we know, victimized by rapidly changing economic and technological realities, the minor leagues largely collapsed during the 1950s. Still, the Dodgers steadily maintained a size advantage as both organizations wound down their minor league investments until they finally stabilized in the mid-1960s at (interestingly) a level essentially identical to where they'd begun 30 years earlier. For the 1946-60 period in which farm systems were at their most impactful, Stoneham's Giants were unable to match their rivals in terms of sheer quantity of minor league teams and players.

But Size Isn't the Only Thing that Matters

While a larger field grows more cornstalks, the quality of the produce is important, too. Let's compare the two organizations in terms of how well all those minor leaguers performed, by adding up system-wide minor league winning percentage on an annual basis over ten-year periods.

Years	Giants	Dodgers
1936-1945	.510	.501
1946-1955	.508	.541
1956-1965	.500	.497
1966-1975	.501	.522
Grand Total	.505	.515

We see only a minor difference between the systems. The Dodgers achieved an advantage in the late '40s/early '50s, but couldn't sustain it. Both systems were rather good insofar as they typically came in above the .500 mark, but neither organization performed better or worse than the other over this long span. Thus, it would seem that although Stoneham was for many years unable to forge a farm system equal to that of his primary rival in terms of scale, the quality of the minor league teams in each organization was more or less equal.

But was it? This may be an inadequate method of assessing farm system quality. The strategic purpose of a farm system, after all, isn't to deploy successful minor league players, but rather to develop and produce successful major league players. Thus, the question isn't how well each system's prospects performed in the minors, but rather how many, and most importantly how good, were the major league players each system graduated.

So let's add up the major league performances of all of the significant players each farm system delivered. As the measure of performance, we'll use Wins Above Replacement (WAR) as presented on Fangraphs, and to focus on significant players—that is, those whose presence meaningfully contributed to the success of major league teams—we'll count only those players who accrued a total of at least five career WAR. There were a total of 141 such players arriving in the majors from these two systems from 1936 through 1975, 69 by the Giants and 72 by the Dodgers.

We'll count the career WAR total of each player in the year in which he arrived in the majors to stay as a member of the 25-man regular season roster (thus, we aren't putting him in the year he may have arrived as only a September call-up). And to smooth out the volatile year-to-year fluctuation that's present in a sample this small, instead of examining each year's total discretely, we'll look at rolling five-year averages, which gives us a clearer picture of the value being produced by each system, the total "area under the curve." To start off, let's focus on the first decade or so of Stoneham's tenure:

Five-Year Periods	Giants	Dodgers
1936-40	11.0	8.4
1937-41	7.5	8.4
1938-42	11.5	7.2
1939-43	23.8	4.8
1940-44	26.5	4.8
1941-45	27.3	1.3

Neither system was churning out a great deal of talent in these years. But despite the fact that the Dodgers system was larger, it was the Giants who delivered better players. Giant products arriving in this period included Sid Gordon (35.5 career WAR), Willard Marshall (17.4), Harry Gumbert (16.5), Sal Maglie (16.2), Dave Koslo (15.8), and Cliff Melton (15.2), while the Dodgers' farm yielded Pete Reiser (20.9),

Goody Rosen (9.9), Vic Lombardi (9.4), Bob Chipman (7.8), and Harry Eisenstat (6.1).

Now let's see what happened when both organizations truly ramped up the farm investments following World War II (See Figure Two).

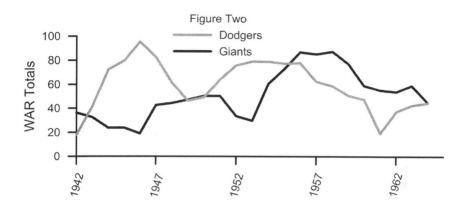

Figure Two

The modest advantage the Giants had gained was immediately wiped out in the late 1940s, as the Dodgers system burst forth with a flood of remarkable talent. Dodgers products arriving between 1946 and 1950 included Duke Snider (63.1 career WAR), Jackie Robinson (58.7), Gil Hodges (40.7), Carl Furillo (31.8), Roy Campanella (31.6), and Don Newcombe (26.8), while the Giants countered only with the likes of Bobby Thomson (30.0), Whitey Lockman (14.6), Hank Thompson (11.5[1]), and Wes Westrum (10.7).

But Stoneham and Hubbell weren't standing idly by. Hubbell's first staff in 1944 included eight scouts. From 1946 through 1951, Hubbell never employed fewer than 25, and the Giants' scouting staff in those years was larger than the Dodgers', even though the Brooklyn organization was stocking more minor league teams.

Most significantly, the Giants worked to gain presence, knowledge, and credibility in the Latin American and African-American baseball communities to a degree that the Dodgers didn't. In 1946, the Giants hired their first Spanish-speaking scout, Pedro Vasquez. And in 1952, they officially named Alejandro "Alex" Pompez to their scouting organization, a position he would hold until his death in 1974.

Pompez had long been familiar to Stoneham, because Stoneham was his landlord: Pompez owned the New York Cubans Negro League team, which played its home games in the Polo Grounds. And as a Spanish-speaking Cuban-American, Pompez had expertise, contacts, and influence throughout both Latin American baseball and the Negro Leagues. Via Pompez, the Giants were also able to hire Pedrin Zorrilla—a Puerto Rican—and Horacio Martinez—a Dominican—onto their scouting staff.

The achievements of this trio in identifying, assessing, and securing Latin American and African-American talent were extraordinary. They signed the following players for the Giants: in 1954, Tony Taylor (20.0 career WAR); in 1955, Willie McCovey (60.7), Orlando Cepeda (46.1) and Felipe Alou (39.2); in 1957, Juan Marichal (58.2), Matty Alou (21.5) and Manny Mota (16.1); and in 1960, Jose Cardenal (16.9).

And it was the Giants' sending scout Eddie Montague in 1950 to check out a Negro League player named Alonzo Perry (whom they never signed) that enabled them to stumble across none other than Willie Mays (150.8 career WAR). Other African-American standouts the Giants signed and developed in the early 1950s included Bill White (35.3), Leon Wagner (9.8), and Willie Kirkland (8.0).

Though the Dodgers had been the first to racially integrate, through the 1950s they were unable to keep up with the Giants in leveraging these talent pools. The Dodgers system produced just two significant Latin American players through this entire period, Roberto Clemente (89.8) and Chico Carrasquel (19.2)—neither of whom would play a major league inning for the Dodgers—and the best African-Americans they developed were Willie Davis (56.8), Jim Gilliam (37.7), Maury Wills (37.5), and Tommy Davis (16.7), fine ballplayers, but not comparable to those the Giants produced.

Therefore, in the early 1950s, the Giants' organization began to catch up in farm production. They briefly caught up with the Dodgers (that was primarily the impact of Mays) before falling back again, but beginning with the 1956-60 five-year cycle, the Giants' output surpassed that of their rivals, and the Giants would hold that advantage for many years to follow, even as the yield of both farms declined with their shrinking systems through the 1960s.[2]

The End Game

Through their final years in New York, the Dodgers maintained an attendance edge over the Giants, and once both teams moved west that advantage only increased. Walter O'Malley's operation always had significantly more revenue to work with than did Stoneham's.

And when in 1968 the Athletics arrived in the Bay Area, Giants' attendance became a serious problem, plunging toward the bottom of the league. By the early 1970s, the Giants were in dire financial straits and would remain so until Stoneham was forced to sell and retire. This was the period in which the franchise sadly sold off its high-salaried stars, including Mays, McCovey, and Marichal.

Yet, despite the cash-flow crisis, Stoneham's Giants never decreased their heavy investment in scouting. In the mid-to-late 1950s, the Dodgers farm operation (first under the direction of Fresco Thompson, then Al Campanis) began to employ more scouts than the Giants. But in the early 1960s, the Giants' scouting staff again outgrew that of the Dodgers, and would remain larger—generally at least twice as large—until the day Stoneham sold the franchise. Indeed, in 1973, just a couple of years before the bitter end, Hubbell was overseeing 56 scouts—his biggest staff ever—even though the farm system was as small as it had ever been.

This unwavering commitment to the baseball equivalent of Research & Development paid dividends:

Five Year Period	Giants	Dodgers
1965-69	46.4	52.3
1966-70	36.4	61.4
1967-71	54.7	56.3
1968-72	61.6	57.3
1969-73	53.7	80.1
1970-74	57.3	72.4
1971-75	66.9	66.6

The trend of declining farm production that characterized the 1960s was reversed late in the decade, and when Stoneham bowed out it was still climbing. Standouts produced by the Giants in these years included Bobby Bonds (55.7 career WAR), George Foster (41.3), Garry Maddox (34.4), Jim Barr (28.7), Bill Hands (28.2), Chris Speier (27.9), Gary Matthews (27.3), John Montefusco (19.8), Gary Lavelle (18.7), and Steve Stone (16.7).

At the same time, the Dodgers' system, even with its more limited scouting manpower, enjoyed its own renaissance. With its key achievement being a phenomenally successful free agent drafting session in June of 1968, the L.A. organization in these years produced Don Sutton (62.9), Ron Cey (50.4), Dave Lopes (40.3), Charlie Hough (34.8), Steve Garvey (34.4), Doyle Alexander (30.5), Bill Russell (28.6), Rick Rhoden (27.2), Willie Crawford (20.0), Joe Ferguson (19.7), Geoff Zahn (18.6), Lee Lacy (18.5), Bill Singer (17.4), and Steve Yeager (16.6).

Stuffing the Barn, and Going to Market

It is the case, of course, that Stoneham's organizational success at building and sustaining a remarkably productive farm system wasn't coupled with success at converting that productivity into championships. Over his 40-season tenure, Stoneham's Giants captured five pennants and one World Series, while the Dodgers took home 12 NL flags and four World Series championships. All too plainly, the Dodgers were much more adept at trading and otherwise sorting and organizing the talent into effective deployment on their major league roster.

But Stoneham's (and Hubbell's) achievement in systemically identifying and developing raw talent was a success of grand proportion, both in its intensity and its duration. Whatever else he did or failed to do, Horace Stoneham was a profoundly green-thumbed farmer.

End Notes

1. This is one-half of Thompson's career WAR total of 23.0. We grant the Giants half-credit for him, whom they added to their farm after an initial trial with the St. Louis Browns.

2. The Giants' farm production replaced that of the Dodgers as the highest in all of baseball, but that title wasn't one the Giants held for long. Beginning with the 1960-64 period, the Giants' rate of production was overtaken by that of the Cincinnati Reds. Quite like the Giants, the Reds achieved their tremendous farm output primarily through success in signing and developing African-Americans (including Frank Robinson, Vada Pinson, Curt Flood, Lee May, and Tommy Harper) and Latin Americans (including Tony Perez, Mike Cuellar, Cesar Tovar, Tony Gonzalez, Leo Cardenas, and Vic Davalillo).

The Scintillating, and Still Underrated, Satchel Paige

by Sean Smith

Leroy "Satchel" Paige began pitching in the Negro National League in 1927 at the age of 20. He pitched in the Negro leagues (and others) for what anyone else would have considered a long and successful career through 1947. Paige wasn't done at that point, though. He was just getting started.

After the end of baseball's segregation, Paige finally had an opportunity to pitch in the major leagues and became a 41-year-old rookie. He pitched—with success—for five of the next six seasons in the American League. After that, he pitched in the minors with results that were good enough to prove that he still belonged in the major leagues. Paige returned to the majors after his 59th birthday and pitched three more scoreless innings, facing 10 batters and allowing only a double to fellow future Hall of Famer Carl Yastrzemski. The professional record ends shortly after that; he had a less successful outing a year later in the Carolina League. In all, Paige was paid to pitch for over 40 years.

Paige was inducted into baseball's Hall of Fame in 1971, the first player whose accomplishments were primarily in the Negro Leagues to receive that honor (Roy Campanella was inducted in 1969 and Jackie Robinson in 1962, but they are in primarily for their accomplishments as Dodgers). Paige has not been universally considered the best pitcher of the Negro Leagues, though Bill James considered him so in his *2001 Historical Baseball Abstract*. James writes:

> *"In the literature of the league there are numerous places where people say that Bullet Joe Rogan was better than Satchel, or Hilton Smith was just as good ... There was a poll of Negro League veterans in 1952 which picked Smokey Joe Williams over Satchel as the greatest pitcher in the history of the league."*

James then argues that just by the fact that Paige was always used as the frame of reference indicated that he was greatest pitcher. While we don't have as much data to evaluate Negro League players to the extent that we can evaluate major league players, great progress has been made in the last few years. The data we have makes a strong case that Paige was indeed the very best among his peers.

Seamheads.com has focused on adding the earlier seasons; as I write this, the site has data through the 1923 season, including some I didn't think was possible to find. For example, you can visit the site and check out fielding statistics for John Henry

"Pop" Lloyd. Baseball Reference has data through the later years. Since Paige started his career in 1927, Baseball Reference is the source of the data used here.

Pitching in the Negro Leagues

Below are Paige's pitching stats compared to other Hall of Fame Negro League pitchers. Note that there is no earned run average, but instead total runs per nine innings. I consider this a fortunate fact, because total runs is a better statistic than earned runs anyway. Dividing runs into earned and unearned ignores the truth that defensive support has an impact on all runs allowed.

The stat kwERA is an ERA estimate based solely on strikeouts and walks. Tom Tango describes this on The Book Blog. It is necessary to use this instead of Fielding Independent Pitching since the calculation for FIP includes home runs allowed, and we don't know how many home runs each pitcher allowed. To calculate kwERA, just subtract walks from strikeouts, divide by batters faced, and subtract this number from 5.40. The last number can be adjusted based on the conditions of the game. A constant of 5.40 works in 2012, in an era filled with strikeouts and home runs. For the years Paige pitched, a constant of 4.6 is used instead, which sets the kwERA for this group at about 92 percent of total runs allowed.

Pitcher	Born	Years	IP	Hits	K	BB	RA/9	K/9	BB/9	kwERA
Satchel Paige	1906	27-47	1298	994	1170	240	3.23	8.1	1.7	2.24
Leon Day	1916	34-46	427	376	237	110	4.51	5.0	2.3	3.67
Bill Foster	1904	23-37	1675	1348	987	511	3.27	5.3	2.7	3.70
Bullet Rogan	1893	20-38	1454	1292	882	364	3.68	5.5	2.3	3.49
Joe Williams	1885	11-34	1186	1063	726	303	3.79	5.5	2.3	3.49
Hilton Smith	1907	32-48	672	565	398	79	3.44	5.3	1.1	3.04
Jose Mendez	1885	07-26	1315	1041	725	332	3.32	5.0	2.3	3.64
Andy Cooper	1896	20-39	1469	1405	569	248	4.23	3.5	1.5	3.91
Ray Brown	1908	31-45	1150	1115	409	225	4.14	3.2	1.8	4.10

Notice how far above everyone else Paige is in strikeouts, with a rate 47 percent higher than anyone else on the list. He walked batters at a rate lower than all but Andy Cooper and Smith and allowed runs at a lower rate than anyone else. He completely dominates the list in kwERA.

The innings pitched numbers here show how much each pitcher pitched in documented Negro League games but by no means indicate how many innings they actually pitched in their careers. These pitchers pitched in barnstorming exhibition games, winter league games, or lesser leagues if that meant getting a bigger paycheck. The documented league games can be used to get an estimate of pitcher quality against high level competition. If you wanted to estimate how much they would have pitched if they'd had the same opportunities as white major leaguers, the best bet would be to look at the number of years pitched, assume the workload of a top starter, and adjust for effectiveness and known injuries. (For example, Paige would not have pitched much—or at all—in 1939, due to injury.)

One thing I won't try to do here is calculate major league equivalencies (MLEs) for the Negro leagues pitchers. MLEs are most reliable when you have a large sample of players moving from one league to another. Of the pitchers listed above, only Paige pitched in the majors. Other pitchers apeared in both the integrated major leagues and the Negro Leagues, but most had short careers. Sam Jones and Don Newcombe had fairly long careers in the majors but did not pitch much in the Negro leagues (Newcombe pitched in the Negro Leagues for a total of 80 innings as a teenager, then signed with the Dodgers). Outside of Paige himself, the only pitchers to throw at least 100 innings in both the Negro leagues and the majors are Joe Black and Connie Johnson.

In the Majors, 1948-1953

Paige signed with the Cleveland Indians for the 1948 season at age 41. He stuck around for five full seasons, pitching mostly in relief. From a pitcher's age-41 season on, he ranks eighth in major league history in wins above replacement, or WAR, as calculated by Baseball Reference (source: Baseball-reference.com Play Index):

Player	WAR	Years
Jack Quinn	18.8	1925-33
Roger Clemens	17.5	2004-07
Hoyt Wilhelm	16.9	1964-72
Phil Niekro	16.4	1980-87
Nolan Ryan	16.0	1988-93
Cy Young	15.2	1908-11
Randy Johnson	11.4	2005-09
Satchel Paige	9.7	1948-65
Red Faber	7.8	1930-33
Warren Spahn	7.2	1962-65

Jack Quinn was a legal spitballer who was allowed to continue throwing it after the pitch was banned. Hoyt Wilhelm and Phil Niekro were knuckleballers, a class of pitchers who historically peak late and last well into middle age. The other pitchers ahead of him were comparable in that they had legendary fastballs and arms that held up forever. Paige started 25 games during these five years and made 153 relief appearances. In 1952, he led the league in games finished and even received a few Most Valuable Player Award votes, finishing 17th in the AL voting.

If it weren't for Bill Veeck, who signed him to pitch for the Indians, Paige may never have had the chance to pitch in the majors. Veeck sold the Indians after the

1949 season, and Paige was out of a job despite pitching very well (3.04 ERA, 132 ERA+). Veeck returned to the majors in 1950, buying the St. Louis Browns, and brought Paige back for three more years. Veeck soon sold the team to Clarence Miles, who moved the Browns to Baltimore and called them the Orioles. Again, Paige was not retained after Veeck left.

Miami Marlins

Three years after his final game with the Browns, Paige signed with the Triple-A Miami Marlins, at the time affiliated with the Philadelphia Phillies. Paige pitched in Miami for three years and pitched so well that he still could have been a good major league pitcher, if only someone had let him. Estimating his pitching ability is pretty easy in this case, as there are plenty of data on which to base an MLE. Almost all of his teammates during these years pitched in the majors at some point in their careers. In 1956, of the 12 teammates with the most innings for the Marlins, 11 pitched in the majors. In 1957 it was 11 of 13, and in 1958 nine of 11. There isn't much selective sampling to worry about here.

These pitchers walked batters at about the same rate in the majors as they did in Miami. They struck out 15 percent fewer batters in the majors, allowed batters to hit nine points higher on balls in play, and gave up 75 percent more home runs in the majors. Here are Paige's actual stats in Miami:

Year	ERA	IP	H	HR	BB	K
1956	1.86	111	101	4	28	79
1957	2.42	119	98	15	11	76
1958	2.95	110	94	8	15	40

And here are his MLE adjusted stats:

Year	ERA*	IP	H	HR	BB	K	ERA+
1956	3.70	108	110	8	28	67	101
1957	3.59	116	107	20	11	65	107
1958	3.41	107	102	12	15	34	116

*Component ERA based on the translated statistics. ERA+ assumes that his ERA matches his component ERA, and that he would have pitched for the Phillies.

He was over 50 years old and still was better than the average major league pitcher, used as a reliever and spot starter. While he could not throw hard consistently at that point, he still had impressive velocity when he needed it, if this story from Larry Tye's *Satchel* is true:

"Equally amazing was the night the Marlins sponsored a distance throwing contest for outfielders. [Whitey] Herzog, who could play all three outfield spots, managed to peg the ball an impressive 380 feet. "Satchel told me after the contest, 'I can throw farther than that.' The next night he threw damn near to the backstop from home on the fly," or about 400 feet."

Tye mentions a similar bet from Paige's time with the Browns, when he threw a ball 427 feet. The record is 445 feet, set by Glen Gorbous in 1957. Playing around with The Trajectory calculator on Dr. Alan Nathan's website, you can get a range for what kind of velocity the baseball had to travel from his hand. To get an exact answer, you'd need to know his throwing angle, spin, temperature, humidity, elevation, and wind.

Being Miami, we can assume it was a hot, humid day at sea level. Even assuming that an impressive feat like this would have some help from the wind, a 400-foot throw would very likely require low-90s velocity, and a 427-foot throw would take velocity over 95 mph. It would be interesting to see how far Aroldis Chapman can throw one, preferably on a hot day in Denver. By the calculations, he should shatter the record. As hard as baseball players throw today, the only reason Gorbous still holds the record 55 years later is because nobody's willing to risk an injury trying to top it.

Paige is on a short list of pitchers who could be considered the greatest of all time. He was the best pitcher, by a convincing margin, in the Negro Leagues from his debut there until he finally got his chance to pitch in the AL. His record after the age of 41 compares well to Randy Johnson, Cy Young, Roger Clemens and Nolan Ryan—the standards for 40-plus-year-old power pitchers.

There is hope that one day we'll see another like him, especially with the help of modern medicine and conditioning. Clemens is 50 years old, and is threatening a comeback. Bill Lee is 65 and threw a complete game in an independent professional league. Jamie Moyer pitched in the majors, though without much success, at age 49. Still, I don't think we'll ever again see a combination as dominant, amazing, and entertaining as Paige.

References:
- Find Tom Tango's article on kwERA at: http://www.insidethebook.com/ee/index.php/site/comments/lego/
- Larry Tye, *Satchel*
- Bill James, *The New Bill James Historical Baseball Abstract*
- Alan Nathan, http://webusers.npl.illinois.edu/~a-nathan/pob/
- Bill James and Rob Neyer, *The Neyer/James Guide To Pitchers*

Leaderboard: 2012 MiLB kwERA Leaders

Work by Russell Carleton (under the pseudonym Pizza Cutter) demonstrates that while pitcher strikeout and walk rates become reliable over the course of a single season (at 150 and 550 batters faced, respectively), home-run rates require a larger sample. As such, FIP numbers (which include home-run rate) distort what might be called a pitcher's "true-talent ERA." An alternative to FIP is kwERA, an ERA estimator developed by Tom Tango that accounts only for a pitcher's strikeout and walk rates. Below are the top-10 minor-league leaders by kwERA, all with a minimum of 550 batters faced so as to allow a reliable sample size for both of the relevant inputs.

Name	Org	Age	IP	K%	BB%	kwERA
Daniel Straily	Athletics	23	152.0	31.6%	7.0%	2.45
Tony Cingrani	Reds	22	146.0	30.2%	9.1%	2.87
Adam Morgan	Phillies	22	158.2	26.7%	6.2%	2.94
Tyler Wilson	Orioles	22	143.0	24.9%	5.2%	3.04
Cody Buckel	Rangers	20	144.2	28.0%	8.4%	3.05
Brandon Workman	Red Sox	23	138.2	23.4%	4.5%	3.13
John Ely	Dodgers	26	168.2	24.2%	5.3%	3.13
A.J. Cole	Athletics	20	133.2	23.8%	5.2%	3.16
Nick Tropeano	Astros	21	164.0	25.7%	7.1%	3.17
Shelby Miller	Cardinals	21	136.2	26.7%	8.4%	3.20

Notes

Left-hander Adam Morgan is the highest-ranked pitcher on this leaderboard not to have made an appearance at the major-league level this season. A third-round pick out of the University of Alabama by the Phillies in the 2011 draft, Morgan throws an 88-92 mph fastball, curve, slider and change, according to *Baseball America*. He was particularly effective this season at High-A Clearwater in the Florida State League, posting a 28.6 percent strikeout and 5.7 percent walk rate in 123.0 innings (490 batters faced). Those rates declined to 20.3 percent and 7.7 percent, respectively, in six starts (35.2 innings) following an August promotion to Double-A Reading. Despite little fanfare entering 2012, he likely will find himself more highly ranked on various industry prospect lists for 2013.

With a birth date of June 18, 1992, Rangers right-handed prospect Cody Buckel is the youngest pitcher to appear on the minor-league kwERA leaderboard after splitting his 2012 season, roughly speaking, between High-A Myrtle Beach and Double-A Frisco. Because of his height (Buckel is listed at six feet) and athletic, over-the-top delivery, Buckel earns comparisons to Giants right-hander Tim Lincecum, like from FanGraphs prospect analyst Mike Newman, for example, who saw Buckel in 2011. In his report from that visit, Newman suggests that, while the height of Buckel's ceiling likely isn't the highest, he probably features a higher floor than most other pitchers his age.

Both Matt Moore (first) and Tommy Milone (fourth) appear on the 2011 iteration of this leader board. While each is left-handed, the pair feature considerably different approaches: where Moore sits in the mid-90s with his fastball, Milone depends more on command and a strong changeup. Despite their differences, Moore and Milone had remarkably similar results in their respective major-league debuts. Moore posted a 105 xFIP-, 100 FIP-, and 2.3 WAR in 177.1 innings; Milone, a 97 xFIP-, 97 FIP-, and 2.7 WAR in 190.0 innings. The pitchers featured almost identical differentials between their strikeout and walk rates, as well (12.4 for Moore, 12.7 for Milone), leading to almost identical major-league kwERAs (3.91 and 3.87, respectively).

- Carson Cistulli

Examining Umpire Strike Zones

by Chris Jaffe

Oct. 12, 1997—a date that will live in infamy for Braves fans, as well as people who appreciate a properly called strike zone.

It was Game Five of the National League Championship Series, and the Braves began the day tied with the Florida Marlins at two games apiece. Whoever won that day would be in the driver's seat to take the pennant. The Braves knew they were going to have a difficult task against young Marlins phenom Livan Hernandez. But it turned out that Hernandez's biggest advantage wasn't his mid-90s fastball or his slider. It was home plate umpire Eric Gregg.

Long known as an umpire with a big strike zone, on that day Gregg made the plate improbably wide. If a pitch was in the same ZIP code as the plate, Gregg called it a strike. The Braves didn't dare take any pitch near the plate, allowing Hernandez to expand the zone even further. By the end of the affair, the Braves were flailing away at all sorts of out-of-the-zone pitches, yet Gregg still called strikes on nearly half of the ones they let pass. With that help, Hernandez fanned 15 men in a 2-1 win that helped catapult the Marlins to their first pennant. After the game, Gregg said everyone knew he had a big strike zone, so what was the big deal?

That game is remembered as a reminder of how an umpire's strike zone can affect the game. Though strike zones rarely have a substantial difference from umpire to umpire, many umps are known as guys with a big or a small strike zone, while some are more or less likely to call the high strike or the low strike. They also can have different approaches to the outside pitch or the inside pitch.

So that brings us to the question: Which umpires over the course of their careers had the biggest or smallest strike zones? Who were most or least likely to have batters draw a walk or strike out when they called the games?

On the face of it, there's an easy answer. Simply add up all the strikeouts or walks an umpire had over the course of his career. That should settle it, right? Well, not quite. You really need to account for another vital element—era, which also affects the likelihood of a strikeout or walk. Currently, for example, we are in an era of historically high strikeouts. There are several reasons for it—how much hitters are swinging for the fences versus just trying to make contact, the willingness of batters to accept a strikeout, whether a pitcher is giving it 100 percent on every pitch or just wasting a few—but ultimately context matters. If you put Gregg back in the 1920s, he wouldn't be striking out nearly as many batters as he did at the turn of the millennium. It's a different game.

Comparing an umpire against his peers is the only way to do it. Let's adjust each umpire for his era and see who stood out as those with the biggest or smallest strike zones.

Plan of Action

Here's how we'll go about it. Let's use Gregg in 1997 as an example. We'll go through all the games he worked behind home plate and count total strikeouts, walks and plate appearances. For Gregg, that works out to 201 walks and 447 strikeouts over 2,376 plate appearances.

Are those numbers high or low? Well, let's see. Across the entire NL in 1997 (and Gregg was an NL umpire), pitchers faced 87,374 batters, walking 7,704 and fanning 15,320. Rather than just compare Gregg's numbers to those, we can make it a tad more precise. Those overall league numbers include Gregg's games.

Non-Gregg umpires oversaw 7,503 walks and 14,873 Ks in 84,998 plate appearances. That means the other umps oversaw walks in 8.8 percent of all plate appearances. If Gregg called games the same as they did, he'd have 210 walks, so he's nine under. As for strikeouts, you'd expect Gregg to have overseen 416, but he actually had 447—31 more than expected. Yeah, it makes sense that Gregg would have more than an average NL umpire.

That's just one season. Do that for every year of his career, and add up the totals. While we're at it, let's get the full career numbers for as many umpires of note as we can. Then all we need to do is compare the results to see who had the smallest and widest strike zones of any umpire relative to his peers. Then you'll know who had the biggest and smallest strike zones, because you'll know who walked or fanned the most batters relative to his era.

Now, there are some obvious criticisms to be made of this. First, walks, strikeouts, and plate appearances are rather blunt instruments. Ideally, you'd look at data showing which umpires often called pitches two inches outside the plate a strike and who didn't. Yeah, that would be nice, but really precise pitch-by-pitch info exists only for the 21st century. Let's not abandon the largest chunk of baseball history. I can find strikeout, walk and plate appearance info from 1918 to 2011. That's nice.

There's a bigger criticism that can be made. Rating umpires by strikeouts and walks per plate appearance overlooks a giant and rather obvious counterpoint. While umps are one factor affecting strikeout and walk rates, they aren't the only one. For example, there's this guy on the mound—the one holding the ball before each play—the pitcher. He plays a big role in this, too.

What if an umpire happens to see a unexpectedly large number of high-strikeout pitchers? That Nolan Ryan fellow wass fanning an ungodly number of batters every four days during the 1970s. If an umpire by happenstance got Ryan a bunch of times in a season, well, that would make a mess of things. And of course, it's not just the pitcher. What if an umpire calls a bunch of games featuring the league's hardest (or easiest) lineup to fan? Wouldn't that skew things notably?

Sure, it could, but the more you look into it, the less there is that meets the eye. One vital feature greatly minimizes any possible disastrous impact of this: sample size.

Let's look at back Gregg. In his career, Gregg called balls and strikes during 48,930 plate appearances. Do you have any idea how big a number that is? That's nearly double Cy Young's career total for batters faced: 29,565. The gap between Young and Gregg is almost exactly equal to Tom Seaver's career. Only two pitches faced half as many batters as Gregg called pitches for, and fewer than 50 pitchers made it a third of the way to 48,930.

Ever heard the phrase, "Things will wash out in the long run?" Well, with a sample size this big, that's what happens. Imagine how many times Gregg would have to call a Ryan game for it to notably distort his career numbers. Keep in mind umpires aren't intentionally lined up with particular teams. And even if they get a team a large chunk of times in a season, you still need to line up the umpire's turn at the plate with the pitcher's turn on the mound. I've heard of managers lining up pitchers to face particular lineups, but not a manager lining up a pitcher to face a particular home plate umpire.

Those 48,930 plate appearances would seem to add up to a pretty impressive number, except that for an umpire it isn't. That doesn't even land Gregg in the top 100 umps since 1918—some are over 100,000.

I'm sure there will always be a slight distortion caused by pitchers or hitters, but it's nothing to worry much about. An umpire who ends his career +220 in strikeouts might really be +210 due to the influence of who the pitchers are, which means that the +220 number illuminates far more than it distorts.

Results

Let's get to the fun stuff: First up, the Gregg types—the umpires who had more strikeouts than expected:

Umpire	Ks	PA	Years
John Hirschbeck	+808	63,395	1983-2011
Lee Weyer	+637	74,057	1961-1988
Doug Eddings	+559	33,072	1998-2011
Harry Wendelstedt	+498	85,938	1966-1998
Paul Runge	+490	59,525	1973-1997

There are two active umpires on the list—Doug Eddings, and our leader, John Hirschbeck, who just destroys the competition. He has had a long career, with three decades under his belt. That really helps his score. But mostly Hirschbeck just has a big old strike zone.

Hirschbeck was especially into strikes at the turn of the millenium. In the four seasons from 1997 through 2000, he called 259 more strikeouts than one would expect. He worked the plate just 114 times in those years, so that's more than two extra two Ks per game. In 1997, he was +83, and then +71 the next year.

On July 13, 1997, Hirschbeck was behind the plate when Randy Johnson and the Mariners dueled Bobby Witt and the Rangers. Johnson and the Mariners bullpen combined for 18 strikeouts, but still lost 4-2 to Texas, whose staff notched 13 Ks.

You'd expect a Johnson-Witt matchup to have a ton of strikeouts. But that same year Hirschbeck worked the plate when David Wells fanned a career high 16 batters. Wells had just one other game with more than 11. Rick Helling struck out a personal best 12 batters in another Hirshbeck start that year.

Hirschbeck's career arc shows that in his first four seasons, he had two with more strikeouts than expected and two with fewer. He was +32 overall in that period. Then, from 1987-2006, something changed. In 614 plate assignments, 767 more batters than expected fanned. What's really remarkable, though, is what happened next. From 2007 onward, he's been almost perfectly even. Whatever happened, the Hirschbeck of today is not the Hirschbeck of yore.

But that's not the real story here. Where is Gregg, the guy famous for having a wide strike zone? Sure enough, he does, but in his career he comes in at "only" +214 Ks. Hirschbeck topped that in just four years.

Again, the story is a man's career arc. From his debut in 1976 until the end of 1984, Gregg scores perfectly evenly. He'd fanned 2,384 batters; you'd expect that number to be 2,384. That doesn't mean he was consistent—actually just the opposite. He'd be up one year and then down the next, but he evened out.

Then Gregg got older and bigger, and as his belt widened so did his strike zone. For the rest of the way, more battters fanned than expected virtually every remaining year with Gregg behind the plate. That said, Gregg was never too extreme. He was normally around +20 per year.

So how do we reconcile that with Gregg's reputation? Let's think it through. Going by popular memory and the numbers, he was a big-strike zone guy. But the popular memory is overwhelmingly shaded by that one playoff game where his strike zone was just goofy big. There's no way he'd have a strike zone that big all the time—it would have too much of an impact on too many games. But because of that key game, and because he normally had a big zone, Gregg has become the archetype for the big-strike zone umpire. It's not entirely fair, but neither is life. Thus, the umpire who ranks 33rd here with +214 Ks is the most famous big-zone umpire of all.

Let's flip it around. What about the umps who saw more walks than expected? Who are they?

Umpire	Walks	PA	Years
Derryl Cousins	+957	86,641	1979-2011
Eddie Hurley	+882	57,718	1947-1965
Randy Marsh	+634	72,159	1981-2009
Bruce Froemming	+621	100,104	1971-2007
Gerry Davis	+460	73,976	1982-2011

Bruce Froemming's inclusion on this list is interesting given the most famous moment in his career. As a young umpire on Sept. 2, 1972, he worked home plate when Cubs pitcher Milt Pappas retired the first 26 batters. With a 2-2 count on the last out of the near-perfect game, Froemming called the next two pitches balls. Pappas got the no-hitter, but 40 years later still hasn't stopped fuming over his lost perfecto. It isn't too surprising that the umpire on that day would end up here.

Two guys stand out well above the others: Eddie Hurley and Derryl Cousins. Hurley was an American League umpire from the late 1940s until the mid-1960s. He debuted in 1947, the season the AL saw a sharp increase in walks. From its founding in 1901 until 1946, the league had just one year in which it averaged one walk per 10 plate appearances. Then it averaged that for five straight years, 1947-51.

No, it wasn't all Hurley's doing. It had far more to do with the rise of a batch of walk-tastic hitters like Eddie Joost, Eddie Yost, and Ferris Fain. But Hurley was the perfect umpire to come up at that period. Even in that walk-prone stretch, Hurley stood out, issuing 229 more free passes from 1947-51 than one would expect. When the league's walk rate returned to more traditional levels, Hurley stayed where he'd been. In 1954, batters got 84 more walks than you'd expect in the 42 games Hurley worked the plate. Every single season of his career, without exception, Hurley had a higher walk rate than the league average. That's a man with a small strike zone.

The better-known name is the only man ahead of Hurley, and that is Cousins. Like Hurley, Cousins has handed out walks at a higher rate than his peers for every season of his career. In Cousins' case, that's more than 30 seasons of work. Cousins' mildest season came in 1995, when he issued just 11 more walks than he'd be expected to. Over 2,443 plate appearances, that's four percent more than an average umpire would've had. Cousins was at his most extreme exactly 10 years later, with 61 more walks than expected.

With Cousins, a high walk rate is just half of the story about his small strike zone. He also fans far fewer batters than one would expect: 919 under par, easily the most. He's the anti-Hirschbeck.

As long as we're going down this route, let's see who has issued the fewest strike-outs and walks relative to his fellow umpires. First, the Cousins' crew—the people who issue fewer strikeouts than expected:

Umpire	Ks	PA	Years
Derryl Cousins	-919	86,641	1979-2011
John McSherry	-765	65,481	1971-1995
Randy Marsh	-724	72,159	1981-2009
John Rice	-626	56,502	1955-1973
John Shulok	-609	60,711	1979-2002

Cousins and Marsh are repeats, as they were also on the other small strike zone list. McSherry just missed that one, finishing in sixth with 395 more walks than expected. Here are the big strike zone guys who issued fewer base on balls than expected:

Umpire	Walks	PA	Years
Larry McCoy	-593	76,889	1970-1999
Doug Eddings	-484	33,072	1998-2011
Lee Weyer	-445	74,057	1961-1988
Ed Runge	-418	50,256	1954-1970
Greg Kosc	-409	61,956	1976-1999

Eddings and Weyer make both big strike zone lists. Hirschbeck surprisingly doesn't, with just 241 fewer walks than expected.

There's another way of looking at this, though. Look back a few lists and you'll see Froemming on the list of umpires most likely to issue a walk, with a mark of +621. On the one hand, that does tell us something about the comparatively narrow size of Froemming's strike zone. But it also tells us about his lengthy career. He is the only umpire of the last half-century to calls balls and strikes in more than 100,000 plate appearances. That longevity gives him an edge in any counting statistic.

So let's convert our data to rate stats. We'll divide the number of walks or strike-outs an umpire called by how many he'd be expected to give out, multiply by 100 and round to the nearest integer. The result will look like the ERA+ or OPS+ numbers at Baseball-Reference, with a score of 100 being perfectly average, higher indicating the umpire was more likely to give out walks or strikeouts, and lower meaning he was less likely to do so. We'll call the new stats BB+ and K+.

Let's start with Froemming, who in his career issued 9,167 walks. Since he had 621 more than expected, that means a typical umpire would have handed out 8,546 free passes. Do the math, and Fromming's BB+ comes out to 107. Of the 238 umps with at least 10,000 plate appearances from their home plate assignments, here are those with the highest BB+:

Umpire	BB+
Eddie Hurley	114
Derryl Cousins	111
Paul Schrieber	111
Kerwin Danley	111
Hal Dixon	110

There has never been an umpire quite like Eddie Hurley. He trails Cousins in the counting stat, 882 to 957, but Hurley trails far more in plate appearances, 57,718 to 86,641. If Hurley had seen as many batters as Cousins, he'd have issued over 1,300 more walks than expected.

That said, the trend above is toward recent umpires. Cousins, Schrieber and Danley are all active. Similarly, the two lowest BB+ are active umpires. Here are those leaders:

Umpire	BB+
Doug Eddings	80
Bill Miller	85
Al Salerno	88
Greg Bonlin	89
Four tied	90

Eddings and Miller are still around, but neither Salerno, Bonlin nor any of the men tied at 90 are still umping.

The lowest single-season score by an umpire with at least 2,500 plate appearances in a season is 71. It's been done twice—both by Eddings, in 2005 and 2006.

Let's look at the K+ leaders:

Umpire	K+
Roy Van Graflan	114
Lou Kolls	112
Doug Eddings	109
Bill Guthrie	108
John Hirschbeck	107
Mark Hirschbeck	107

John and Mark Hirschbeck are brothers—the first pair of brother umpires in baseball history. Clearly they have similar eyesight.

Who is Roy Van Graflan? He was an AL umpire for seven years from 1927-33. Baseball used smaller umpire crews back then, and Van Graflan averaged over 60 plate assignments per year. He struck out a ton during them. In 1931, he issued 486 third strikes, when a typical umpire would be expected to give out 369, a difference of 117. Eat your heart out, Gregg (Gregg, by the way, scores at 103, though typically higher in the last half-dozen years of his career).

In 1931, Van Graflan had a K+ of 128, the highest single-season score ever. In his first home plate assignment of 1931, he saw little-heralded Yankees pitcher Hank Johnson fan 12 in 7.2 innings. Three days later, in his next game behind the plate, Van Graflan called out 12 batters on strikes versus an even less renowned Yankee hurler, Roy Sherid. That set the tone for Van Graflan's season, and entire career.

Now for the lowest K+ umpires:

Umpire	K+
Eddie Hurley	91
John McSherry	91
John Rice	91
Cy Pfirman	92
Six tied	93

That Hurley—there really was no umpire like him. It may not mean anything, but these guys had longer careers than the guys with high K+ scores. Aside from John Hirschbeck, all the high scores had careers around 30,000 plate appearances. The top four here are all over 60,000, as are four of the six tied at 93.

Hall of Famers

What about the most famous umps? How do the Hall of Fame umpires stack up? Let's look at their career numbers. Below are the Cooperstown umpires, with the total plate appearances they saw, how far their strikeouts and walks veer from expected results, and their BB+ and K+ scores.

Umpire	Years	PA	Walks	Ks	BB+	K+
Bill Klem	1905-1941	130,304	76	371	101	104
Bill McGowan	1925-1954	128,783	-65	-389	99	96
Al Barlick	1940-1971	91,619	142	-147	102	99
Doug Harvey	1962-1992	89,932	292	-514	104	96
Jocko Conlan	1941-1965	81,657	-275	99	96	99

Umpire	Years	PA	Walks	Ks	BB+	K+
Nestor Chylak	1954-1978	74,269	-191	-131	97	99
Cal Hubbard	1936-1951	66,889	-172	143	97	102
Billy Evans	1906-1928	47,708	164	-59	104	98
Tommy Connolly	1898-1932	35,442	157	76	105	103

We have only partial data for Klem, Evans and Connolly, who began before 1918.

By and large, these famed umpires were fairly average in their tendencies, which makes sense. The main exception is Doug Harvey. When I first saw Harvey's career score, I had a theory as to what happened. He's the only really recent Hall of Fame umpire; he worked in the NL from the 1960s to 1990s. I remember that by the 1980s, people complaining that umpires had moved the strike zone from the rulebook definition to a lower and more outside strike zone. Maybe the veteran Harvey was just calling the old school strike zone while his younger peers did something differently, and that led to Harvey's score. Former umpire Ron Luciano noted in one of his books that Harvey was known for calling a textbook strike zone.

However, when you look at the year-by-year data, that theory doesn't explain Harvey's numbers. In fact, Harvey's scores are largely the result of his first 12 seasons. From 1962-73, Harvey walked more batters than expected every year while fanning fewer than a normal ump would. In both cases, there was no exception to the trend. By the end of 1973, Harvey had issued 335 more free passes and 340 fewer strikeouts than expected. At that point, his BB+ was 111. For the rest of his career, Harvey was actually below average with walks, handing out 43 fewer than a typical umpire would have, which works out to a BB+ of 99 from 1974 onward.

One last question to consider before moving on—who are the most even umpires of them all? Well, three have a K+ and BB+ of 100—and they're all fairly recent: Terry Tata, Jerry Neudecker and the still-active Marvin Hudson. Hudson has probably the most impressively neutral scores. In nearly 32,000 plate appearances umped, he's issued 12 more walks and just one more strikeout than one would expect.

That said, being extremely neutral doesn't make for a great or even a good umpire. CB Bucknor has a BB+ of 99 and a K+ of 100, and he is among the most-often criticized current umpires. Just because overall he's got the right numbers doesn't mean he's always making the calls correctly. His overall numbers hide the fact that he jumps around from year to year.

Players and people around the game tend to prize consistency in umpires' strike zones. People want to know a pitch is going to be a strike when it's thrown in a certain place or that it's going to be a ball. An overall neutral score doesn't necessarily mean an umpire is always calling the same pitches balls or strikes.

For a strike zone to be so big or so small that it causes notable criticism, it has to distort the game itself—much as it distorted Game Five of the 1997 NLCS when Gregg called seemingly everything a strike.

This little study really has nothing to do with identifying the best or worst umpires. Too many other factors come into play. But it does shed light on who the most and least pitcher-friendly umpires in history were. Surprisingly, Gregg isn't one of them.

Examining Umpire Strike Zones Addendum

Chris has done a tremendous job examining something that I don't believe has been examined at this level before. I'm going to take Chris' analysis one last step and ask the ultimate question: Which umpires most favored the batters through their strike/ball calling, and which ones most favored the pitchers?

To answer this question, I'm going to do a simple thing. I'm going to multiply Chris' findings by the standard run impact of a strikeout and walk. The source for my standard run impact is *The Book: Playing the Percentages in Baseball,* by Tom Tango, Mitchel Lichtman and Andrew Dolphin (required reading for all mathematically inclined baseball fans).

According to page 26 of *The Book* (and roughly verified in countless other studies), a walk is worth 0.323 runs and a strikeout is equal to -0.301 runs. Both numbers are compared to an average offensive event. I multiplied these two numbers by the number of walks and strikeouts above/below average on each umpire's watch (see Chris' article). So a total positive number means that the umpire was friendlier to batters; a negative number means that he was friendlier to pitchers.

Here are the 10 umpires who were the most hitter-friendly, expressed as the total runs above average for his strikeout and walk totals:

Umpire	Runs	TBF	Runs/38 TBF
Derryl Cousins	586	86,641	0.257
Eddie Hurley	452	57,718	0.297
Randy Marsh	423	72,159	0.223
John McSherry	358	65,481	0.208
Gerry Davis	306	73,976	0.157
Bruce Froemming	284	100,104	0.108
Tim McClelland	271	78,238	0.132
Bill Stewart	265	80,899	0.124
Doug Harvey	249	89,932	0.105
John Rice	245	56,502	0.164

As you can see, I added a couple of columns: Total Batters Faced (TBF) and Runs per 38 Total Batters Faced. Thirty-eight is about the average number of plate appearances in a game these days, so this figure gives you a rough idea of how many runs each particular umpire may have impacted on a per-game basis.

As Chris pointed out in his article, Derryl Cousins and Eddie Hurley stand head-and-shoulders above everyone else as the most hitter-friendliy umpires ever. On the chart, their estimated impact ranged from 0.25 to 0.30 runs per game.

Their actual impact may have been far greater. When umpires are known to have narrow strike zones, pitchers probably feel that they have to be more precise with their pitches. This may lead to fatter pitches for the hitter, resulting in more line drives for hits and more home runs. There's more to uncover in this particular data set.

With those caveats in mind, let's list the 10 pitcher-friendliest umps:

Umpire	Runs	TBF	Runs/38 TBF
Lee Weyer	-335	74,057	-0.172
Doug Eddings	-325	33,072	-0.373
John Hirschbeck	-321	63,395	-0.192
Larry McCoy	-310	76,889	-0.153
Greg Kosc	-262	61,956	-0.161
Ernie Quigley	-252	84,775	-0.113
Bill Miller	-248	34,633	-0.272
Bob Engel	-233	69,062	-0.128
Charlie Berry	-225	67,578	-0.127
Paul Runge	-204	59,525	-0.130

Chris didn't talk much about Lee Weyer in his article, but Weyer's combination of career length, 106 strikeout rate and 93 walk rate make him the bestest friend of pitchers ever. This isn't a surprise; Weyer was known for his wide strike zone when he worked the National League (1961 until his death in 1988). Reportedly, when teaching umpires, Weyer said "Don't be afraid to call strikes. A big strike zone gets the hitters swinging, making for more outs and a quicker game."

On per-game basis, however, no one can touch Doug Eddings. In fact, no umpire—whether favoring the batter or pitcher—matches Eddings' walk/strikeout impact on a per-game basis. This isn't a total surprise either. In a Hardball Times artcle last January, Josh Weinstock used PITCHf/x data to show that Eddings has the widest strike zone in the majors (see references).

This math is pretty generic. In more detailed studies, the weights given to runs could change from year to year, as could the average number of plate appearances in a game. Another caveat is that intentional walks were included in total walks here, because we don't have the data to separate them for every year. Ideally, they would be separated, since the umpire has no control over intentional walks.

So someday, someone may want to replicate this study with more fine-tuned numbers. A more refined study would probably change these rankings a little bit. In addition, as I said before, the impact of a home plate umpire almost certainly extends beyond the number of strikeouts and walks. There's a lot more to study.

For now, I hope that you pay a little more attention to the umpire behind home plate when you go to your next ballgame—especially if it's Doug Eddings.

- Dave Studenmund

References

- Josh Weinstock's article is available at: http://www.hardballtimes.com/main/article/which-umpire-has-the-largest-strikezone

Fishing for Expansion Supremacy

by Marc Hulet

The Colorado Rockies and Florida (now Miami) Marlins joined the National League via expansion in 1993 and took similar approaches toward player development, focusing on young, close-to-big-league-ready talent with some veteran players sprinkled in. But which club did the better job at identifying talent and igniting long-term success?

We are going to answer this question by analyzing each club's expansion efforts, including all the transactions that branched out from the original rosters. I call this the "family tree" approach. Starting with each player selected in the expansion draft, we will follow the individual tree branches for each throughout his Rockies or Marlins career and then each related player connected via trade, until that path comes to an end.

By using the "family tree" approach rather than simply stopping with those players directly taken during the expansion draft, we get a better grasp on how the selections actually impacted each organization. Players such as Kevin Reimer and Trevor Hoffman had little to no impact on the Rockies and Marlins, but were integral to future success. Some of those players were actually drafted with the goal in mind of trading them for other pieces of the expansion puzzle.

We will judge the original expansion draft's impact on the organization through both Wins Above Replacement (WAR) and accumulated plate appearances (for hitters) or innings pitched (for pitchers). The chosen statistics allow us to gain a solid understanding of how each player—and the draft as a whole—impacted each organization.

When I began this exercise, I suspected—from observation only—that one team had significantly out-performed the other with its approach. As it turns out, I was correct.

And it's not even close.

In 20 years, the Colorado Rockies have never finished higher than second place and have made the playoffs just three times in their history. They lost the league division series (LDS) twice—to the Atlanta Braves (1995) and to the Philadelphia Phillies (2009)—and were swept in the World Series by the Boston Red Sox in 2007.

The win-now approach that the Rockies employed worked, to a degree, in the beginning. After finishing sixth in its inaugural season, the club came in second or third over the next four seasons. Then the wheels came off, and the organization found itself mired in a nine-year slump during which it finished no better than fourth place.

The Rockies possessed the first overall pick in the expansion draft and selected a 23-year-old pitcher, David Nied, out of the Atlanta Braves organization. The Braves were busy building one of the best starting rotations in the history of major league baseball, with the likes of young pitchers John Smoltz (age 25), Tom Glavine (26), Steve Avery (22) and Pete Smith (26). That offseason, the organization also added a 26-year-old named Greg Maddux via free agency at the expense of the Chicago Cubs.

Nied was an interesting choice to leave unprotected for the draft because, in his first taste of big league action during the 1992 season, the right-hander posted a 1.17 ERA and struck out 19 batters in 23 innings. Perhaps the Braves knew something no one else did about the rookie, or he simply fell victim to explosive offensive environment in Colorado. Nied pitched only 218 innings for the team and compiled 2.7 WAR. His big league career ended after the 1996 season, and he made just six appearances for Colorado.

Second baseman Eric Young Sr. was the club's sixth pick of the draft—and the 11th overall pick. He was selected out of the Los Angeles Dodgers system. The Dodgers used a number of second baseman in '92, including Young, Mike Sharperson and Lenny Harris, before committing to former Red Sox shortstop Jody Reed for the 1993 season, making the young second base prospect expendable.

Young spent parts of five seasons in Colorado, playing both second base and the outfield. He compiled 2,450 plate appearances and 10.1 WAR before being traded back to the Dodgers in August 1997 for Pedro Astacio. Young managed 5.2 WAR in another two and a half seasons in L.A., but it was another misstep for the Dodgers.

Astacio, just 28 at the time of the trade, was one of the most successful pitchers in Colorado history during his five-year run with the club. He pitched 827 innings and compiled 16.7 WAR despite the disadvantages he faced playing roughly half his games in Colorado. He was then sent to the Houston Astros at the trade deadline in 2001 in exchange for pitcher Scott Elarton.

Elarton made four starts for the Rockies that year and then missed all of 2002 due to injury. Over the next two seasons he made just 19 appearances (18 starts) before being released in May 2004. In total, he pitched 116 innings with -0.3 WAR.

With their fifth selection of the first round, and ninth pick overall, the Rockies selected outfielder Kevin Reimer from the Texas Rangers. This was one of the best choices the organization made in the draft, even though Reimer never played a game for the club. That same day, in what was likely a pre-arranged deal, the Rockies flipped Reimer to the Milwaukee Brewers for a 29-year-old outfielder who had played parts of five seasons in the majors—Dante Bichette.

Reimer played just one season for the Brewers and accumulated a negative WAR in 125 games. Bichette, on the other hand, spent seven seasons in Colorado and compiled 4,352 plate appearances and 8.0 WAR. He hit 201 of his 274 career home runs for the Rockies, and was the poster boy for the Crooked Number Club. He was traded to the Cincinnati Reds in October 1999 for pitcher Stan Belinda and outfielder Jeffrey Hammonds. Belinda, who was diagnosed with multiple sclerosis in 1998, never pitched for the Rockies and was released in July of 2000. Hammonds spent one year in Colorado (511 PAs) and compiled 1.9 WAR. He left after the season and signed as a free agent with the Milwaukee Brewers.

Joe Girardi is now better known as the manager of the New York Yankees, but he also played 15 seasons in the big leagues as a catcher. After parts of four seasons with the Chicago Cubs, he was selected 19th overall in the expansion draft. He spent three years handling the Rockies pitching staff and had 1,217 plate appearances. Girardi compiled 0.6 WAR before he was flipped to the Yankees for reliever Mike DeJean, who was a key member of the bullpen for four seasons. He pitched 256 innings for the Rockies and added 2.6 WAR.

DeJean then went to Milwaukee in a six-player deal that sent pitcher Mark Leiter and infielder Elvis Pena to Wisconsin. Colorado added pitchers Juan Acevedo and Kane Davis, as well as utility infielder Jose Flores, who never played for the club.

Acevedo, who provided 32 innings, and Davis, 68, each compiled 0.3 WAR for the club. Acevedo was later swapped for infield prospect Josue Espada, who never reached the majors in 10 pro seasons. Davis' only full major league season came with the Rockies in 2001, and he was then traded to the New York Mets in February 2002 for minor leaguer Corey Brittan, who failed to suit up for Colorado.

For anyone who followed the Rockies in the 1990s, it will come as no surprise that third baseman Vinny Castilla had the biggest expansion-related impact on the organization. The Rockies dipped back into the Braves system (each club could only lose one player in each of the three rounds) for its seventh pick of the second round, and the draft's 39th overall selection.

Castilla was 25 at the time of his selection and had played mostly shortstop during his three seasons in the Braves system. He played 21 games at the big league level with Atlanta over two seasons, 1991 and '92. Castilla went on to play seven seasons in Colorado, accumulating 3,781 PAs and 14.1 WAR. After hitting no more than 14 home runs in any one season in the Braves system, Castilla hit 40 or more home runs in three straight seasons between 1996 and '98, and totaled 239 dingers in his Rockies career.

In an effort to save money following the 1999 season, the organization traded Castilla and his hefty contract to the Tampa Bay Devil Rays for Cuban pitcher Rolando Arrojo and infielder Aaron Ledesma. Arrojo, 31, made 19 starts and struck out 80 batters in 101.1 innings; his ERA was 6.04. He was then traded to the Boston Red Sox in July 2000 (along with pitcher Rich Croushore and infielder Mike Lansing) in exchange for pitchers John Wasdin, Brian Rose and Jeff Taglienti and infielder Jeff Frye. Taglienti never pitched a game for the Rockies. Frye played 37 games, mostly at second base, before departing later that year as a free agent.

Rose and Wasdin combined to pitch 123 innings for the club and compiled 1.6 WAR. The latter pitched 60 of those innings and was then released in early June 2001. Rose was traded to the New York Mets in March 2001 for Mark Leiter. He was then flipped to the Milwaukee Brewers in a six-player deal with the Brewers.

Reliever Curtis Leskanic was taken with the 65th overall selection in the third round; only seven players were selected in the expansion draft after him, but he ended up having one of the largest impacts on the organization of anyone picked. A former eighth-round draft pick of the Cleveland Indians, Leskanic spent just one year in the Minnesota Twins system after coming over in a trade for first baseman Paul Sorrento before being plucked away by the Rockies.

He was a mainstay in the bullpen for much of his seven years in Colorado, and pitched 470 innings. His 7.5 WAR was impressive from a reliever, and Leskanic did a decent job of neutering the Colorado effects on his pitching line. He was later traded to the Brewers in late 1999 for fellow reliever Mike Myers.

Myers played for Colorado for two seasons and appeared in a whopping 151 games. As a lefty specialist, though, he pitched just 85.1 innings and added 1.9 WAR. The trade route was then explored once more, with the veteran reliever being dealt to the Arizona Diamondbacks for two young players: catcher J.D. Closser and outfielder Jack Cust.

Closser became the Rockies "catcher of the future" and played the part in his first season by hitting .319 in 36 games. In his final two seasons, though, he failed to hit more than .219, and was unceremoniously placed on waivers in October 2006 (and nabbed by Milwaukee). In total, he managed 0.5 WAR.

Cust appeared destined for a killer career in Colorado, given his prodigious raw power. Despite that, he wasn't given a very long rope by management, and totaled just 78 plate appearances in 2002. He batted .169 and struck out 32 times with just one homer, good for -0.5 WAR. Before the 2003 season, Cust was sent to the Baltimore Orioles for Chris Richard, who appeared in 19 games, compiled -0.1 WAR and failed to have his contract renewed following the '03 season.

In total, the Colorado Rockies' expansion efforts were good for a total of 111.4 WAR. The pitchers managed 5,387 innings; the hitters provided 16,474 plate appearances. The Curtis Leskanic selection impacted the organization for the longest amount of time; he joined the club for the 1993 season and later turned into Mike Myers, then Jack Cust, J.D. Closser and Chris Richard. With the release of Closser in 2006, the organization sawed off the final limb of the original expansion family tree, 14 years after the initial draft.

The numbers seem respectable, but were they good enough to best the Florida Marlins?

The Florida Marlins, now known as the Miami Marlins, have enjoyed a fairly successful two decades in the major leagues given the organization's perennial belt-tightening ways.

With that said, the organization has never finished higher than second place in the National League East, and has made just two playoff appearances. However, in those two appearances the Marlins wound up World Series champions. The organization has had more than one opportunity to build a dynasty around a big league roster, but fell victim, instead, to ownership fire sales and constant retooling.

In 1992, though, everything was fresh and new for the Marlins organization and its fan base. The club had the second pick of the draft and selected a young Toronto Blue Jays outfielder—Canadian native Nigel Wilson. He was a 22-year-old coming off a Double-A season that saw him hit 34 doubles and 26 home runs, but Toronto was in the middle of its back-to-back World Series championships and was fielding a veteran team with the largest payroll in baseball. The win-now mentality made Wilson expendable.

He spent most of 1993 in Triple-A—appearing in just seven games with the big league club—and then all of 1994 back at the same level. He was then selected off waivers by Cincinnati after posting an .875 OPS and .309 batting average at the highest level of the minors.

The Marlins' third selection, and sixth overall player taken in the draft, was second baseman Brett Barberie, previously of the now-displaced Montreal Expos. The Expos already had 23-year-old Delino DeShields entrenched at the keystone. DeShields, a former first-round draft pick, was coming off a 46-steal season, and the organization was quietly building a playoff contender.

Barberie, 25 in 1993, spent two years as the Marlins' starting second baseman and received 830 plate appearances. He compiled 3.5 WAR. With Quilvio Veras ready to take over second base in 1995 (more on him later), Barberie was dealt to Baltimore for rookie reliever Jay Powell, who spent parts of four seasons in Miami and pitched 195 innings.

Unfortunately, he had a negative WAR of -0.5. He was pawned off on the Houston Astros (along with a minor league pitcher) in mid-1998 for young catcher Ramon Castro. He was a prospect with impressive raw power who ended up spending parts of six seasons with the Marlins, but his career was marred by off-field issues, injuries and inconsistency. He compiled 1.1 WAR over 531 plate appearances. Castro was granted free agency in the fall of 2004 and signed with the New York Mets.

To be successful, an organization has to have reliable pitching. Pat Rapp was just that for the Marlins organization during its early years. He wasn't flashy, but he pitched for parts of five seasons with the club and was an innings-eater, managing 5.9 WAR over 665 innings. Originally selected from the San Francisco Giants organization with the 10th overall selection, he was later traded back to his original club at midseason in 1997 for two minor league pitchers who never played for the Marlins, Bobby Rector and Brandon Leese.

If there is one thing the Marlins organization knew how to do, by design or not, it was acquiring impact, high-leverage relievers. Bryan Harvey was one of three big-name closers to find his way to the organization through fallout from the expansion draft. He was grabbed out of the Angels organization with the 20th overall selection.

He was coming off an injury that saw him appear in just 25 games for the Angels in 1992, but he had saved 46 games in '91 and finished fifth in the Cy Young award race. A large, multi-year contract made him somewhat unattractive, but Florida saw an opportunity to add some experience at the back end of the 'pen. He saved 45 games for the Fish in '93, but then injuries hit again and he collected more than $8 million over the next two years while spending most of the time on the disabled list. He was granted free agency at the end of 1995 and re-signed with the Angels. In his three years with the Marlins, Harvey accumulated 2.8 WAR. Unfortunately, he managed just 79 innings of work.

Jeff "Mr. Marlin" Conine spent parts of eight seasons with Florida—but that came over two different periods. His first tour of duty came between 1993 and 1997, when he compiled 2,852 at-bats and an impressive 15.1 WAR. He hit more than 20 home runs twice, and also batted more than .300 during two different seasons. Conine finished third in the American League Rookie of the Year voting in 1993 after hitting .292 with 79 RBIs. Selected from the Kansas City Royals during the expansion draft, he was dealt back to K.C. in late 1997 for minor league pitcher Blaine Mull, who managed to pitch just nine games above Single-A.

With its first pick of the second round of the draft (28th overall) the Marlins selected outfielder and Florida native Carl Everett from the New York Yankees. He managed just 74 plate appearances with the organization over two seasons and was then sent to the Mets in late 1994 for the aforementioned Quilvio Veras, a young second baseman. He manned second base for the Marlins for two seasons and managed 4.1 WAR in 846 plate appearances.

Veras was then sent to San Diego in late 1996 for a former third overall draft pick (1994) in pitcher Dustin Hermanson. He was then flipped to Montreal before the 1997 season along with veteran outfielder Joe Orsulak for the promising—but injury-riddled—Cliff Floyd. He was a very good player for the organization, with 17.3 WAR over 2,569 plate appearances. Floyd was then sent back to his original organization in mid-2002 along with infielder Wilton Guerrero and pitcher Claudio Vargas for pitchers Carl Pavano, Graeme Lloyd, Justin Wayne and Donald Levinski and infielder Mike Mordecai.

Hurlers Lloyd, Wayne and Levinski complied just 87 innings for the Marlins at the big league level. Lloyd was granted free agency in late 2002; the other two pitchers were cut loose with little fanfare.

Mordecai carved out a nice career in parts of four seasons with the Marlins as a pinch-hitter and back-up infielder. He was granted free agency at the end of 2005, but failed to catch on with another club. He tallied 279 plate appearances with a negative -0.3 WAR.

Pavano was the gem of the Floyd deal. The young pitcher, 26 years old at the time of the trade, spent parts of three years with the organization and won 18 games in 2004. Pavano then reached free agency and signed a lucrative contract with the New York Yankees. He threw 485 innings during his Marlins career and had 8.7 WAR.

There have been a few pitchers by the name of Cris (Chris) Carpenter in the major leagues. The one who fits here was a fairly nondescript reliever, a former first-round draft pick who spent parts of five seasons with the St. Louis Cardinals before being selected with the 38th overall pick of the expansion draft. He pitched just 37 innings with a 0.5 WAR for the Marlins, but he had a huge impact on the organization's history.

Carpenter was traded to the Texas Rangers right before the trade deadline in 1993 for two young pitchers: Kurt Miller and Robb Nen. Miller played parts of three seasons with the Fish before being passed on to the Chicago Cubs. Nen, an inconsistent minor league hurler, was the steal of the deal.

In Florida, he was immediately placed in the bullpen. The move was pure genius, as he compiled 108 saves for the club over five seasons. He was good for 5.4 WAR during 314 innings of work. Although he was still in his prime, Nen and his large salary were then dumped on the San Francisco Giants for pitchers Mike Pageler, Mike Villano and Joe Fontenot. Only Fontenot appeared in the majors, providing just 42 league average innings.

Danny Jackson was selected from the Pittsburgh Pirates organization during the third round of the draft, 54th overall. That same day, though, The Marlins flipped Jackaon, a 10-year veteran, to the Philadelphia Phillies for bullpen depth in the form of Joel Adamson and Matt Whisenant. Adamson, 24, appeared in just nine games, totaling 7.0 innings. He bounced around the system until November 1996, when he was traded to the Milwaukee Brewers for minor league reliever Ed Collins.

Whisenant did not pitch much for the Marlins either. Control issues kept the left-hander from reaching the majors until 1997, at the age of 26. He appeared in four games and pitched just 2.2 innings. He spent most of the first half of the season in Triple-A before being dealt to Kansas City in July for catcher Matt Treanor. It was a weird bit of luck—or perhaps great scouting—that the organization was able to turn Whisenant into Treanor. At the time of the deal, Treanor was a 21-year old catcher who was hitting just .198 in 80 Single-A games. He didn't reach the majors until seven years later, in 2004. He then spent the next five seasons as the back-up catcher for the big league club. Treanor compiled 832 plate appearances and 1.4 WAR. He was released in December 2008 and signed with the Detroit Tigers.

Perhaps the most talented player to be selected in 1992 expansion draft was minor league hurler Trevor Hoffman, who was picked eighth overall by the Marlins out of the Reds organizations. Hoffman, a former 11th-round draft pick out of the University of Arizona, had split 1992 between Double-A and Triple-A. He had spent just two years in the minors, and had yet to play a game at the big league level.

The right-hander made the Marlins' Opening Day roster in 1993 and appeared in 28 games, posting a 3.28 ERA with 26 strikeouts and 19 walks in 35.2 innings. In June of that year something occurred that could have put a black mark on the organization for years to come: Hoffman was traded to the San Diego Padres along with two other players, Andres Berumen and Jose Martinez. He went on to spend 16 years in San Diego, appearing in 902 games, saving 552 games and recording 22.3 WAR.

However, two players came back to Florida. The first was reliever Rich Rodriguez, who was in his fourth big league season. He appeared in 36 games for Florida, pitching 46 innings. He earned an ugly -0.9 WAR for his efforts. He was released at the end of spring training in 1994 and caught on with the St. Louis Cardinals.

The second player who came to the Marlins in the Hoffman deal was an inconsistent and cantankerous—but extremely talented—young outfielder named Gary Sheffield. Just 24 at the time, he already had five-and-a-half seasons of major league baseball under his belt, including a 33-home run, 6.8 WAR season that resulted in a third-place finish in the National League Most Valuable Player voting. He went on to spend parts of six seasons in Miami and had 2,358 plate appearances. In 1996, Sheffield hit 42 home runs and drove in 120 runs. He also walked 142 times with just 66 strikeouts. His season resulted in 6.5 WAR. During his entire Marlins career, Sheffield earned 14.9 WAR.

His time in Florida ended in May 1998, less than a year after the Marlins won their first World Series title. Sheffield, along with Charles Johnson, Bobby Bonilla, Jim Eisenreich and Manuel Berrios, was sent to the Dodgers for future Hall of Fame catcher Mike Piazza and infielder Todd Zeile. Zeile compiled 270 plate appearances before being traded to the Texas Rangers in July '98 for minor league pitcher Daniel DeYoung and infielder Jose Santos. Neither player appeared in the majors with the Marlins.

Piazza appeared in just five games for the organization before he was again traded, this time to the New York Mets. In return, the Marlins received three young players in pitchers Geoff Goetz and Ed Yarnall and outfielder Preston Wilson. The young outfielder, 23 at the time of the deal, didn't get his big league feet under him until 1999, when he finished second in the rookie of the year voting to Reds hurler Scott Williamson.

Wilson slugged 26 home runs that year and began a run of five seasons with at least 23 taters. He hit 31 long bombs with 121 RBIs for the Fish in 2000, but he also struck out 187 times. The Marlins and Rockies worked out a deal for Wilson in November 2002, sending him west along with catcher Charles Johnson, infielder Pablo Ozuna and pitcher Vic Darensbourg for pitcher Mike Hampton and outfielder Juan Pierre.

Hampton was traded to the Atlanta Braves two days later for pitchers Ryan Baker and Tim Spooneybarger. Barker did not pitch for the Marlins, but Spooneybarger threw 42 innings for the club before injuries ruined his career. He was later released by the Marlins in 2005.

Pierre was in the prime of his career at the time of the trade. The speedy outfielder played for the club for three seasons and managed more than 200 hits twice, while stealing a total of 167 bases. He accumulated 2,214 at-bats and 11.2 WAR. As with nearly every other talented player who collected a paycheck from the organization, he was dealt away. Pierre was sent to the Cubs in December 2005 for three pitchers: Renyel Pinto, Sergio Mitre and Ricky Nolasco.

Pinto battled injuries and command issues during his five-year Marlins career, but he still managed to pitch 231 innings. Unfortunately he was good for only a -0.6 WAR. He was released in June 2010. Mitre battled inconsistencies during his time in the organization and compiled just 190 innings pitched, but managed 2.4 WAR. Released in September 2008, he was picked up by the New York Yankees.

Nolasco was the gem of the bunch. He appeared in 35 games (22 starts) during his rookie season with the Marlins in 2006, but then missed most of '07 due to an injury. He then came back and pitched more than 200 innings the next year, and has been a mainstay in the rotation ever since. To date, Nolsaco has provided 1,100-plus innings of work and 18.1 WAR. And the motor is still running, as he is not set to become a free agent until after the 2013 season.

Returning to the Piazza deal, one of the two young pitchers acquired in his swap was not through impacting the organization. Goetz, selected sixth overall in the 1997 amateur draft, never pitched for the big league club after battling injuries and inconsistencies. However, Yarnall—who also never pitched for the Marlins at the big league level—was later traded to the Yankees, along with pitchers Todd Noel and Mark Johnson, for third baseman Mike Lowell.

A 25-year-old third baseman at the time of the deal, Lowell had just 15 big league plate appearances before he played his rookie campaign with the Marlins in 1999. He held his own at the plate, which was most impressive considering that he had been diagnosed with testicular cancer in February of that year.

Lowell went on to play seven seasons in Florida, acting as a guiding force in the infield and earning a Gold Glove in 2005. He also appeared in three All-Star games and hit 32 home runs in 2003. Overall, he compiled 4,005 PAs and 19.4 WAR.

But. looking to save money in 2005, the organization dealt Lowell, along with young pitcher Josh Beckett and veteran reliever Guillermo Mota, to the Boston Red

Sox for three young pitchers: Anibal Sanchez, Jesus Delgado and Harvey Garcia, as well as a highly regarded infield prospect named Hanley Ramirez.

Delgado battled injuries and appeared in just two games for the Marlins. He was claimed off waivers by the Seattle Mariners in 2009. Garcia appeared in eight games with the Fish, but was also let go in '09. Sanchez, though, was a diamond in the rough. He battled through injuries during the early part of his Marlins career and did not appear in more than 18 games during any one season from 2006-2009. He then made 32 starts in each of the next two seasons.

Sanchez entered 2012 with the Marlins, but was traded to the Detroit Tigers on July 23—along with veteran infielder Omar Infante—for a package of young players including pitchers Jacob Turner and Brian Flynn, as well as catcher Rob Brantly and a compensatory 2013 draft pick. All three players will look to continue this limb of the expansion family tree for years to come. Sanchez ended his Florida career with 794 innings pitched and 13.4 WAR.

The other player in the deal, Ramirez, just 22 during his rookie season in 2006, was named the NL Rookie of the Year after hitting .292 with 51 steals and 119 runs scored. He flashed some serious power for a shortstop over the next four seasons, never hitting fewer than 21 dingers and topping out at 33. He finished second in the 2009 MVP voting when he hit .342 and topped 7.0 WAR for the second straight season.

Like Sanchez, though, Ramirez's time with Florida ended with another 2012 salary dump. After years of being highly sought after by a number of teams, including Boston, who originally traded him away, the three-time All-Star shortstop was sent to the Los Angeles Dodgers organization for a modest return that included young pitchers Nate Eovaldi and Scott McGough. Both pitchers were with the organization at the time of this writing. Despite his tumultuous time with the Marlins, Ramirez left behind a legacy in Florida after making 4,150 PAs and accumulating 32.5 WAR.

All totaled, it sounds like the Marlins had a very successful expansion draft, but just how good was it compared to the Colorado Rockies'?

———

Both clubs did a solid job of drafting their original rosters. Colorado received more value from the players actually selected during the draft process, but Florida did a better job of valuing and trading its original expansion assets for future gain. In fairness, Colorado was at an inherent disadvantage due to its inability to attract free agent pitchers and develop pitching assets due to the "Colorado effects."

It is a little hard to believe that the Marlins organization is still feeling the impacts of the original expansion draft more than 20 years later. Six players linked to the selection of the future closer known for his killer change-up are still playing for Miami. The loss of future Hall of Famer Trevor Hoffman certainly seems disastrous on the surface, but he was just the beginning of an eye-popping family tree limb that included numerous big-league stars.

Hoffman's selection was perhaps the single most important move ever made by the Marlins franchise. Although he found much success with the Padres, he was directly (and indirectly) responsible for future Marlins stars such as Gary Sheffield, Mike Piazza, Preston Wilson, Juan Pierre, Mike Lowell, Anibal Sanchez, Hanley Ramirez and Ricky Nolasco. Those eight players earned the Florida Marlins 117.5 WAR during their careers—and that number is still growing.

Florida's hurlers managed 6,031 innings, while Colorado's pitchers compiled 5,387 innings—a modest difference of 644 innings. The Marlins hitters, though, managed 30,923 at-bats, compared to the Rockies' 16,474—resulting in a whopping 14,449 more plate appearances for the Fish, almost double that of their expansion counterparts.

If that isn't enough to swing the Marlins' expansion efforts into the win column over the Rockies, consider that the organization has received 202.3 total WAR from the original draft, compared to the Rockies' 111.4. That means that the Marlins received 90.9 more WAR than the Rockies. That number is still climbing—and could continue to do so for years to come.

The history books have already been closed on the Colorado Rockies' expansion efforts but the story is far from over for the Florida (Miami) Marlins.

Leaderboard: 2012 HR per Ball in Air

Because it's subject to human judgment—and because humans are notoriously fallible and biased and flawed—batted-ball classification (i.e. distinguishing between fly balls and line drives and ground balls) is prone to some inconsistencies. Broadly speaking, it's not a giant problem; however, if one's ambition is to announce with some measure of authority this or that player's home-run rate on fly balls, that same "one" has to account for the potential biases therein. And yet, home runs per fly ball is a pretty good proxy for Most Powerful Hitter, and the identity of the Most Powerful Hitter is need-to-know information. "What to do?" we ask.

One way of circumventing the problem is to consider that same player's home run rate on all batted balls in the air (HR/BIA). While there's some overlap between fly ball and line drive classification, ground balls are less prone to scorer bias—owing to how they're on the ground, one assumes. Therefore, if we look simply at home runs on all batted balls that weren't grounders, we get a more reliable figure.

Below are the leaders from 2012 in home runs per ball in air among those with a minimum 300 plate appearances, at which sample size home-run rate becomes reliable, according to work by Russell Carleton.

Name	Team	PA	HR	BIA	HR/BIA
Adam Dunn	White Sox	649	41	212	19.3%
Giancarlo Stanton	Marlins	501	37	196	18.9%
Mike Napoli	Rangers	417	24	138	17.4%
Wilin Rosario	Rockies	426	28	162	17.3%
Josh Hamilton	Rangers	636	43	255	16.9%
Pedro Alvarez	Pirates	586	30	185	16.2%
Justin Maxwell	Astros	352	18	112	16.1%
Curtis Granderson	Yankees	684	43	271	15.9%
Jose Bautista	Blue Jays	399	27	172	15.7%
Chris Davis	Orioles	562	33	212	15.6%

Notes

Adam Dunn's 2011 season was awful in pretty much all the ways a season could be awful. He set a career-high 35.7 percent strikeout rate, a career-low 59 wRC+ (that is, offensive production relative to league average, where 100 is average), and a very career-worst -3.0 WAR. Another bad part of it (and partial cause of it) was his career-worst HR/BIA rate. While he had generally posted figures in the 15-16 percent range, Dunn hit home runs on only 6.8 percent of his balls in air in 2011. A big part of his 2012 rebound was his recovery in terms of power. After his poor 2011, Dunn posted a league- and career-best figure in 2012.

These figures aren't park-adjusted, so naturally any player who does the majority of his hitting in an above-average offensive environment will have some advantage in terms of home run hitting. That said, there's only one full-time catcher on this list and only one rookie, too, and they're both Colorado Rockies rookie catcher Wilin Rosario. Rosario, who played all of 2012 as a 23-year-old, doesn't necessarily have excellent control of the strike zone, as he posted a 25:99 walk-to-strikeout ratio in 426 plate appearances. What he does have, pretty clearly, is both raw and in-game power.

Despite the fact that he was a rookie, it's not entirely suprising to see Rosario's name on this list, given the power he showed in the minors. In fact, a full nine of the players here are reasonable in one way or another. Here's the surprising one: Justin Maxwell. A one-time prospect in the Nationals system, Maxwell played in 2011 with the Yankees Triple-A affiliate, showing decent power there (16 home runs in 204 plate appearances) but losing the majority of the season to a shoulder injury. In an attempt to sign every minor-league player, the Astros claimed him off waivers in April. Then Maxwell finished among the league leaders in home runs per ball in air.

- Carson Cistulli

Surprise! The Seasons Nobody Saw Coming

by Brandon Isleib

The Nationals, Orioles and Athletics came out of nowhere this year, didn't they? Or did they? What about the Pirates? Did their 2011 contention run prepare us for this year? What do we mean by nowhere?

Consider the 1959 Dodgers and 1991 Braves. The Braves surprised everyone by going from last place to the World Series in one year. The Dodgers were similarly impressive, placing seventh in 1958 and winning the pennant the following year. But were the Dodgers, after winning six of the previous 13 pennants, a complete surprise in 1959? If we're trying to tell team stories through pennant races—and that's how we experience a season, a day and a game at a time—we'd say the Dodgers "rebounded" in 1959. So how similar are those Dodgers to the 1991 Braves? Looking at two seasons by themselves, very similar. Looking beyond that, not at all. It's not just about looking up won/loss records; it's about franchise résumés, about reputations, about momentum.

The 1959 Dodgers and 1991 Braves "feel" different because of their previous successes, or lack thereof. It's easy just to call it an impression and move on. But while team reputations are somewhat relative and based on intuition, those notions come from the daily unfolding of pennant races. So we can quantify that "feel" if we can quantify days in contention as a continuous impression of that team's ability.

The Statistic to Do That Thing I Just Described

Over the last couple years, I've developed a stat I call Momentum; for this article I'll call it the Reputation Estimate (RE), because that's what it's measuring—how we'd estimate each team's reputation, by itself and against other teams. RE is best at stratifying teams and tracking their gradual rise and fall. I'll give the math basics—the appendix will tell all—and use this season as an example.

Teams generate momentum, and therefore RE, when they're in contention. I've defined contention as being over .500, and at least one of the following:

- In first place or within three games of it;
- Leading the first Wild Card or within two games of it; or
- Leading the second Wild Card.

The three-games idea is based on typical series length. If two teams are within three games of first and they start a series against each other, the media may size up both teams before the series, hype it as must-win for both teams, and so on. The point is that both teams are in the spotlight. You don't have to measure this at three games, but it's a common sense place to do so.

The number of points a team gets for being in contention depends on the era. Looking at schedules prior to division play, a day in contention generates four points of RE. In the two-division era, a day in contention generates three points. For all games in 1994 or later, a day in contention generates two points.

Because of the league structures, there only had to be one team in contention per league in the old days, but in 2012 there have to be at least five teams in contention, so the different point totals are intended to reflect the lower bar. In every era, a team loses a single point of RE when it's not in contention, stopping at zero. Teams can carry their RE from one season to the next, though the amount that is carried over depends on the number of teams that had high RE scores. The idea is that more excitement carries over when there are more teams worth talking about.

That's a lot of mathy abstraction. Here's an example. Entering 2012, these were the top six teams in American League RE, as well a team in the doldrums:

Team	RE
Yankees	653
Red Sox	596
Rangers	501
Tigers	430
Angels	351
Rays	289
Orioles	0

The Yankees and Red Sox were perennial contenders—we were going to watch them regardless of what they did, because their reputations were strong. The Rangers were on the cusp of joining them, and the Tigers and Angels were good teams trying to break into that top three. The Orioles, second from the bottom every season since 2006, were at zero (only the Royals were worse) and had a long way to go.

Of course, the season was wild, with half the league involved in playoff races going into September (none of it aided by the second Wild Card). The Angels were up and down, the Rays were mostly up, and the Red Sox were so high-profile that everybody watched them crash, contend for a couple weeks, and then crash again. Those seven teams' REs throughout the season:

Team	May 20	June 20	July 20	Aug. 20	Sept. 20
Yankees	665	715	775	837	899
Red Sox	572	565	550	519	488
Rangers	549	611	671	733	795
Tigers	424	393	378	440	502
Rays	337	399	417	443	472
Angels	327	311	371	406	375
Orioles	48	110	161	205	267

RE captures all their stories. The Red Sox's off-year put them in the Tigers' and Rays' tier and put a huge gap between those teams and the top. The Angels were in with that group briefly, but fell off the pace. And it took all season, but the Orioles' persistence got them some recognition eventually.

To answer the questions at the top of the article, by RE the Nationals, Orioles and Athletics came out of nowhere this year, because they started 2012 at zero. The Pirates started at four points, which isn't much better, but enough to put them above eight zero-point teams.

So I'm going to use this system to answer a fun question: What have been the most surprising seasons? Which seasons most bewildered us by having the most unexpected pennant contenders? I'm going to answer that question by looking at the highest percentage of days in contention by teams entering the season with zero RE—teams out of nowhere, so to speak.

Taking out the seasons too affected by league instability or disparity—everything before 1907 (the 1906 Cubs started at zero but were a .601 team in 1905) plus seasons affected by the Federal League or World War II—gives a diverse and intriguing set of seasons, all of which indicate that RE is measuring what we want it to measure.

If we label all zero RE teams entering a season as "surprise teams," here are the eight most surprising seasons of all time.

No. 8: 1993 AL

- 63 percent of contention from surprise teams (492 days out of 777)
- Surprise teams' days in contention: White Sox (159)/Yankees (127)/Tigers (77)/ Royals (66)/Angels (59)/Mariners (4)

Despite sporadic contention since 1990, the White Sox entered 1993 with no RE. The A's and Twins had taken the last six division titles, and had been the only teams in the West within three games of first place since June 1992. RE shows Chicago's difficulties well: To become the alpha team of a division or league, the existing alpha team has to fall. If the White Sox, A's and Twins were in the race in 1993, then the

A's and Twins would have kept their profiles and the White Sox would be a distant third, gaining ground only on the also-rans.

1992's stable pennant races, along with repeat winners in both AL divisions for the first time since 1978 meant that if the top teams went under, someone contending from the start could get noticed quicker than usual. But the league was turned upside down by pitching woes—every A's pitcher in 1993 who threw at least 10 innings for them in 1992 saw his ERA rise by at least a run, with the exception of Rick Honeycutt (down 0.8) and Bobby Witt (up 0.8)—and of the seven AL teams entering 1993 without RE, an astounding six of them contended at some point. The East featured the high-profile Blue Jays, the finally-rebuilt Yankees under Buck Showalter (it's hard to think of the Yankees as coming from nowhere, but Spike Owen and Dion James probably don't spring to mind as starters either), and a different team seemingly every month—the Tigers in the first half, the Orioles in the second half, and the Red Sox (who wound up 80-82) in May, July and August.

In the West, the White Sox didn't take charge until after the All-Star break; everybody was playing .525ish ball until then, including the Angels (who ended 71-91), the Royals and Rangers, both of whom hung in for awhile, and even the Mariners, though the latter was more from division weakness than team quality.

Though 1993 is the start of the modern Yankees, it isn't the White Sox's or the Yankees' rise by themselves that makes this season a surprise; it's the entire narrative, with the Tigers, Royals and Angels joining them—completely unpredictable in any year and altering several teams' reputations. The Twins entered 1993 third in AL RE and ended 10th. A dying team gets buried quicker with more shovels, and 1993 was one of the quickest burials in history.

No. 7: 1984 National League

- 69 percent (419/602)
- Surprise teams: Padres (157)/Cubs (150)/Mets (92)/Reds (20)

The NL in the '80s tended to be uniquely egalitarian; entering 1984, RE ranked the Dodgers, Phillies, Braves, Expos and Cardinals in descending order, but for all intents and purposes it was a five-way tie. And unlike the 1993 AL collapses, all five teams were in the conversation through Memorial Day. But they all wound up close to .500, their depth frustrated by the front-line talent emerging in Chicago, New York and San Diego. Though nothing was settled in June, by July it was down to that trio apart from a last gasp (for the decade) from the Phillies.

For the Cubs and Padres, it was the coming-out party for future Hall of Famers, as Ryne Sandberg and Tony Gwynn took their games to the levels we associate with them; the Cubs supported Sandberg with 16-1 Rick Sutcliffe, while the Padres flanked Gwynn with rookie breakout Kevin McReynolds. The Mets outperformed their Pythagorean expectation by 12 games and were outscored, but rookie manager Davey Johnson revamped the pitching staff by just letting the kids play. The rotation in 1983 featured Tom Seaver, Mike Torrez, Ed Lynch, Walt Terrell and Craig Swan; in 1984 it transformed to Terrell, Dwight Gooden, Ron Darling, Sid Fernandez and Bruce Berenyi. That didn't change the pWAR, largely because the bullpen in 1983 was superb, but it gave upside and direction for 1985.

As pennant races went in the two-division era, these weren't the most involved. But that the East was led by both its previous doormats (the Cubs and Mets had brought up the rear together since 1980) in an era when the other teams in the division didn't even collapse makes 1984 a surprise from any angle.

No. 6: 1967 NL

- 70 percent (166/237)
- Surprise teams: Cardinals (135)/Cubs (26)/Braves (5)

In 1966, the Giants dynasty, the Dodgers dynasty and the Pirates' attempt at a dynasty combined for 360 days of contention—93.3 percent of the league total. In 1967 they were all irrelevant. The Reds started off 26-11, with vastly improved pitching around a great offensive core, by which point the Cardinals were the only team within five games of them. The Cardinals hadn't mattered since their 1964 pennant; in 1966 they were a well-balanced team with legitimate stars—Lou Brock, Orlando Cepeda, Tim McCarver, Bob Gibson—but the supporting cast couldn't hit. In 1967, players like Curt Flood and Julian Javier had a resurgence, and better performances from their stars and bench compensated for Gibson's midseason injury.

As the Reds tanked in June, the Cubs—a team that went 59-103 in 1966 but had a good offense—challenged the Cardinals, thanks to improved up-the-middle defense (Glenn Beckert and Don Kessinger totaled -2.0 in dWAR in 1966 but 2.7 in 1967) and an ace in Ferguson Jenkins. But the Cardinals beat the Cubs five times over two series in August; by the end of those contests the Cubs were in fifth and the Cardinals had a 10.5-game lead over the Braves, who went 15-32 the rest of the way.

This race is a good example of how fast starts from unexpected teams can change the rest of the landscape. The Pirates and Giants made a good run of it for awhile, but the Reds and the Cardinals were too hot for the established teams to have enough time to look for answers. A 21-7 September from the Giants didn't matter because the team was 13 games back at the start of the month.

No. 5: 1956 NL

- 74 percent (333/451)
- Surprise teams: Braves (133)/Reds (121)/Cardinals (44)/Pirates (35)

Since June 13, 1954, only the Dodgers and Giants had gained any RE, and in 1955 the Dodgers' record left second place closer to sixth than first. The Dodgers didn't fold in 1956, winning the pennant only five games behind the 1955 record. But without the 22-2 start of 1955, the Dodgers let the league into the mix. As of June 22, the fifth-place Pirates were only three behind first (they would finish seventh); by month's end it was down to the Dodgers, Braves and Reds to fight the season out.

And fight they did, as the three teams were never separated by more than six games. This was the first Dodgers team in a decade without Jackie Robinson, but they were largely the same team otherwise. The Braves got back into contention thanks to a rebounding Lew Burdette and a full season of Joe Adcock. The Reds' big changes were Rookie of the Year Frank Robinson in left field, as well as reclamation project Brooks Lawrence, who lowered his ERA three runs and achieved a 19-10 record after a 3-8 mark for the Cardinals the year before. But the Reds' 16-game swing was only a four-game swing in their Pythagorean record; they underperformed severely in 1955 and overachieved moderately in 1956.

This pennant race took a page from every style of excitement. It was chaotic in the early going, with teams that collapsed after a great start, and it settled down to a few teams who never shook each other off: the established dynasty; the soon-to-be dynasty; and the surprise team with the Hall of Fame rookie and the scrap-heap ace (Cincinnati also tied a league record with 221 team home runs). This season is remembered best for being the Dodgers' last pennant in Brooklyn, and for Don Larsen's perfect game in the World Series, but the season that led to it was no less exciting.

No. 4: 1926 NL

- 76 percent (282/370)
- Surprise teams: Reds (146)/Cardinals (86)/Cubs (35)/Dodgers (15)

The story lines always returned to the Giants, Cubs and Pirates. The Giants had spent more time in and around first place than five teams combined. Branch Rickey's first on-field accomplishment was taking the Cardinals from hapless to perennial contender—something no NL team had managed from scratch since Frank Selee's Cubs. So the 1926 Cardinals are historically important as the first fruits of Rickey's innovations. But to label this season as all about the Cardinals, whose primary changes from 1925 were putting defensive whiz Tommy Thevenow at shortstop (3.9 dWAR) and deepening the pitching staff, is to ignore the Reds, who had been over .500 eight of the previous nine seasons with only one pennant.

The Reds of this era were unusual in several ways. First, they featured many former AL players, rare given the restrictions around interleague trading at the time. Carl

Mays and newly purchased Wally Pipp were more famous as Yankees, Val Picinich was an offseason purchase from the Red Sox, and outfielder Rube Bressler was a starting pitcher on Connie Mack's 1914 A's. Second, most of the team's improvement from 1925 is masked by league trends, as the NL scored 0.5 runs per game fewer in 1926, while the Reds scored 0.3 runs per game more.

The 1926 Reds also blazed quite the trail against left-handed pitching. In 1926, Cincinnati was 65-62 against right-handed started pitching, but 22-5 (.815) against lefties—a better clip against southpaws than the 1906 Cubs, 1998 Yankees and 2001 Mariners. NL lefties weren't the highest caliber in 1926—the Reds had two of the best ones in Eppa Rixey and Jakie May—but that's still ridiculous. And Cuckoo Christensen/Bressler in left field was the only platoon. The Reds just happened to be a bunch of lefty mashers:

Triple-slash platoon splits for important right-handed batters, 1926 Reds:

Player	Versus RHP	Versus LHP
Rube Bressler, LF	.347/.399/.455	.400/.554/.582
Hughie Critz, 2B	.261/.295/.347	.314/.410/.486
Chuck Dressen, 3B	.254/.321/.381	.318/.412/.455
Bubbles Hargrave, C	.341/.392/.500	.411/.476/.643
Val Picinich, C	.260/.321/.320	.275/.431/.575

That's right—the Reds had an outfielder and two catchers with an OPS over 1.000 against southpaws. It was a fluke of a season, but what a fluke.

As for the pennant race, six teams were within three games of first place on June 17—everybody but the Braves and Phillies—and those teams were separated by only 4.5 on July 18. By the end of July, rookie manager Joe McCarthy's Cubs dropped a touch behind the Reds, Cardinals and Pirates, remaining a hot streak away all season from re-entering the race. The Pirates last led on Aug. 30 and the Reds on Sept. 16, as the Cardinals held a small lead. It was a rough-and-tumble race remembered most for being the start of the Cardinals and McCarthy, but it was excitement from start to finish that highlighted some frequent bridesmaids.

No. 3: 1912 AL
- 77 percent (141/183)
- Surprise teams: Red Sox (132)/Senators (9)

The 1910-11 A's won the league by over a dozen games each year, even though the Tigers started 1911 with a 27-5 record. Before then, the AL race was routinely chaotic, as 1906, 1907 and 1908 were four-team races. The next year, 1909, was primarily the A's and Tigers, with an indescribable challenge from the Red Sox—indescribable not just from the talent disparity in the lineup (Tris Speaker plus meh) and dugout (Connie Mack/Hughie Jennings versus... Fred Lake?) but from the complete lack of a rotation: Frank Arellanes was the only Sox pitcher with more than 19 starts. For the Red Sox, 13 pitchers started at least five games, but only five of those made at least 10.

One of those five pitchers was Smokey Joe Wood, just 19 years old in 1909. He would become one of the best pitchers in the league over the next two years. In 1912, with the opening of Fenway Park, while Walter Johnson posted a better ERA+ than did Wood—240 to Wood's 179—Wood posted a 34-5 record, better than Johnson's 33-12 mark. Though the White Sox started off 21-5 and the Senators—supporting Johnson with breakout offense from corner infielders Chick Gandil and Eddie Foster—won 17 in a row to enter the race (and distance themselves from 1911's 64-90 team), the Red Sox took first place for keeps on June 15.

So what made 1912 as bold a statement for the Red Sox as the A's made in the four surrounding years?

Pitching WAR of various Red Sox and A's in 1912:

Smoky Joe Wood, Red Sox	10.0
Ray Collins, Red Sox	5.2
Buck O'Brien, Red Sox	5.2
Eddie Plank, A's	4.3
Hugh Bedient, Red Sox	4.0
Rest of the Red Sox	0.4
Rest of the A's	0.0

The Sox couldn't have predicted a rotation this deep. O'Brien started minor league play at age 27, went 5-1, 0.38 in 1911 for the Sox, carried that success into 1912, then went 4-11 in 1913 and was out of the majors. Bedient, 21-20 over two minor league years in Fall River and Providence, and Collins, already a solid number two behind Wood, both would be done in the majors after 1915. Every team dreams of finding aces out of nowhere; the Red Sox pulled it off and pointedly interrupted the AL's first dynasty.

No. 2: 1939 NL

- 82 percent (148/180)
- Surprise teams: Reds (142)/Bees (6)

Books on managers cover Bill McKechnie in welcome depth, and the Reds are his most famous project. He turned every concern to defense, got Paul Derringer's career on track, and made Bucky Walters an ace after acquiring him from Philadelphia. But what matters here is how thorough that turnaround was in the face of several other quality teams. The Cardinals generally had faded by this point, in between talents at several positions and especially in the rotation, but still were decent, and 1938's pennant race was another Giants/Cubs/Pirates-a-thon, though the Reds spent a week in June trying to break up the troika and were only four back in September. It wasn't enough to gain them any RE, but they looked like a real team in 1938.

Aside from a late charge by the Cardinals, who improved across the board from 1938, the only teams to gain RE in 1939 were the Boston Bees and the Cubs, all in mid-May before anybody got hot. The Reds ended July with a 14-1 run that only the Cardinals kept up with. The 180 days of RE, of which the Reds had 142, is the lowest NL total in between the war-shortened or affected seasons of 1918 and 1944. There was no race at all.

But that speaks to how effectively McKechnie could shape a team. Though the Giants had a talented rotation, they struggled, particularly Hal Schumacher; the Pirates, with no talent in their rotation, saw Russ Bauers and Cy Blanton develop sore arms (the other starters in 1938 were Jim Tobin and Bob Klinger; that might be the most anonymous front four of any successful team); the Cubs had several key players age, and breakout number two starter Clay Bryant turned up with a sore arm himself.

Like many of the seasons in this article, it looks transitional, but the transition was extremely important. Just as 1926 marked the end of an era dominated by three teams, so 1939 quashed its revival. The Giants, Cubs and Pirates were each .500 or better in 26 seasons from 1901-1938; since then, it's only happened five times (1945, 1967, and 1969-71). The 1926 season added the Cardinals permanently to the mix, which was a big deal by itself, but the Reds' dominance in 1939 dismantled the old guard.

No. 1: 1959 AL

- 97 percent (341/353)
- Surprise teams: White Sox (143)/Indians (111)/Orioles (56)/Tigers (21)/Senators (6)/A's (4)

From 1956-1958, AL teams other than the Yankees spent only eight days gaining RE after the All-Star break. In 1958, Yankees dominance was even clearer. The Senators had 61 wins, the Yankees had 92, and the other six teams were bunched between 73 and 82. That bunching implied that should the Yankees falter, something interesting would happen. Not that anyone rational would expect the Yankees to falter, but the parity-nee-mediocrity of the rest was unusual.

As noted about 1993 and as shown in 2012, streaks do funny things to season narratives. The 1959 Tigers started 2-15, depositing the Indians, White Sox and A's in first through third by May 2. The Yankees were 7-10 at that point, but they were about to face Detroit, so things were looking up ... except that the Tigers swept the Yankees twice in May, leaving them tied for last on May 20. By May 26, the Indians,

White Sox and perennial doormat Orioles were within 2.5 games of each other at the top; everybody else was seven to 9.5 back.

The Indians let the league back in with a 2-11 slump, including losing two to the Tigers and three of four to the Yankees. On June 9, last place was 5.5 behind first, with the 24-25 A's only three back and the Yankees and Tigers at .500. The Indians responded to their created problem with a seven-game winning streak against the Orioles, Senators and Red Sox, knocking the latter two out of contention for good. The A's lost seven in a row to fall back. By the first All-Star break, the Indians and White Sox were at the top, with the Orioles, Yankees, and .500 Tigers about five back. Coming out of the break, the Indians finished July with a 15-10 run, and the White Sox went 16-5, putting permanent distance between them and third place (the A's were in third on Aug. 1 at 51-50, but would go just 15-38 the rest of the way).

The White Sox swept the Indians in a four-game series at the end of August to stay ahead for good; they led the Indians by five games at season's end, so it essentially was that sweep alone that separated them. Similarly to 1958, only five games separated third from sixth, but the Yankees weren't anywhere near the top this time. And although the Yankees would win the next five pennants, all but 1963's were hard-fought until at least to September. The Yankees would be a good team for several years, not *the* good team; and 1959 revived the AL's relevance above being the Yankees' tune-up for October.

So what changed that year? For the White Sox, it was Jim Landis' breakout year as a premier defender in center field, giving the team three elites up the middle with Nellie Fox and Luis Aparicio, which aided the resurgence of Early Wynn and the bullpen. The Indians, who if they had won the pennant would be the only non-wartime team until the 1984 Tigers to make the World Series without a Hall of Fame player (Alan Trammell or Jack Morris threaten to pass this to the 1991 Braves, who after Tom Glavine or John Smoltz would pass it to Curt Schilling's 1993 Phillies), had a suddenly deep lineup. Rocky Colavito and Minnie Minoso were backed by Woodie Held and Tito Francona, who fulfilled their promise after sporadic productivity for other teams.

For the Yankees, no one player cratered, but 1958's depth was 1959's indifference:

Offensive/defensive WAR for the Yankees' MVPs in 1958-59:

Player	1958	1959
Mickey Mantle	9.0 / -0.7	6.1 / 0.3
Norm Siebern	3.3 / 0.6	1.2 / -1.1
Yogi Berra	2.6 / 0.8	3.6 / 0.8
Elston Howard	2.6 / 0.7	1.5 / 0.0
Gil McDougald	2.2 / 1.0	1.3 / 1.6
Andy Carey	2.5 / 0.6	0.1 / -0.1

Player	1958	1959
Hank Bauer	1.7 / 0.2	-0.2 / -0.9

Not all of those players were equally responsible—Berra improved and McDougald was about the same—but it's difficult to replace all your depth at once. Hector Lopez and Bobby Richardson tried, but that was a lot of value to replace.

Conclusion

Seasons out of nowhere generally require that the slate of expected contenders falter after extended periods of dominance, whether it be one or several teams. In those voids, either a team is ready to dominate and does so (1912 Red Sox, 1939 Reds) or the league falls into an exciting disarray (1926 NL, 1959 AL). History will always love a surprise team, but sometimes the conditions are right for surprise seasons, and Reputation Estimate measures just that.

Appendix: Calculating Reputation Estimate

A team gains RE when, after at least 20 games of its season, it is over .500 and:

- It is in first place or within three games of it;
- It is leading the first Wild Card or within two games of it; or
- It is leading the second Wild Card.

Otherwise, a team loses RE, a point per day until it reaches zero. Days start for each team in a league when at least one team in that league starts gaining RE—in both leagues in 2012 that date was April 27. The 20-game starting point is connected to the within-three-games qualification; a 4-3 team is within three games of a 7-0 team, but neither record says much at that point.

Offseason "decay" for each team is caluclated as:

(RE on final day of season)/(2-x)

Where x is the league median for RE divided by league mean. If x > 1, 1 is used instead.

Because divisional play has increased both the ease of being in contention and the amount of playoff spots available, RE gained per day changes by era; for the same reasons the league "median" has to adjust downward slightly. These adjustments serve primarily to keep RE totals and team rises and falls comparable across eras. Here's the chart, with the second Wild Card messing things up since it came before the Astros' league switch:

Year Range	Points Gained Per Day	League Median for x
1871-1968	4	Median
1969-1993	3	Median
1994-1997	2	8th place
1998-2011, AL	2	8th place
1998-2011, NL	2	9th place
2012, AL	2	Mean of 8th and 9th place
2012, NL	2	Mean of 9th and 10th place
2013-	2	9th place

Two examples of how this works. AL teams with positive RE ending 1999:

Indians	638
Yankees	630
Rangers	545
Red Sox	456
A's	32
Blue Jays	27

All other teams had no RE. The median here was 0, so x was 0, meaning that each team's RE was halved over the offseason. This clearly is not a balanced league; anybody but the top four doing anything would be inherently more interesting.

On the other hand, thanks to two years of chaotic pennant races, the 2008 NL ended with x = 1.41, the highest season-ending figure and the second-highest figure for any stretch of history save for a week in the August 1961 NL. Everybody kept their RE entering 2009, but the low, flat and historically strange distribution makes it clear why:

Cardinals	698
Mets	596
Phillies	469
D-backs	461
Cubs	455
Dodgers	449
Padres	403
Brewers	399
Braves	394
Marlins	159

I handle the 1892 and 1981 split seasons as teams gaining RE starting 20 games into each half, and losing RE in between. That's everything you need to calculate this stat from July 8, 1871 onward.

Economics & Analysis

The New CBA: Steps in the Right Direction

by Dave Cameron

For several decades, Major League Baseball and work stoppages went hand in hand. In 1972, players initiated the first strike in U.S. professional sports history, erasing the first several weeks of the season. That was followed by lockouts in 1973 and 1976 that each lasted a couple of weeks, and then an eight-day strike in 1980 that simply delayed negotiations over free agency until the following season. In 1981, the sport lost nearly two months of the season due to a strike, which forced the All-Star Game to be played in mid-August.

The rest of the 1980s brought some labor peace until the owners colluded to hold down player salaries from 1985-1987, and then spring training was wiped out by a lockout in 1990. Finally, the fighting between the players and owners came to a head in 1994, when the season was cut short in August and the World Series was not played for the first time in 90 years.

The reverberations of that decision still echo through the sport. The face-off between the two parties damaged the game's reputation in a way that neither side had intended. The strike-shortened season put a hole in the game's history, and both the owners and players felt the repercussions. Average attendance dropped by more than 6,000 fans per game in 1995.

Fans made their displeasure known, and the message got across loud and clear. MLB hasn't had a work stoppage since.

The willingness of both sides to compromise and work together to avoid the mistakes of the past has never been more obvious than in the negotiations over the newest Collective Bargaining Agreement, which was reached on Nov. 22, 2011. This agreement is impressive not only for the civil tone of the negotiations, but for the sweeping changes to the game they brought about without either side threatening to take the game away to gain the upper hand.

We're not talking about just a few tweaks here and there. This CBA institutes some of the most dramatic structural changes the sport has seen since the resolution of the 1994-1995 strike. The Houston Astros were re-assigned to the American League, which brings daily interleague play to the sport for the first time. A second Wild Card team was added, and the playoffs were re-tooled to give a greater advantage to division winners. Free-agent compensation was overhauled, with the old system thrown out entirely. HGH testing was implemented, as was random testing of players during the offseason.

Yet while all these changes are the largest in any new CBA, they are all dwarfed by the drastic overhaul of the systems that govern teams' acquisition of domestic amateur players and foreign professionals.

New Systems for New Talent

As signing bonuses for elite talents have continued to rise, MLB has been pushing for several years for a more controlled atmosphere in the draft and in the international market. The commissioner's office went so far as issuing "recommendations" for each draft slot, but had no formal power to punish teams for going over those recommendations; any franchise could ignore them entirely in the pursuit of young talent. In 2011, the final year under the old system, the Pittsburgh Pirates spent $17 million in signing bonuses by going after players who were deemed to be difficult signings (including Gerrit Cole, whom they selected with the first overall pick). That total smashed the previous record set by the Washington Nationals, who broke the bank the previous year to get Bryce Harper under contract. The league was set on getting these costs down—or, at the least, gaining control over the rate of growth—but needed the MLB Players Association to agree on enforceable spending caps.

For years, the players had refused to agree to such limits, but with the sport doing very well financially, no one was in the mood to bite the hand that was generously feeding them. And so, in exchange for a 16 percent increase in the league minimum salary—it went from $414,000 in 2011 to $480,000 in 2012, with further escalation in future years—the players agreed to allow MLB to enforce spending limits on the draft and international free agency. They stopped short of agreeing to a hard cap, but the penalties for going over the limits are harsh enough that the rules amount to de facto spending limits.

Before we go any further in discussing the changes, let's lay out exactly how the new system operates.

For the amateur draft, each pick in the first 10 rounds is given an assigned bonus amount, with the scale for 2012 ranging from $7.2 million for the top overall selection down to $125,000 for the 30th pick in the 10th round. The assigned values of these picks are then added together for each team based on the selections that it holds, and the total amount becomes that team's pool allocation for the draft. With 13 picks, including the No. 2 overall selection, the Twins had the largest 2012 pool allocation at $12.4 million, while the Angels' total pool was the lowest at only $1.7 million—the penalty of forfeiting their first- and second-round choices to sign free agents Albert Pujols and C.J. Wilson.

Teams are allowed to sign players for any amount they desire, but they are heavily taxed for every dollar spent over their pool allocation: a 75 percent tax on each dollar up to 110 percent of their limit, and then a 100 percent tax for every dollar beyond that mark. However, the real deterrents aren't financial—they are the penalties enforced upon the team's next draft. Once a team spends 105 percent of its pool allocation, it forfeits the right to sign any player in the next draft to a bonus of more than $500,000. If a team goes over 115 percent of its pool allocation, that becomes a $250,000 limit.

The value assigned to the 95th selection in 2012 (the final pick in the second round) was $500,000. So any team that goes more than five percent over its limit is essentially punting its top two picks in the following draft; it would have to draft a player willing to sign for the equivalent of third-round money. Perhaps some agent will eventually have the stones to argue that his client is worth paying the overage tax, but it's essentially impossible to argue that any prospect is worth forfeiting the next year's draft. About the only leverage an agent has is to get a club to borrow from the assigned values of its other selections.

However, here's where the new rules get even stickier: Any team that fails to sign a player drafted in the first 10 rounds forfeits the money that was assigned to its pool allocation from that slot.

In prior years, teams would often take talented players with strong college commitments in later rounds, then use them as leverage in negotiations with their earlier selections. If their top pick decided not to sign, they would then take that bonus and give the kid who thought he was going to college enough money to change his mind. Under this new system, that no longer flies—if your top pick doesn't sign, you don't have any money to reallocate to those later picks. Your pool is reduced as though you'd never had that pick at all.

In practice, this change has led to a dramatic shift in how teams approach their draft selections. While the stated intention of the new policies is to reduce the effects of signability, it actually increases the need for teams to understand exactly what price a player will sign for before the draft ever begins. Given that pre-arranging contracts with amateur players and their "advisers" is still technically prohibited, this isn't something that teams can be open about. Knowing these costs ahead of time can dictate strategy all the way through the draft, and the interconnected nature of the pick values means that one misstep could drastically impact every other selection a team makes.

The Astros showed how this kind of informed decision-making can work to a team's advantage when they held the No. 1 overall selection last summer. The assigned value for that pick was $7.2 million, but the Astros also held the 41st pick in the draft, and they suspected that at least one highly regarded player was going to slide to that spot because his bonus desires didn't line up with the pick value of where he would go in the first round based on talent. The Astros took a calculated risk by using the first overall pick on Carlos Correa—rated by *Baseball America* as the No. 6 player on its pre-draft list—knowing that they could get him signed for significantly less than the assigned value of the No. 1 overall pick, which would give them bonus flexibility with the 41st pick and subsequent selections.

Things played out exactly as hoped when Lance McCullers Jr.—rated No. 13 by *BA*—fell to the Astros at No. 41. While their assigned value for that pick was only $1.26 million, they ended up signing McCullers for $2.5 million, which put him squarely between the values of the 12th and 13th picks. They were able to over-spend on the 41st selection because Correa signed for $4.8 million, 67 percent of the assigned value of that top pick.

In essence, the Astros traded down. In the National Football League or the National Basketball Association, it's common to see a team swap a high pick for a slightly lower pick and an additional valuable selection. Trading draft picks is still not allowed by MLB, but the Astros effectively swapped the No. 1 overall pick for something like the No. 6 and No. 13 picks, if you go by *BA's* rankings. Houston saw an opportunity to use the system to its advantage and planned its strategy accordingly.

In other words, the noble goal of having each pick based solely on talent has not yet been accomplished. Signability is still a huge issue in the draft structure.

In fact, the new system can actually punish teams that ignore signability and select the best player available. The Astros' decision set off a chain reaction that led to Stanford right-hander Mark Appel—generally considered to be the best prospect in the draft—sliding out of the top seven picks. While reports on his requested bonus vary, Scott Boras (Appel's advisor) made it clear that his client expected to be paid at a level commensurate with a premium selection.

Once Appel got past Minnesota at No. 2, however, that premium paycheck became untenable. The slot values decelerated quickly, going down $1 million each step from No. 1 through No. 4, meaning that the fifth overall selection had an assigned value of just $3.5 million—less than half of the value given to the first overall pick. While both the Baltimore Orioles and Kansas City Royals were known to be coveting college pitchers with the fourth and fifth picks, both passed on Appel to select lower-rated NCAA pitchers who were willing to sign for something close to the assigned value.

The Orioles' entire draft pool was $6.8 million; the Royals' pool was $6.1 million. If Appel was set on getting a signing bonus close to the $7.2 million value of the No. 1 overall pick, both teams would essentially have to give him their entire draft pool, then punt every pick from rounds 2-10 on guys they could sign for $99,000 or less. When faced with the option of the best college pitcher and a slew of 11th-round picks or the next best college pitcher and the right to proceed as planned with the draft, both teams understandably took the safer route, causing Appel to fall out of the top five.

Finally, the Pirates—big spenders in the draft just a year before—stepped up and selected Appel with the eighth overall selection. They certainly couldn't have planned on having him available, so this was a last-minute audible that required a quick decision. With just $2.9 million assigned value to the pick and a total pool of $6.6 million, the Pirates were in essentially the same position as the Orioles and Royals,. But with less interesting options available, they went for the high-risk, high-reward gamble and hoped they could convince Appel to begin his pro career for less than his stated salary goal.

By all public accounts, this is not what MLB wanted the new draft system to encourage. They wanted top prospects like Appel to go at the top of the draft based on their talent, instead of sliding down to the bottom of the first round where they could be picked off by higher revenue teams. The draft is designed to funnel talent to losing teams to promote competitive balance—one could argue over whether that is its primary goal, but it clearly is a goal. Ensuring that teams that need premium prospects get to draft them was promoted as a positive byproduct of the new system.

The Pirates were not willing to punt their entire draft to sign Appel, so they proceeded to select players as they would have had things gone according to their original plan. Thus, they used their next 10 selections on players who were worth something close to the value of their selection. In fact, with their fourth-round pick, they selected Brandon Thomas, who was projected as perhaps a third-round player heading into the draft. This put an even greater strain on their bonus pool: Now, two of their top four players expected to receive more than the Pirates were given to sign players taken in those slots.

The story doesn't have a happy ending for Pittsburgh. Appel and the Pirates both stuck to their guns, and he returned to Stanford for his senior season. The Pirates not only failed to sign the player they selected eighth overall, but because they also lost the $2.9 million in value from that selection, they also weren't able to come to terms with Thomas, who also is back in school for the 2013 season.

The Pirates ended up spending just $3.2 million of their bonus pool, signing just three of their top five selections, despite following the "best player available" model that the draft is supposed to encourage. The Pirates will receive a compensatory selection in the 2013 draft for not signing Appel, but in retrospect, they clearly would have been better off passing on Appel and selecting someone whose expectations more closely aligned with the assigned value.

This raises a bit of a dilemma for MLB, however. The Appel example shows that players who are expected to go in the top few picks can become virtually unsignable outside of the top five, so an elite prospect could theoretically slide to a position where drafting him simply doesn't make sense for any reason other than taking a flier and calling the kid's bluff. While top prospects slide in the drafts of every major sport—remember Aaron Rodgers sitting alone in the green room at the NFL draft in 2005?—their day eventually ends with a chance at redemption.

A top-three major league prospect who falls out of the top 10 has essentially been told that he's going back to school, and his professional career will have to wait unless he takes a bonus that is a fraction of what comparable talents signed for. A system that was supposed to help small market teams sign the best available players can actually prevent them from doing just that, and as a byproduct, can delay the major league careers of some of the most talented players in the sport.

This is a big problem. Having players fall in the draft is nothing new, but forcing players back to college is. While one can truthfully say that it is the player's choice not to sign, and Appel was the one who decided not to accept $2.9 million from the Pirates, these are choices that are really no choice at all. Appel's market value is far greater than $2.9 million, and with another good season at Stanford, he has a strong chance of going No. 1 overall next summer, when he can once again ask for $7 million and point to the assigned value as justification for his position.

One could point out that Appel would have been a rich man either way and a year closer to lucrative arbitration and free-agent payouts had he signed, but that argument allows one to argue in favor of essentially any bonus limitations MLB wants to enforce. The agreement the MLBPA entered into was not to give MLB the freedom to drastically drive down signing bonuses for top picks, but to maintain the standard and hold the rate of growth. Appel is just one player, but it is unlikely that either the league or the players are happy with how his situation unfolded, and the next CBA— which won't go into effect until 2017—will likely need some modifications to allow teams like the Pirates to draft top players who slide a few spots.

Dealing with the Rest of the World

International free agency also was overhauled in the new CBA, and if you think the Pirates' situation was problematic, you haven't seen anything yet. While MLB continues to push toward an international draft, the new system uses a similar model of pool allocation to level the playing field for foreign free agents under the age of 23.

For 2012, the playing field was completely even, with every team given a spending pool of $2.9 million to spend on players beginning July 2—the start date of international free agency. The same taxes and penalties that apply in the draft apply here, so teams have heavy disincentives to spend more than 105 percent of their total pool.

While 20 of the 30 organizations spent less than $3 million in this market in 2011, the teams that were active internationally were extremely active. For instance, the Texas Rangers spent $13 million on these types of international free agents in the final year under the old system. The Toronto Blue Jays ($8 million), Seattle Mariners ($7 million) and Royals ($7 million) also spent lavishly and were forced to make extreme cuts in their 2012 spending.

For future years, each team's signing pool will be based upon its major league record in the prior year, with losing teams getting significantly smaller pools than winning teams. I hope you can spot the issue here.

Teams that don't have the economic resources to compete with the big boys in payroll find that developing cost-controlled players through the farm system is essentially the only path to contention. Some teams have excelled at player development, and they have placed a significant emphasis on Latin America or emerging markets such as Asia and Europe. However, under this new system, the success of a low revenue team will hinder its ability to continually invest in that farm system, through giving that team lower draft choices and limiting its international spending pool. Previously, a low-revenue team could simply shift money from the draft to international prospects if its success resulted in lower draft positions, but now that avenue will be closed off as well.

Penalizing success at the player development level is a potential source of concern. While losing the ability to sign a premium prospect or two for a year may not be a death knell, a sustained wave of success from a low-revenue team—like what the Tampa Bay Rays have accomplished the last five years—could do real damage to an organization's base of prospects. Everyone should agree that the new CBA should not penalize franchises like the Rays or Oakland A's for their success. These are the teams that MLB should be trying to help the most, but basing the sliding-scale pools on a team's win-loss total puts these overachievers in harm's way.

The Playing Field Still Tilts

Overall, the net effect of these changes is a more level playing field in prospect acquisition. On its face, a that sounds like a good thing, but we must note that it holds true only in one specific aspect of player acquisition. When it comes to major league payrolls, we are nowhere near a level playing field: Opening Day payrolls in 2012 ran from $198 million (New York Yankees) to $55 million (San Diego Padres). Even with luxury tax penalties pushing the top payrolls down, there is still a huge disparity in what teams spend on their rosters.

Reducing potential advantages in prospect acquisition simply increases the emphasis on payroll, as the new rules have made it more difficult in some circumstances for low-revenue teams to be more aggressive in the draft or international free agency. As we level all of the playing fields except for the one with the greatest disparity, we only make that disparity more important.

And that's where I fear the new CBA went off track. MLB is enjoying a time of labor peace not seen in generations, but the new agreement included compromises that may not be in the interests of the game long-term.

Unfortunately, the MLBPA does not care deeply about these issues. Competitive balance isn't the players' primary concern, or even a significant secondary issue. The owners are going to have to recognize that their own agenda created some negative byproducts, and work to restructure their creation without an external force pushing them to do so.

There were a lot of good things in the new CBA. I, for one, am a big fan of the new playoff system, and think that many of the changes that were implemented are indeed benefits to the sport. The fact that such sweeping changes were enacted without acrimony or even the thought of a work stoppage is heartwarming to any fan who just wants to see baseball every spring.

And yet, I hope that we can acknowledge that this new agreement has some wrinkles that need to be ironed out. No agreement of this scale will ever be perfect, but it would behoove MLB to review some of the unintended consequences of the new draft and international rules, and see whether they pass the test of actually helping promote competitive balance.

More Complex Than a Salary Cap: Financial Disparity in MLB

by Adam Dorhauer

In 1994, Major League Baseball ground to a halt. The Collective Bargaining Agreement was about to expire, and negotiations for a new one were at an impasse. The owners united (with a few dissidents) under new leader Bud Selig and threatened to unilaterally impose a salary cap if the players wouldn't agree to one. The players wouldn't agree to one, which included not agreeing to play under the un-agreed-upon cap. I think you can see the issue.

The owners contended a cap was necessary because the chasm of financial disparity between the haves and the have-nots had become untenable. Without a cap, most teams couldn't keep up, couldn't pay market rates for players anymore, and would be left running deficits just to tread water in the second division. The players countered that a cap was not the only solution, and that the league could address its financial problems with revenue sharing alone.

After months of negotiations and no real progress had wiped out half a season, the World Series, and Opening Day, the whole thing went to the courts, and the order for the league to resume, with no salary cap, finally came down from the Supreme Court itself. (Okay, so the ruling judge, Sonia Sotomayor, wasn't actually on the Supreme Court when she heard the case, but she is now, so half-credit, right?)

Now, nearly two decades later, MLB is surging financially. Revenues and team values continue to grow steadily each year, and teams are almost universally profitable. The latest CBA was negotiated last offseason with relatively little tension. Selig's concern over inequity has turned to praise for league-wide parity and the overall state of the game. Problem solved, right?

Meanwhile, the New York Yankees opened 2012 with a payroll north of $200 million for the fifth straight year (all payroll figures courtesy of Cot's Baseball Contracts and Baseball Reference). The Oakland A's opened 2012 having just traded two of their best starting pitchers, as well as their closer, for prospects, and had a rookie (Yoenis Cespedes) as their highest paid player.

The Yankees had all their key pieces locked up coming into spring training, including one-time Oakland star Nick Swisher. With pretty much everyone of significance returning from 2011, they casually dropped another $10 million on Hiroki Kuroda and called it a day. The A's watched their best hitter, Josh Willingham, leave for Minnesota, the latest in an endless exodus of high-priced talent from Oakland.

There is some consolation for Oakland, however. The A's managed to extract some level of revenge for Swisher by signing Yankees cast-off Bartolo Colon for $2 million (plus, presumably, the research and development costs on a drug powerful enough to restore Colon to 2005 form). They outdrew the Yankees (139,000 to 137,000) in their opening home series; although, to be fair, the A's opened with a four-game series while the Yankees played only three, and two of those Oakland games were played in Tokyo, where they drew 88,000 fans. When you're spending about as much on your whole team as the Yankees spend on the left side of their infield, though, you take what you can get.

Oh yeah, and the A's, like the Yankees, won their division and reached the postseason.

In 2011, the National Basketball Association locked out its players in an attempt to lower player salaries. The league found itself in the same position MLB was in back in 1994, saying that half the teams were losing money and that slashing player salaries was necessary to keep the league viable. Only the NBA already had a salary cap, and had had one since the 1980s.

According to estimates by *Forbes*, 15 of the 30 NBA teams lost money in the final year of the old CBA. The year before that, the magazine estimated that 17 teams were in the red. In each of those same seasons, *Forbes* only had three MLB teams losing money.

Granted, the *Forbes* estimates are not exact. Team financial records are private, and any public estimates have to simply make do with limited available information. On top of that, even if the records were public, different accounting approaches can yield very different results. For example, rival analyses by the owners and the Major League Baseball Players Association reached wildly different conclusions from the same data during the 1994-95 strike. Things can get especially complicated when teams are partnered with, owned by, or own other businesses (such as television networks, for example), and profits can get shifted between the related entities with creative accounting.

So when Forbes says half the teams in the NBA are losing money, maybe they are, maybe they aren't. Who knows? For the sake of discussion, though, we'll take the Forbes numbers at face value.

Even with half of NBA teams losing money, league-wide profits were estimated at around $180 million in each of the last two seasons before the lockout. The reason so many teams are losing money is not that the league itself is unprofitable and can't sustain player salaries; rather, unlike MLB, which has found a way to divide up its profits in a way that benefits each of its member organizations, the NBA concentrates massive profits in the few highest revenue markets at the cost of everyone else.

The Knicks' profits for 2010-2011, when the league said it was in financial straits, were estimated at $75 million. The year before that, they made $64 million. The highest profits estimated for any MLB team in those two years were $30 million in 2011 (Cleveland) and $37 million in 2010 (San Diego). MLB pulls in about 60 percent more revenue than the NBA, yet the most profitable NBA team is turning twice the profits of any team in baseball.

In the NHL, another salary cap league, the issue is even more stark. With league revenues less than half of MLB's, the NHL's top team, the Toronto Maple Leafs, pulled in $82 million in profits last year. The Rangers and Canadiens also topped $40 million in profits. The NHL just locked out its players for the second time in eight years.

This is what the MLBPA feared when it opposed a salary cap as a financial panacea in 1994: that the owners would use the cap primarily to keep player salaries down rather than to fix financial issues. Without a salary cap, MLB owners have figured out a way to take league-wide profits and divide them up so that every team has a good shot at finishing in the black, and the owners and players alike have seen steady growth in their share of revenues. The NBA and NHL have implemented salary caps, but have failed to translate league-wide profits into success for individual teams. Instead of following MLB's lead in working out financial issues between owners, they have again put the onus on players conceding more in terms of a lower cap, even in the face of work stoppages.

Two Separate Issues

There are two problems with financial disparity in sports. One is the issue of competitive balance: that teams with higher revenues can buy better players and have a better chance of being competitive. The other is the issue of profitability: that teams with lower revenues can struggle to pay market wages for players without losing money. While the former issue is generally more prominent in the public discourse, the latter has played a more significant role in labor negotiations.

In general, a salary cap addresses the first issue but not the second. In fact, a cap/floor system can actually exacerbate the issue of financial viability for some franchises. In MLB, even with revenue sharing, some teams still generate significantly more revenue than others, but teams are allowed to tailor their spending as best they see fit. Low-revenue teams, or teams with a lot of low-cost talent, are under no pressure to up their spending beyond their ability to cover the costs.

We see the opposite in the NBA and NHL models. Their cap/floor systems flatten team payrolls within a fairly narrow band, but their revenue sharing components are much more conservative, leaving large discrepancies between team revenues. This means that teams like the Knicks and Maple Leafs rake in huge profits because they can't spend nearly up to their revenue, while teams in smaller markets have to divert whatever profits they could otherwise make into spending up to the floor. As a result, the system effectively shifts profits away from low-revenue teams toward the top handful of teams, which is the exact opposite of what it should be doing.

The Tampa Bay Rays have been consistent contenders for the past five years despite having one of the lowest payrolls in the majors. After spending their first decade as the American League's doormat, the Rays finally exorcised their losing ways and broke through in 2008, making it all the way to the World Series. Since then, they've become something of a spiritual successor to the Oakland teams of the early 2000s, the ones whose success inspired a best-selling book and a Hollywood movie.

Success dried up for those A's teams, however. They fell into prolonged mediocrity when their talent outgrew their budget. One by one, the players who made them great disappeared: Jason Giambi to the Yanks, Tim Hudson to Atlanta, Miguel Tejada to Baltimore, Mark Mulder to St. Louis, Barry Zito to San Francisco, Eric Chavez to the disbaled list. They weren't even necessarily bad baseball moves; Dan Haren, the centerpiece pitcher Oakland got back for Mulder, was both better and cheaper than Mulder would ever be after the trade. Zito came nowhere near providing the value it cost the Giants to sign him.

The budget concerns that led to the constant departures, though, meant constantly having to find undeveloped talent in the amateur ranks and in other organizations, and having to turn that into productive major league talent. It's hard to win that way, and it eventually caught up to Oakland. The same thing happened to Minnesota, another low-budget contender that quickly fell in the standings once its cheap stars got expensive, even as the Twins raised payroll to try to keep those stars around. The same thing will probably happen to Tampa Bay if its farm system hits a dry spell.

The Yankees don't have that problem. They've gone nearly two decades now without breaking stride. When they lose talent, they simply retool, and they keep competing. Of course, money doesn't guarantees success. The Mets have been one of the top spenders over the past decade or so, and have had little to show for it. Ditto the Cubs.

Money helps, though. It helps winning teams keep winning, and it helps losing teams stop losing. To a team with money, terrible means a lot of handwringing over a few losing seasons while it waits to shed salary so it can load up on talent again. It means not having been to a World Series since 2000 for the Mets. For the Red Sox, having three bad years (two of which were 89- and 90-win seasons) is like the second leaving of Babe Ruth.

Meanwhile, the Pirates have endured 20 straight losing seasons, and despite strong starts the past two seasons, they once again dropped under .500. The Royals are, well, still the same old Royals they've been since the mid-'90s. I'm sure these teams are encouraged by the Oaklands and Tampas of the league, but they are also painfully aware that money, while not a prerequisite for success, does still matter.

Competitiveness aside, all major league organizations, excluding the post-Madoff Mets, are making money. MLB's model has corrected the profitability issue at least by implementing revenue sharing with no floor or cap (though there is a luxury tax threshold that acts as a soft cap for the top handful of teams, currently set at $178 million). However, even with revenue sharing, large financial disparity remains.

Currently, teams pay 34 percent of their local revenues into a pool to be divided evenly among all 30 teams. Because teams put in more money the more revenue they generate, this redistributes money from the rich teams to the less-rich teams. This forms the base plan of MLB's revenue sharing. Additionally, there is a supplemental plan that divides revenue based on pre-calculated "performance factors." (I don't actually know what "performance factor" means, other than there is a table of each team's factor attached to the CBA. As far as I can find, the CBA doesn't fully explain what it means or how it is calculated.)

The obvious solution would seem to be simply increasing the level of revenue sharing. MLB has been doing this gradually over the years anyway: in the previous CBA, the amount of local revenue shared was 31 percent, and before that it was in the 20s. Theoretically, you could set the figure at whatever you wanted. If you want teams to be on more level footing, you can have each team split 50 percent of its revenue, or 60 percent, or 100 percent if you want everyone to have the exact same resources. The problem with that is that increasing the amount of revenue sharing does not necessarily have the impact on competitive balance you might expect, and it has some non-obvious side effects on player salaries.

From a purely economic perspective, teams buy more production and improve their talent level because winning more games translates to increased revenue. At some point, though, buying more talent stops producing as much revenue as it costs, so there is no financial incentive to keep spending on talent.

Let's say that in an unrestricted market, each projected win of improvement costs $7.5 million. And let's say the Yankees have determined that they can add up to 20 wins worth of talent at that price before they start losing money investing in more. They buy their 20 wins for $150 million, and that investment is covered by their expected growth in revenue.

Now, let's introduce revenue sharing. Under MLB's base plan (we'll ignore the supplemental plan for illustrative purposes), each extra dollar of revenue a team generates means an extra 34 cents it has to put into the revenue sharing pool, so it really gains only 66 cents for every dollar generated. That means the Yankees can no longer afford to spend $150 million, because they can no longer generate enough revenue to cover the costs. However, 20 wins won't cost $150 million anymore, because the market can no longer afford to pay $7.5 million per win. Since teams are getting only two-thirds the return on those wins, they are going to bid no more than $5 million per win.

As a result, the Yankees can still buy 20 wins; they just buy them for $100 million instead of $150 million. The result, if everyone is just trying to maximize profits, is that competitive balance remains unchanged. Since teams are paying less money into the player market to get the same level of production, team profits go up and player salaries go down. The new profits get directed out of the revenues of the richest teams to the lowest revenue teams (at the expense of the players), and you get proper financial balancing between teams.

In reality, revenue sharing does affect competitive balance, because teams don't necessarily act only to maximize expected profits. Many teams see on-field success as a goal parallel to making money, and so are willing, at least to some extent, to dip into their profits to win more games. From that perspective, creating additional profit for low-revenue teams to work with does give those teams a competitive boost and allows them to spend enough to compete, while remaining profitable.

The competitive effect is muted by the diverging incentives of profits and wins, however, and the further you push the revenue sharing model toward an equal split, the more at odds you put those two incentives. With high levels of revenue sharing, teams will either (a) spend much less on player salaries in response to the reduced economic incentive or (b) lose significantly more money in revenue-sharing payments than they make up in added revenue when buying talent, to the point that the most profitable action is to just not buy any talent . Or (c) both will happen to some extent.

We can see evidence of this at the current level of revenue sharing in the *Forbes* estimates. Teams with lower revenues tend to have higher profits, which suggests that teams might be spending more to add talent than they recoup in revenue. This extends beyond player costs, by the way. Anything teams spend money on to increase their revenue potential, be it marketing, stadium construction/renovation, whatever, will be affected by the altered incentives. The more you make teams give up their revenue gains, the less they will be willing to spend to grow their revenue.

Any attempt to increase competitive balance through increased revenue sharing has to take into account and attempt to correct for both of these problems: the reduced economic incentive to invest in revenue growth, and the suppression of player salaries.

This is where a cap/floor system might make sense. As implemented in the NBA and NHL, restrictions on team spending hinder profitability, but if you flatten revenue across the league, the floor can be necessary to keep teams from pocketing the guaranteed revenue as extra profit rather than investing in the on-field product. The cap itself becomes fairly unnecessary because the economic incentives are already limiting team spending, but you can implement one anyway if you want to stop some magnate from buying a team and totally eschewing profits for the fun of owning a kickass team (this actually happens with European soccer teams).

The key to this is that the cap and floor have to be set far enough apart to accommodate the level of revenue sharing the league implements. For MLB's current structure, that basically means no cap and no floor. The cap and floor become tools to counter the altered market incentives of revenue sharing; they are not solutions in and of themselves.

Of course, if we did all that, Hank Steinbrenner would throw a fit and brand us all a bunch of Commies (even moreso than he already has). More importantly, and less amusingly, the cap/floor system relies on a direct relationship between spending and success that doesn't exist in MLB's unique salary structure.

In baseball, as with most sports, success is measured in wins. Players and teams will do anything to win: go weeks without shaving or doing laundry, breathe through their eyelids, or even hire Bobby Valentine (okay, so it doesn't always work). Most importantly, teams spend money to win. More money buys more talent, and more talent leads to more wins.

Except something gets lost at each step, and one state doesn't translate so cleanly into the next. Money can buy talent, but not all talent is available to be bought. Not all talent costs that much money either. Talent influences wins, but it doesn't guarantee them.

Instead of a simple chain from point A to point B to point C, the reality is that baseball is rife with detours between the money a team starts with and the record with which it finishes. You can be Jerry Dipoto and one minute you're barreling full-speed ahead, turning dollars into talent into wins by the hundreds of millions, bringing in Albert Pujols and C.J. Wilson, not even caring that your predecessor traded away Mike Napoli for Vernon Wells and the $81 million left on his contract. It's just another hole out of which you can spend. Everything seems pretty straightforward. You're L.A. of A. You just banked $3 billion to broadcast your games on television. Now, you turn that into wins.

Then, suddenly, you take a sharp left turn and find yourself spending as much on an enfeebled Jason Isringhausen as you are on budding superstar Mike Trout. Then, several months later, you take a U-turn and find yourself behind the Oakland A's in the standings.

What happened?

There are two major detours in the path from money to wins in the majors. The first is random variation in a team's record, which is a factor in every sport but especially important in baseball because of how close most teams are in talent. The second is the role service classes play in distorting the relationship to talent in MLB's salary structure.

In 2008, Tampa Bay won 97 games with the second-lowest payroll in baseball. The next year, payroll jumped from $44 million to $63 million ... and the Rays won just 84 games and missed the playoffs. Both the high win total in 2008 and the big drop in 2009 are particularly jarring from the perspective that money equals wins, but we can make sense of these facts by incorporating the two points above.

First, a 13-win drop seems like a lot because it makes such a huge difference in the standings. However, in terms of the random variation inherent in team records, it is not really that much. Even if a team's talent does not change at all from one year to the next, its record will still swing by at least 13 games 15 percent of the time just from random variation (because of changes in talent, nearly a quarter of teams actually see their records swing by at least 13 wins from one year to the next). Half of the time, two teams with equivalent talent will finish at least six games apart.

As hard as it might be to believe, it is entirely possible the Rays' talent level was just as high in 2009 as it was in 2008. After all, they had mostly the same players, and the team would bounce back to win 96 games in 2010. Baseball Prospectus' PECOTA projection system projected the Rays talent level at 90-92 wins before each season from 2008-2010 (see references).

If random variation means that two teams with the exact same talent will still finish 13 games apart 15 percent of the time, think of the implications on the final standings. That is really a reflection of how tightly major league teams are bunched in terms of talent: that over a 162-game season, 13 games is a huge difference in the standings. It's one reason we see some really surprising teams reach the postseason, teams like the 2011 Diamondbacks or 2009 Rockies, or the Baltimore Orioles this year.

Random variation aside, though, we still have the issue of how the Rays actually became good, and have stayed good for the past five years. This relies more on the second factor listed above, that player salaries do not always have a clear relationship to talent.

For salary purposes, there are three distinct classes of major league players based on how much service time a player has: pre-arbitration, arbitration-eligible, and free agent. Each class of players has its own distinct relationship between talent and salary, and only the free agent class presents a clear advantage for wealthier teams.

Pre-arbitration players: Teams have a certain amount of young major league-ready talent already in the organization, usually developed from the team's farm system, though it can also be acquired from other organizations through trades, the Rule 5 draft, etc. Teams get complete control of these players for their first three seasons in the majors at a salary close to or at the league minimum. These players can range anywhere from role players up to superstars, but all get paid at the same level as waiver claims or spring training invitees. This is how Trout can cost the same as Isringhausen.

Because these players provide production at essentially no cost, they are valuable commodities, even if they aren't particularly good. This is why teams that sell off their veteran stars usually seek prospects in return, and why a trade like this year's

Dodgers-Red Sox blockbuster can be a coup for the Sox even though L.A. got far more talent in the deal.

For pre-arbitration players, there is essentially no relationship between salary and production/talent. Approximately 50 percent of players, accounting for about 40 percent of the playing time in the majors, are in the pre-arbitration class.

Arbitration players: After the first three years, teams still have another three years of control over a player, but at an increased cost. As long as the team offers the player a contract, he cannot sign with any other team, but the team must now give the player the option of having his salary determined by an arbitration panel. Player salaries typically increase over each of these three seasons, and they depend on how well the player has performed in previous years. Role players can continue to make near-minimum salaries, but the biggest stars can make tens of millions over their arbitration years.

While these players make considerably more than they did in their first three years, they still make considerably less than free agents. The general rule of thumb is that a player gets about 40 percent, 60 percent and 80 percent of his free agent market value in his three arbitration years, respectively. At this level, salary is directly related to talent, but at a much more gradual slope than at the free agent level. Approximately 25 percent of players (30 percent of the playing time) are in this service class.

Free agents: Finally, any player with at least six full years of major league service who does not already have a contract can sign with any team at whatever price the market determines he is worth. Most of the highest-paid players in the game are in the free agent service class. Free agent salaries are directly related to talent, with a steep increase in cost as talent goes up. Approximately 25 percent of players (30 percent of the playing time) in the majors have enough service time to qualify for free agency.

Additionally, some players don't fall cleanly into any of the above three classes because they sign multi-year contracts that bridge multiple categories. Evan Longoria, for example, signed a long-term deal a week into his major league career. Longoria now has enough service time to have been arbitration eligible for each of the last two seasons, but has made $7 million combined in those seasons. Even accounting for Longoria's service time, that is a huge bargain for someone of his caliber.

For comparison, at the same point in Ryan Howard's career, he had already won a $10 million salary in arbitration and signed a contract covering the rest of his arbitration-eligible years for $18 million a year. Longoria is already under contract for two more arbitration years plus two free agency years for an average of $9 million per year, or less than the salary Howard got in his first year of arbitration. As free agents, both of these players would have gotten well over $20 million a year and several years guaranteed. Howard is actually on a five-year $125 million contract now that he qualifies for free agency, and he is not as good a player now as when he got $10 million in arbitration.

Longoria-type extensions can be the most valuable commodity to major league teams, because they capitalize on the discount value of pre-arbitration players for several years after they exit that service class, in exchange for offering players long-term security. Longoria, for example, has topped FanGraphs' annual list of most valuable trade assets in every year since 2008—when he first signed his current contract—through 2011.

The full details of service classes are a bit more complicated than that, but that's all you really need to know for this discussion. See the appended list of recommended articles for more information.

Incompatibility of a Cap

You might notice two things in particular that disrupt the usefulness of the cap/floor system:

(1) The majority of major league players (pre-arb and arb-eligible players) can't be bid for on the open market

(2) There is no relationship between talent and salary for half of the players in the majors, and half of the remaining players are controlled by one team for close to half their open-market value.

Teams can have vastly different starting points before they start paying market price for talent, and for most teams, success depends as much on how much talent they can develop, as well as how much talent they can buy. Because of this, it makes sense to allow teams some freedom in setting their budgets based on their situation.

The Rays' Opening Day payrolls over their run of success have floated from the low $40 millions to the low $70 millions, depending on how much talent they had in each service class. When their talent moved up from pre-arb to arbitration-eligible, they raised payroll to cover it. When they graduated new talent from the farm system and let expensive veterans go in free agency, payroll dropped accordingly.

Given that they were able to assemble contending talent on those payrolls, it wouldn't make sense to force them to spend up to $80-$90 million just to meet a salary floor, and it wouldn't make sense to make them spend up another $30 million on their cheaper teams just to dump it off again to make room for the advancements in service time. The cap/floor system falls short here, because it fails to account for the non-straightforward relationship between the talent and salary of baseball players.

Because of its incompatibility with MLB's salary structure, the cap/floor system is not the right tool to correct the distorted market incentives of an aggressive revenue sharing plan. Instead, a plan that aims to further level the financial disparity in baseball should attempt to do so without altering the market incentives in the first place.

Market-based Revenue Sharing

One way to do this would be to to base the revenue sharing model on a team's local market rather than its revenue. Instead of each team paying a set percentage of its revenue into the pool, each team pays a set amount based on a valuation of its market.

A key advantage of tying revenue sharing payments only to market attributes and not to actual revenue generated is that no matter how aggressively you divide revenues, you don't eliminate market incentives. For example, if you value the New York market at $100 million more than the bottom markets, you can have the New York teams contribute the full $100 million beyond what the small-market teams pay, and they still get full value out of growing their revenue. I came up with that figure by replicating a Voros McCracken study from 2002 (see references) with 2010/2011 data. Teams will still have the same market incentive to add as much revenue as they can as if there were no revenue sharing.

This makes it much easier to remove the inherent financial advantages that some markets enjoy over others. Unlike revenue sharing based on actual revenue generated, this system can't ensure every team has roughly equal revenue every year, but the differences that remain will be more linked to team performance than to the market the team occupies.

Using the Detours

Another option would be to leave the revenue discrepancies alone and instead take greater advantage of the factors that already blur the relationship between money and success. These factors are quite powerful as is, as a team's market value already has less bearing on its final record than random variation. Teams from across the payroll spectrum contend for playoff spots, even if they don't do so with equal frequency. While the effect of market size is certainly there, it's not that big a factor.

So if you want to further reduce the effect a team's market has on its success, it makes sense to push those obscuring factors even further. MLB has done this in the past by increasing the number of playoff teams. Since the results of a playoff series are less closely linked to talent than a team's season record is, using more playoff rounds to determine the league champion enhances the role of unpredictable variation around each team's talent level.

We can see the impact by comparing actual pennant winners to the teams with the best record in the regular season (the presumed pennant winner with no playoff structure). Since the playoffs expanded to four teams from each league in 1995, the average payroll index (team payroll divided by the league average) of league champions has been 1.29. The average payroll index of the teams with the best regular season records those same years is 1.39. The expanded playoff structure has effectively diminished the relationship between financial resources and success.

Similarly, anything that weakens the link between talent and team success, such as a shorter season, will shrink the competitive gap between high- and low-payroll teams by increasing the role of random variation in team results.

The other, more important factor disrupting the money-to-wins translation is, as we've seen, the role of service classes. Even if the Rays don't have the money that the Yankees do, Tampa Bay can still buy just as many wins if it gets enough value from pre-arb players and the Yankees have to buy enough wins on the free agent market. At some point, it is going to even out.

The minimum major league salary is just under $500,000. With 25 roster spots, that works out to a minimum Opening Day payroll of $12 million. Most players who make near the minimum are pre-arb players, who are assigned that salary regardless of how good they are, but there are also players who are freely available at that price simply because they are near the bottom of the acceptable talent level in the major leagues: waiver claims, designated-for-assignment players, minor league free agents, Quad-A-type players who can be had cheaply in a trade, etc; basically roster filler for most teams. Those players are good enough that a team full of them would still probably win 45-50 games.

So the minimum starting point for every team is $12 milllon in payroll obligations and about 45-50 wins worth of talent. Beyond that, teams add cheap wins by graduating better-than-marginal players out of their farm systems before they start paying more for wins. The more wins teams add at that level, the less they have to pay overall for wins.

Compare the Rays' sources of production to the Yankees'. The following table shows how much production each has gotten from the three service classes through 146 games this year, along with the amount paid above the minimum:

Salary Class	Rays	Cost	Yankees	Cost
Pre-arbitartion	13.2 WAR	-	4.0 WAR	-
Arbitration	17.2 WAR	$30.4M	4.5 WAR	$16.3M
Free agent	4.6 WAR	$17.9M	31.8 WAR	$170.7M

For all the production the Yankees bought from free-agent-class players, the Rays got just as much out of their pre-arb and arbitration players at a fraction of the cost.

Now say you make the Yankees pay free-agent rates for all their players. Rather than picking up an extra eight or nine cheap wins, they can buy maybe three more wins at their payroll, or else balloon spending by tens of millions to levels even the Yankees have never reached. Three wins on top of their free agent wins would put them about even with Tampa Bay right now.

To achieve this, all you have to do is expose all Yankees players to bidding on the open market. If someone thinks Brett Gardner is worth $10 million, then they can bid $10 million for him, and the Yankees have to either match that or let him go. This is the same concept as restricted free agency in other sports.

Of course, you can't have pre-arb players making $500,000 for most teams and then making $10 million for the Yankees. Instead of the $10 million going to Brett Gardner, you have $500,000 go to him, and then you do something else with the rest of the money. Since that money is effectively coming out of the budget teams spend on free agents, it would make sense to redistribute it back to free agent players. You could also redistribute it to small market teams as a revenue-sharing component of the plan.

This same plan can be adapted to other markets as well. For example, say you want to manipulate the cost per win for the L.A. market, but you don't want to make those teams pay full-market price for everyone like New York. Instead, you have the same bidding process for L.A.'s pre-arb players, but the L.A. teams only have to match 50 percent of the winning bid or else let the player go to the highest bidder. Then for Chicago, you only have to match 40 percent, and on down the line (by the way, this same system can be used to replace the current arbitration system, much as MLB replaced the Elias rankings for free agent compensation in favor of an open-market system. Instead of leaving arbitration decisions up to panels using outdated valuation models, you determine the market value of each player by letting other teams bid on him, and then letting the team choose between matching a set percentage of the winning bid or letting the player go to the highest bidder).

There are bound to be side effects of any drastic change to the system. For example, eliminating or reducing the benefit of pre-arb players to large-market teams greatly reduces their incentive to spend on scouting and player development, so maybe you can't make New York pay full market price for pre-arb players. You have to give those teams enough benefit at least that they don't just shut down their development system. At the same time, reducing the incentive for large-market teams to spend on development can help small market teams better control the amateur market, which in turn would help them stay competitive.

This is not meant as a takedown of MLB's current system. I'm not an economist, and I don't know all the ins and outs of the system (performance factors, anyone?). It seems to be working pretty well as is in any case. Not perfectly, but well enough that teams like Tampa Bay and Oakland have a much better chance to reach the postseason than their payrolls would suggest.

This is also not meant as a comprehensive appraisal of the options available. There are countless issues to discuss, from relocation to division alignment to the matter of whether and why large-market teams should subsidize small market teams in the first place (Hank Steinbrenner says no, I say yes, but we're already nearly 7,000 words in, so we'd best leave that alone).

No, this is just a cursory evaluation of financial inequity in the context of MLB, a look at how much it matters, and why the solution is not as simple as cutting salaries or capping spending. It's about understanding the strengths of the current system that caps in other leagues have failed to achieve, and how the unique nature of baseball alters the equation.

Any potential solution should acknowledge and consider these factors. That means getting more creative than just adding a cap. Otherwise, you risk ending up back where you started 18 years ago, where the NHL is now and the NBA was last year, with a lot of strife over profits and labor rights, and with no baseball being played.

References and Recommended Reading

- 2008-09 PECOTA projected wins are from a Feb 16, 2009 article on MLB.com. 2010 projected wins are from a Jan. 30, 2010 article on i-Yankees.com.
- In 2002, Voros McCracken published a regression estimating the effects of market size and income on revenue on BaseballThinkFactory.org: "Makin' Money: Estimating Teams' Revenue Using a few Simple Numbers." Using the base market values estimated by Voros' method, the following standard deviations show the effect of each factor on season W% since 2000:
    - Market value: 3.5 wins (9 percent of the total variance in team win pct)
    - Random variation: 6.4 wins (30 percent)
    - Talent variation, corrected for market value: 9.0 wins (61 percent)
    - Talent variation, uncorrected for market value: 9.7 wins (70 percent)
    - Total: 11.6 wins (100 percent)
- Business of Baseball Glossary, entries for Service Time, Arbitration, and Super 2 on BizOfBaseball.com
- Major League Baseball Players Association: Frequently Asked Questions on MLB. com (contains updated info on Super 2 requirements for the new CBA)
- Kristi Dosh, "Why MLB Does NOT Need a Salary Cap" on ItsASwingAndAMiss.com
- Sky Andrecheck, "WAR, Salary, and Service: Estimating Dollars Per Win" on BaseballAnalysts.com
- Tom Tango, "True Talent Levels for Sports Leagues" on InsideTheBook.com

Case Study: Kyle Lohse

The Cardinals made the playoffs in large part due to an offense that was second in the National League in runs scored, but their starting rotation was a major contributor as well. Adam Wainwright returned from Tommy John surgery to pick up right where he left off. Jaime Garcia pitched effectively despite having an injury-plagued campaign. Jake Westbrook did his typical, league average thing, and Lance Lynn's name is bound to pop up on Rookie of the Year ballots. However, it was Kyle Lohse who stuck out the most.

Lohse pitched 211 innings and finished with career bests in WAR, ERA, FIP, xFIP, SIERA, bases-on-ball percentage and a litany of plate discipline metrics. He also posted his highest strikeout rate since 2006, when he spent half the year pitching out of the Twins bullpen. As a full-time starting pitcher, this was by far the best season of Lohse's career. And his continued success at stranding runners and limiting the conversion of hits on balls in play, in connection to his altered approach, suggests that he hasn't simply been lucky.

In 2011, Lohse seemed to be pitching decently while overperforming his peripherals. However, his performance this season sheds more light on his 2011 campaign, and firmly points to his breaking out and establishing a new level of production.

Lohse's 2011-12 seasons have garnered attention for the wrong reasons, which obviously means the right reasons have largely gone overlooked. Among NL pitchers with at least 300 innings thrown, he is tied for sixth with Roy Halladay in wins, and tied with Shaun Marcum for the fewest losses. Yes, Lohse has posted a 30-11 record over the last two seasons, including a 16-3 mark this past season that may garner him some bottom-ballot support for the Cy Young Award. He also managed a 3.11 ERA over the same span, which ranked ninth among the 40 qualifying pitchers, right behind Jordan Zimmermann and slightly ahead of Halladay.

His rank in these far less meaningful statistics obscured his improvement in strikeouts, walks and home runs allowed. His W-L and ERA also pulled focus from his changing pitch repertoire, his ability to induce more swings both in and out of the zone, and his reduction in contact allowed (relative both to himself and the league average).

By traditional metrics, Lohse has pitched like an ace, and he finally started living up to his lucrative multi-year contract the past two years. By advanced metrics, the story is far more interesting. At first, it appears that Lohse had been pitching over his head. His strand rate (LOB%) improved from 59.6 percent in 2010 to 71.3 percent in 2011, and he—or he and the defense—held batters to a measly .269 BABIP. Given his career .300 BABIP against and sub-70 percent strand rate to that point, it didn't seem like his career-best 91 ERA- in 2011 was sustainable.

Then he went out and finished the 2012 season with a .262 BABIP and a 77.2 percent LOB%. One year with a mark that low is probably an aberration. Two straight years like that and it's foolish to instantly write it off without delving deeper. Lohse started to make analysts wonder if he actually had skill in these departments, as his ridiculously low BABIPs over the last two seasons aren't explained by the Cardinals defense.

Cardinals pitchers have posted a .297 BABIP since 2011, which is right around league average. Lohse's BABIP has been over 30 points lower. Compare that to, say, Jeremy Hellickson, who had a .261 BABIP this past season for a Rays team that led baseball with a .277 BABIP. Since WAR is based on FIP, and Lohse has vastly outproduced his FIP, it stands to reason that his WAR value has been understated over the past two years.

Luckily, FanGraphs breaks out the various components of pitcher WAR, which provides a snapshot of what a pitcher's total would look like under different lenses. If RA/9 instead of FIP drove WAR, Lohse would have been worth 8.5 WAR over the last two seasons, good for 10th among the 164 NL pitchers who threw at least 100 innings. By current standards, his 6.1 WAR ranks 19th in the same leader board.

How has he gotten to this point? The major cause is a change in approach, especially with runners on base. Lohse previously threw his slider 14-17 percent of the time, but upped that to 23 percent of his total offerings. He relied less on his curveball and fastball, while continuing to throw about 20 percent change-ups. As a result, he elicited more swings than ever before, and reduced contact on those swings.

The league average rate on out-of-zone swings over the last three seasons is 30 percent. Lohse jumped from 24 percent to 29 percent in 2011, and again up to 31 percent this past season. He is now right in line with the league; he was previously well below average in this regard. His slider is a big part of why batters have increased their propensity to swing at these pitches. He has also caught up to the league on in-zone swings, improving from 59 percent to 61 percent to 64 percent in a 64 percent league.

His overall contact rate has dropped from 87 percent to 84 percent since 2010. His first-pitch strike rate jumped from the 58-61 percent range to 68 percent over the last two seasons. His swinging strike rate has improved as well, from 5.3 percent in 2010 to 5.9 percent last year, all the way up to 7.1 percent in 2012. Again, he is below average in several of these categories, but the extent to which the average bests him is reduced.

Mix these ingredients together and Lohse is attacking the zone at the same rate over the last three seasons, but batters are fooled more often and are making less contact. The added use of his slider has kept the opposition on its toes, leading to more first-pitch strikes—especially on pitches out of the zone—and more overall swings and misses. This has become even more important with runners on base, where Lohse is among the leaders with a .292 wOBA against.

Lohse is an impending free agent whose case figures to be interesting. By traditional runs-allowed metrics, he is one of the best starters in the NL. On the other hand, fueling those numbers are Verlander-esque BABIPs. With almost 400 innings of a .265 BABIP now under his belt, it's time to start asking if Lohse's improvements are for real. However, he would still be pitching better than ever before even if his BABIP normalized and his ERA more closely resembled his FIP, xFIP and SIERA.

- Eric Seidman

The Curious Case of the Washington Nationals

by Vince Gennaro

L et's re-imagine the past year, starting with the offseason. Pay attention and take notes. You may be asked for your input.

It is January, 2012. The National League East division is in the throes of major change. You can throw out the old adage, "The rich get richer and the poor get poorer." It has no relevance in the NL East. The dominant, star-laden Phillies seem to be aging at a pace that jeopardizes their long-term competitiveness. They are also staring down some serious financial decisions: Can they afford the payroll expense to retain Cole Hamels as a third "ace" on their staff? With the new Collective Bargaining Agreement (CBA), baseball's new magic number is $189 million—the threshold in coming years for the luxury tax. The onerous penalties for exceeding the threshold provide strong incentives for teams such as the Phillies to rein in their payroll spending. While the Phillies have dominated the division in recent years, their ability to sustain this dominance is certainly in question.

The New York Mets are an interesting case study. Their new mantra seems to be, "It may get worse before it gets better." The ownership group's financial difficulties have resulted in a slashing of payroll and shedding of star talent, albeit generally under-productive star talent. While departed shortstop Jose Reyes had a banner 2011, his frequency on the disabled list over the past several years would qualify him as a second-year medical student in some states. The Mets can only hope that former Cy Young Award winner Johan Santana can regain his pre-surgery form and lead a young Mets pitching staff back to prominence while Lucas Duda, Daniel Murphy, and Ike Davis fulfill their promise.

Ironically, while the two NL East franchises in the biggest, most lucrative markets seem to have some question marks, the Marlins, Braves, and Nationals are on the upswing. A new stadium in Miami has served as a shot of adrenaline for the Marlins. Armed with new revenues and a shiny new ballpark, with an all-important retractable roof, the Marlins' offseason spending spree ensures they will be competitive in 2012. Adding free agent Reyes to join Hanley Ramirez rivals a younger Derek Jeter and Alex Rodriguez for star power and offense on the left side of the infield. Adding Mark Buehrle and closer Heath Bell to the pitching staff to complement their young, talented team gives Marlins fans every reason to be optimistic. Atlanta is also expected to be a factor in the division, particularly if top pitching prospect Julio Teheran joins the rotation on a full-time basis and has the expected impact. The Braves missed qualifying for the 2011 postseason by the narrowest of margins, and their young team and stocked farm system should propel them to be competitive for the next several years.

Despite the glorious futures of the Braves and Marlins, this may be the Washington Nationals' decade. The young talent that is congregating in D.C. may be the best in all of baseball. Their formula has been simple. It begins with playing .393 winning percentage ball over a three-year stretch to amass the top draft choices, and do it in years when this generation's most highly touted pitcher and most heralded position player are entering the draft. Give the Nats ample credit for not squandering those precious assets—top draft choices—by trying to save money by drafting highly "signable" players. Instead, they recognized this as a golden opportunity to acquire two once-in-a-generation players as the anchors of their franchise for years to come. As we calibrate where the Nationals stand in the spring of 2012, we see that Stephen Strasburg has recovered from his Tommy John surgery and looks to be on track to fulfill his pre-injury expectations. Bryce Harper has enjoyed a great start to his pro career, but there is a consensus among Nationals' management that he needs to begin the 2012 season in the minor leagues.

To augment their young talent of Strasburg, Harper, Drew Storen, and the Zimmerman(n) boys—Ryan and Jordan—the Nats were active this winter. In addition to extending their star third baseman Zimmerman through 2019 and acquiring lefty starter Gio Gonzalez in a trade with Oakland, they signed Mark DeRosa, Brad Lidge, Chien-Ming Wang and Edwin Jackson in free agency. Should any of the NL East mainstays falter, the Nationals may be poised to capitalize on the opportunity and find themselves in a pennant race.

Case studies have long been a tool used in academic circles to blend the teaching of theories or critical thinking skills with the "real world." I use case studies regularly in my teaching in graduate sports management programs, particularly in my business of baseball course, which has a heavy focus on baseball analytics. Over the last year, I've taken cases—focused on classic baseball operations issues, such as a trade decision, free agent signing, draft strategy, or prospect valuation—beyond the classroom. These events have been greeted positively by student participants, school administrators, and Major League Baseball front office executives, with each seeing benefits from a different vantage point. Students see it as an engaging way to apply their analytical skills and critical thinking, while showcasing their talents to major league team executives. School administrators view it as a way to build enthusiasm for "skill building" within their student population. MLB team executives see the events as a scouting combine for their future analytics talent, as well as a window into some fresh approaches to solving the complex issues that face a baseball general manager.

Our case is set at 7 p.m. on Sunday, July 8, and the top major league players from around the country are en route to Kansas City for the All-Star Game. For major league team front offices, the trade deadline "season" has arrived. Over the past few weeks, teams have been sizing up their chances for a berth in the postseason, and trade feelers have been floated. But the All-Star break is a perfect time for a team to solidify its position and increase the seriousness of the discussions with targeted clubs. For some, it's still too early to determine if they are "buyers" or "sellers," but other clubs recognize the trend towards deadline trades occurring early in July.

Brewers GM Doug Melvin, along with his trade partner, Indians then-GM Mark Shapiro, helped change the paradigm of waiting until the last few days of July to consummate a trade. Melvin secured the services of Cleveland Indians ace CC Sabathia on July 7 for his stretch run at a postseason spot in 2008. He reasoned that Sabathia had more value to him the sooner he received him. By striking early, Melvin was able to squeeze 17 starts out of the lefty ace and narrowly earn entry into the playoffs for the Brewers. If Melvin had waited three weeks, not only would he have lost three or four starts—potentially a quarter of the "value" provided by the big lefty—but he might have lost Sabathia altogether to another suitor. Melvin made it clear that he would adjust his trade package of prospects to reflect the declining value of Sabathia as the clock continued to tick.

The Nationals braintrust is gathered to examine the landscape at the All-Star break—a unique freeze-frame in a baseball season that has few pauses. The Nats are fresh off a home win against the Colorado Rockies earlier in the day, which raised their record to a respectable 43 wins and 44 losses. Below are the NL East standings on the evening of July 8:

Team	Wins	Losses	Win %	GB
Philadelphia	55	32	.632	---
Atlanta	53	32	.624	1.0
Miami	49	37	.570	5.5
Washington	43	44	.494	12.0
New York	36	50	.419	18.5

In addition to the three division rivals that sit on top of the Nats, there are seven other NL teams with better win-loss records than Washington:

- In the NL Central—St. Louis is 50-35, Milwaukee is 47-37, Pittsburgh is 43-43
- In the NL West—San Francisco is 53-34, Arizona is 49-35, Los Angeles is 46-38, Colorado is 44-43

The expanded playoff format—the addition of a fifth playoff team via a second Wild Card—begins this year, adding a wrinkle to the decision process as teams try to sort out whether or not they are in contention.

As the Nationals discuss this situation, it's important to take notice of how they arrived at their 43-44 record. Strasburg has been brought along slowly in his recovery from Tommy John surgery. Although his velocity is in the mid-90s and there are no red flags, the Nats decided to apply an unusual form of an innings limit on his treasured right arm. Instead of planning to truncate the pitcher's season in August, they used him sparingly in the first half of the season. Strasburg made only 10 starts through July 8 so that he could pitch on normal rest and shoulder a full load for the second half of the 2012 season. In several of his first-half starts, he was dominant and shows promise to improve on his 5-2 record and 3.20 ERA (2.95 xFIP) for his expected 15 starts in the second half.

Both Ian Desmond and Danny Espinosa have had slow starts to the season, and the Nats are beginning to be particularly concerned about Desmond's lack of offense. In 2011, he logged a .298 on-base percentage and a .358 slugging percentage, with just 40 extra-base hits in 639 plate appearances. His 2012 first half was more of the same, as his OPS for 2012 stands at .635. On a good day, Desmond is a league-average shortstop, so his future as a starter is in question. Second baseman Espinosa, who played shortstop throughout his minor league career, displays considerably more power but has struggled with his batting average, which stands at .235 at the All-Star break. Desmond is hovering around replacement level, and Espinosa is at 1.0 WAR (wins above replacement) through the All-Star break.

Left-handed starter Gonzalez missed a portion of the first half of the season with a series of minor injuries that limited him to only eight starts and a 2-3 record with a 4.45 ERA (4.10 xFIP). In his last three starts he has been extremely effective, pitching 21 innings, yielding 15 hits and striking out 20, while walking only five batters. Another piece of good news for the Nats is the accelerated development of Harper, who has been torching Double-A pitching during May and June. The Nats will soon decide either to allow him to run away with minor league player of the year honors or call him up to the big club. His power bat could ignite the club's offense, if not the entire nation's capital. Furthermore, Jayson Werth began with a weak April, but his May-June production seems to be more akin to when he was on the Phillies. So while the Nationals navigated their way to a 43-44 record at the break, they did it with more than a fair share of adversity.

The big story for the Nationals' first half has been Jackson. Given the price of pitching, one might have expected Jackson to sign a three-year, $40-million deal this past offseason. Either the market never materialized, or agent Scott Boras overplayed his hand, but in February, Jackson chose to settle on a one-year deal with the Nationals for a reported $11 million. Many considered Jackson the winter's best signing, since pitchers of Jackson's caliber are seldom available for a one-year deal, particularly when that year is the flame-thrower's age-28 season. So far, Jackson has not disappointed. He came out of the gates strong—on a mission to prove his value to next year's suitors—and worked his way to an overpowering 9-3 record with a 3.11 ERA (2.88 xFIP) in 17 starts. According to FanGraphs, he has already accumulated 3.2 WAR for the season through July 8, putting him already close to his career high of 3.9 WAR with nearly half a season remaining. In his 107 innings pitched, he has 104 punchouts and only 28 walks. He continues to average 94.5 mph with his fastball, but the big difference versus previous years is the rise in his strikeout rate, from 6.7 per nine innings pitched in 2011 to 8.7 for the first half of 2012.

If it were not for Jackson's stellar performance in his 17 starts, the Nationals baseball operations team might be able to catch its breath at the All-Star break. But instead, they are working hard to analyze some key decisions that lie in front of them.

In March of 2012, I produced a Case Competition at the Society for American Baseball Research (SABR) Analytics Conference in Phoenix that described a hypothetical critical decision period for the Washington Nationals. Fourteen schools competed, entering teams of four to five students in a two-day competition held amidst a conference where major league team owners, presidents, general managers and others spoke to a group assembled—including representation from 18 major league teams—to discuss the state of baseball analysis and explore leading-edge innovations. The student teams, which were a mix of undergraduate teams and graduates school teams, received the 6,000 word case three days in advance of their arrival in Phoenix and their scheduled presentation to a panel of judges. The judging panel included MLB executives from five clubs, including Tom Garfinkel, president of the San Diego Padres, and prominent baseball writers/authors such as Rob Neyer from SB Nation, as well as the managing editor of The Hardball Times,

Dave Studenmund. The format included 30-minute presentations by each student team and a question-and-answer session with the judging panel. The participating teams were:

Undergraduate Case Participants

- Arizona State University
- Siena College
- Tufts University
- University of South Carolina
- University of Waterloo (Canada)
- Yale University

Graduate School Case Participants

- Elon University-Love
- Manhattanville College-Sports Management
- New York University-Tisch
- Northwestern University-Kellogg
- The University of Chicago-Booth
- University of California Berkeley-Haas
- University of Florida-Hough
- University of Portland-Pamplin

Ultimately, two winners were selected: The University of Chicago—Booth (graduate business school) narrowly edged out the Kellogg school at Northwestern to be the overall winner, while Yale University was the undergraduate division winner.

Sometimes when a team asks, "Are we buyers or sellers in the midseason trade market?," no one cares. However, for the Washington Nationals, that is not the case. There are many interested parties lining up for an answer to the question—are you buyers or sellers? Such a simple question, yet such a complicated process to determine the rational answer. Nats general manager Mike Rizzo is focused on making the best decision—the one with the highest probability of success, and one that ultimately deploys the organization's assets in a way that allows the Nationals to win most efficiently, both today and in the future.

The questions they need to address are: What is the probability of reaching the postseason at various win totals now that a second Wild Card has been added? How well can the team be expected to perform in the remaining 75 games of the season? On the one hand, one of the big problems with the first half of the season was Washington's record in interleague play—4-11, including 1-8 in American League parks, where the designated hitter was employed, which means the Nats' record against NL competition was a solid 39-33 (there are no interleague games remaining in the 2012 regular season). Furthermore, nearly half of their remaining 75 games are against division opponents who are ahead of them in the standings, giving them plenty of head-to-head opportunity to make up ground. On the other hand, Washington is currently positioned well back in the pack, and needs to jump over six teams with better winning percentages just to slide in as the second Wild Card.

Washington's three choices are: 1. Stand pat, 2. Be buyers, or 3. Be sellers. On the "buy" side, an interesting proposition has caught the Nationals' attention. The Cincinnati Reds were beset by a poor start and a rash of injuries and quickly fell out of the race for a playoff spot. The Reds' two-time All-Star and three-time Gold Glove-winning second baseman, Brandon Phillips, is in the final year of his contract and will become a free agent at the end of the season. The Reds are interested in getting some value for Phillips by trading him to a contender. From the Nats' perspective, he provides a strong right-handed bat, solid infield defense and an overall upgrade at one of their weakest positions on the field. Phillips is working under a club option for 2012 of $12.25 million. As of July 8, he has about $6 million remaining on his contract. The two options available to the Nationals are: 1. Washington provides Cincinnati with minor league pitcher Tanner Roark—a 25-year-old right-handed starting pitcher who spent 2011 in Double-A—in exchange for Phillips; or 2. The Nats receive Phillips, and the full $6 million he is owed, in exchange for Robbie Ray—a 20-year-old left-handed starting pitcher, a former 12th round pick in the 2010 draft.

If the buy-side option isn't enough to ponder, the sell-side options are even more vexing. First, the D-backs have made a nice run in the first half, powered by big years from Paul Goldschmidt and Justin Upton and a stellar season from Stephen Drew as he heads towards free agency in the fall. Despite Arizona's stellar 49-35 record, its starting pitching has been spotty. Offseason acquisition Trevor Cahill has been disappointing in the first half, and Ian Kennedy is far off his near-Cy Young form of 2011. The D-backs covet Jackson, a former D-back they dealt to the White Sox at the trade deadline in 2010. Their fondest memory of the hard-throwing righty is June 25, 2010, a 149-pitch no-hitter for Arizona at Tampa Bay. Given the way he is pitching this season, he may be the key to a deep run into the postseason for Arizona. The D-backs have offered a choice to the Nats, middle-infield prospect Chris Owings or third base/left-field prospect Bobby Borchering, in exchange for a half season of Jackson.

Over in the AL, the Texas Rangers, are anxious to finally seal the deal—for a World Series championship. After losing the fall classic in two consecutive years, and with Josh Hamilton in his walk year, the Rangers are all in this season. They replaced the departed C.J. Wilson with Yu Darvish, but their homer-happy ballpark has caught up with flyball pitcher Colby Lewis, and the Rangers feel they are still one starting pitcher away from going the distance. They believe that Jackson may be their man. To test the seriousness of Texas' interest, the Nationals demanded right-handed relief pitcher Tanner Scheppers, who has been known to hit triple digits on the radar gun. Only his spotty command and his past injuries stand in the way of his potential to be a big league closer. After much back-and-forth, the Rangers agreed to include him in the deal if the Nationals would also pick up $2.5 million of Jackson's $5 million in remaining salary.

Finally, another AL contender, the feisty Toronto Blue Jays, are also in play. Toronto sits seven games over .500, and is making a run at the second (or possibly first) Wild Card; the Jays are just five games behind the No. 2 Wild Card slot and seven games behind the Wild Card leader. The Jays would like to bolster their young rotation with some maturity from a pitcher who has "been there, done that," and Jackson fits the bill. Toronto is willing to send one of two players to the Nats in exchange for Jackson. Washington's choices are outfielder Moises Sierra or lefty pitcher Griffin Murphy. Sierra profiles as a corner outfielder with a cannon for an arm. The Dominican-born youngster is coming off of a solid year at Double-A ball. Murphy was a late signee as a second-round draft pick in 2010, so he did not make his pro debut until last year. He only made 11 starts and has shown mixed results. The Jays are willing to trade either of these players for Jackson, providing the deal gets done within the next 48 hours—by the All-Star Game—so that Jackson could fit 16 starts into a tight second-half schedule. Toronto is battling in a highly competitive AL East division, and every game counts. The Blue Jays clearly recognize that doing a deal closer to the July 31 trade deadline could reduce the value of Jackson (or any player they acquire) by as much as 25 percent. So, if the deal is not done by July 10, the Blue Jays have made it clear they will not part with their prospects. Also, the Nationals are well aware that both the Jays and Rangers are actively in talks with Oakland about acquiring Brandon McCarthy and the Twins about Carl Pavano, who is having a surprisingly strong season.

If the Nats hold off on dealing Jackson, it might mean they miss the window and he remains with Washington for the entire season. If that were the case, they could make him a qualifying offer, which he presumably would decline, and receive draft-pick compensation. Under the new CBA, the first 10 draft picks are protected, which means if a team that finishes in the bottom one-third of the standings signs Jackson after the season, the Nats would receive the signing team's second-round draft pick. In all other cases the Nats would receive the team's first-round draft pick. The other possibility is that the market heats up for a front-line starting pitcher once we approach the deadline. Based on the Nats' survey and analysis of the trade market, the odds are in favor of the market weakening rather than strengthening. In other words, they would expect to receive proportionately less for Jackson as they approach the end of the month.

The case participants, who were asked to view this case entirely from the perspective of the Washington Nationals' front office, were judged on the quality of the analysis and answers to key questions embedded in the case, including:

- Their assessment of the probability of the Nats reaching the postseason
- Their estimate of the dollar value of a Nats postseason appearance
- The translation of scouting report data into prospect valuations and the resulting evaluation of each trade option
- The way in which "risk" is incorporated into their ultimate decision to buy, sell, or hold

The ultimate recommendations made by the case participants were far from unanimous. Of the 14 student teams in the competition, nine recommended the Nationals act as sellers, dealing Jackson to the Toronto Blue Jays, the team that offered the preferred prospect package. Three participant teams suggested Washington should be buyers, recommending the acquisition of the Reds' Phillips in exchange for a Nats pitching prospect. Two case teams made the curious recommendation that Washington should act simultaneously as a buyer and a seller, dealing Jackson in exchange for prospects while acquiring Phillips. The argument for the dual strategy centered on the opportunity to balance future assets (prospects in exchange for Jackson) while still not bailing completely on the playoff chase (the acquisition of Phillips), but it failed to gain acceptance among the panel of judges.

An important consideration that weighs into the "buy or sell" decision is the financial impact on the team of reaching the postseason. The Nationals' finance team has modeled its club's financials and created a schedule of expected revenues should the team reach various stages of postseason success. The revenues are largely in the form of increased season-ticket sales, single-game sales, sponsorship fees, and broadcast ratings and revenue increases resulting from the increased popularity and fan sentiment about a playoff-bound team. When a team reaches the postseason after many years of non-competitive baseball, the positive fan reaction can be dramatic from both new fans and the increased spending level of existing, loyal fans. Incremental revenues would spike for the 2013 season, but the "carryover effect" tends to be significant—particularly in the form of season ticket holder retention rates—and it can have a lasting financial impact for up to five years. The finance team has expressed its estimates as the present value of the future revenue stream resulting from several alternative playoff scenarios. They are as follows:

- $8 million—qualifying for the Wild Card but losing in the one-and-done play-in game
- $14 million—winning the Wild Card play-in game but losing in the NL Division Series
- $25 million—winning the NLDS, but being eliminated in the NL Championship Series
- $38 million—winning the NLCS, but losing the World Series in six games
- $55 million—winning the World Series

In addition to knowing the payoff from reaching the postseason, the Nats need to estimate their likelihood of qualifying, which is a function of their expected win total for the season and the probability of qualifying for the playoffs at various win totals. The Nationals' baseball ops group needs to assess these factors to ultimately estimate the expected value of becoming a "buyer." Not only is it an important input into the buy/sell decision, but also to help evaluate the specific deals on the table.

Another important input into Washington's decision is its scouting evaluation of the prospects offered from the various Jackson suitors. The Nationals need to accumulate and review all of the scouting information available from their pro scouting department and also their amateur scouting records, particularly for a recent draftee such as the Blue Jays' Murphy. The club has a strong stable of respected scouts, who are the lifeblood of any baseball organization. In a business whose product quality is largely dependent on the players on the field, talent evaluation is of paramount importance.

In the old days, the Nats simply would have asked their scouts what they thought of the prospects and viewed their raw scouting reports. But in today's business, that approach is too "top-line" and is susceptible to overlooking some important considerations, ranging from the systematic biases of individual scouts to the relative importance of various skill ratings. For example, for pitching prospects the Nats have learned that fastball command—the ability to locate a pitch—has a much higher correlation with the ultimate success at the major league level than fastball movement. In fact, young pitchers with a lot of movement on their fastball often have a difficult time controlling their pitches, leading to high walk rates and excessive pitch counts. This has led the Nationals to assign a higher weight to "command" ratings than to "movement" when analyzing its scouting reports.

Washington's quantitative analysis of their scouting reports also has led the Nationals to acknowledge the relationship between a scout's projections and the age and minor league level of the prospect. If a 19-year-old pitcher in the rookie league gets the same rating as a 21-year-old pitcher in Double-A, the historical data suggests the latter is more likely to succeed at the major league level.

Of course, the team cannot omit the prospect's minor league stats in estimating his ultimate major league performance projection. The better the player performs relative to his league's average, the more likely he is to succeed at the major league level. Once the Nats have the performance projection of the prospect, his performance needs to be converted to a dollar valuation. Ultimately, Washington wants to place an asset value on each prospect. The asset value creates a common denominator and nets out the player's performance potential and his age, adjusts for the scouts' biases, factors in the minor league level of the player, and incorporates his positional value. This last point reflects the reality that a left-handed starting pitcher is generally valued at a rate higher than a second baseman, even if they historically perform at relatively the same level. While one could argue that a team should be indifferent to a "three-WAR" pitcher or second baseman, the secondary markets are not. The free agent market valuation, as well as the trade value, of a left-handed pitcher consistently exceeds that of a second baseman. Perhaps it speaks to a flaw in the measurement of a players' WAR or an inefficiency in the market, but it is a reality the Nats should capture in their dollar valuation of the player as a team asset.

Another important consideration is an assessment of each player's "makeup"—his intangibles—which includes his commitment to baseball as a profession, his aptitude for learning, his overall attitude, how he handles failure (and success) and how he is expected to withstand the pressure of a tense big league moment. These factors are important considerations in all trade and player acquisition decisions, even if they cannot be easily quantified. However, for all of the trade scenarios on the table, the prospects' intangibles have been reviewed and determined to be remarkably similar to one another. In other words, the Nationals have decided that the player's makeup would not be a differentiating quality in this particular case, so they have been omitted from consideration.

The baseball ops department needs to make a recommendation to GM Rizzo about each of the players offered by potential trade partners based on the estimated asset value of the prospects to the organization. The asset value calculation, along with all the relevant formulas, will be provided to you. They involve a multi-step process of analyzing the scouting reports, converting the reports into player performance projections, and placing a dollar value on those performance projections.

The first issue facing student teams was the evaluation of how the Nats would perform over the full 2012 season given their hypothetical results through July 8. What would be the Nats projected win total and the resulting likelihood of reaching the postseason? If the probability of reaching the postseason was high, then the Nats might be buyers; if it was low, they might be sellers; and if it was somewhere in between, they might stand pat and wait for more information (e.g., games played) to make a decision. One factor working against delaying the buy-versus-sell decision is the calculation of the amount of value a player can add if he is acquired in early July versus the end of July. Decision makers constantly balance the information value of delaying a decision versus the steady reduction in the value of a trade asset over time—an impact player who can help a team reach the postseason in the current year.

Forecasting Washington's full-year win total included consideration of its remaining schedule and the expected performance of the team's key players. The case depicted the hypothetical first-half performance of many of the Nationals' key players, which has implications for the second-half forecast. Case teams translated bottom-up forecasts for the Nationals' key players and the balance-of-year schedule into an estimated win total for the club. The winning case team—The University of Chicago-Booth—differentiated itself from other participants by its methodology to assess Washington's playoff probabilities. The team of graduate business students used Monte Carlo simulations to estimate the Nationals' win total, as well as their playoff chances. After creating a series of assumptions about Nationals' players' performance, the resulting win total and their NL opponents' records for the year, they concluded Washington had only a modest six percent chance of reaching the postseason.

Other case teams, who were less pessimistic about the Nationals' chances, turned their focus to assessing the financial payoff of reaching the postseason. Some used the case data, as well as external sources, to estimate a win curve for the Nationals. Given the parameters of the case, the Nats were expected to gain about $19 million in future revenues from fans' response to a playoff-bound team. The future revenues would come in the form of increased season ticket sales for next season, more aggressive ticket price increases, and the various other revenue streams impacted by winning.

Whether the Nationals were to be a buyer or seller, several prospects needed to be assessed and valued. Rather than rely strictly on statistical data, case participants were given mock scouting report data to include in their prospect valuations. They were asked to apply statistical analysis of the scouting reports and adjust for various scouting biases, including the minor league level at which the prospect was rated. A high rating of a 20-year-old prospect in Low-A is generally not equivalent to the same rating for a 22-year old in Double-A. The students were given adjustment factors for minor league level, player age, and individual fictional scouts. Combined with the scouting report data, these factors allowed students to project a prospect's major league WAR and then apply some valuation parameters to ultimately develop an asset value for each prospect under consideration.

Beyond the major issues that case participants were asked to address, students also were judged on their overall approach to incorporating risk and uncertainty into their analysis and ultimate recommendation. While major league teams, often with the help of independent analysts, have made great progress incorporating analytics into their decision-making, measuring and pricing risk seems to be an area where more advances are needed. One example is in the area of projecting player performance. There is little information value in a point estimate of a player's future performance without the context of the shape and range of the distribution of expected performance. The winning Chicago-Booth team used its approach to risk analysis to select a left-handed pitching prospect—Murphy of the Blue Jays—with a lower mean expected performance but a distribution of expected performance that gave the prospect considerably more upside.

The case competition is a unique way to challenge up-and-coming baseball analysts to apply their skills to real-world baseball operations issues. While it's difficult to match the precise high-stakes conditions that front offices face, problems can be framed, hypothetical details can be provided, and aspiring analysts can try their hands and minds at solving the pressing issues confronting teams. More importantly, major league teams value these tools as both internal teaching tools and evaluation tools for prospective, upstart analysts.

For more information about upcoming Case Competitions, including the competition at the SABR Analytics Conference on March 7-9, 2013 in Phoenix, please contact Vince Gennaro at vince@vincegennaro.com, or visit vincegennaro.com.

Bargain Hunting in the Free Agent Market

by Matt Swartz

The economic structure of baseball's free agent market creates inequalities. When the players union and the league sit down to negotiate, they build a framework that is designed to increase the value and pay of experienced players. Players with at least six years of service time—those eligible for free agent market salaries—get about two-thirds of the total salaries, despite only producing one-third of the value. Players with fewer than six years of service time are often far more cost effective—players with under three years of service time generally get close to the league minimum salary, and even players with three to six years of service time generally have their salaries determined by an arbitration process that pays them less than half as much for the same value as players on the free agent market receive.

So why don't teams just avoid the free agent market altogether? After all, the baseball free agent market is almost rigged to generate enormous salaries for players who reach six years of experience.

Unfortunately, teams can only get so much production from younger players, so they need some free agents to compete for the playoffs. The playoffs often generate huge amounts of revenue, and the salaries of younger players are restricted so heavily that teams have strong incentives to spend money on free agents so they can capture the gold at the end of the playoff rainbow.

Being successful on the free agent market requires efficient spending. Some teams are very good at this—the Cardinals only averaged $3.3 million per Win Above Replacement (our value metric of choice, otherwise known as WAR) from free-agency eligible players from 2007 to 2011. On the other hand, the Athletics spent $13.2 million per WAR, and the Pirates did not even get a positive amount of WAR from free agents.

Everyone knows the *Moneyball* story nowadays: team figures out which players are undervalued, team corners the market on those players, team wins and encourages development of cinematically enticing walk-off home runs. Everyone also knows the epilogue to that story—other teams copy that team, and that team suddenly begins to stink.

Since then, analysts have often discussed the search for the "New Moneyball." Nearly everything has been called the "New Moneyball": defense, PITCHf/x, cornering the market on scouts and many others. I set out to figure out which types of players have actually been underpaid and overpaid through the last five years

(2007-11), a time period which happens to coincide with the post-*Moneyball* Athletics' five-year playoff drought.

What We Already Know

This is not my first time searching for free agent bargains. In my past research, I have identified two large market inefficiencies, and knowing these is important when looking for other types of bargains.

3. *Players who re-sign with their previous teams are, on average, better bargains than players who sign with other teams.*

This was the subject of my article in *The Hardball Times Annual 2012*, and the results were very distinct. Regardless of how you skew the data, teams clearly re-signed the players who were likely to age gracefully and stay healthy.

While there is some evidence that players who re-sign early will give a hometown discount in exchange for security, the far more important reason is that uncertainty is reduced by having inside information, and teams who know their own players better can mitigate the risks.

4. *Equally valuable players are paid more at some positions than others.*

Some of this can be explained by measurement issues in WAR when adjusting for position, but the difference remains important even when this factor is considered. Relief pitchers cost far more per WAR than any other player, and so I analyzed them separately when considering bargains for pitchers later in this article.

Additionally, players who play outfield, first base, and designated hitter cost significantly more than catchers, second basemen, third basemen, and shortstops. This is important to consider when looking for "underpaid" players, since some characteristics are more common among each group. For instance, left-handed batters seem to be overpaid on the aggregate, since there are so few southpaws at catcher, second base, third base, and shortstop, but when you look at each group separately, lefties do not appear to be overcompensated.

The following table shows the average cost per WAR (in millions of dollars, adjusted for the cost of draft pick compensation) at each position for all eligible players from 2007 through 2011:

Position	Cost
C	$4.2
1B	$6.1
2B	$3.3
3B	$4.4
SS	$3.7
LF	$7.0
CF	$5.5

Position	Cost
RF	$6.0
DH	$7.3
SP	$4.8
RP	$13.1

Methodology and Sample

I decided to analyze players two different ways to discover who is underpaid:

Prospective Analysis: I looked at all contracts signed to discover which statistics correlated with higher pay than expected at the time. Using all contracts that began sometime between 2007 and 2011, I used regression analysis to predict salaries based on the previous three seasons of WAR (regressed to the mean), age, and whether the player was re-signed. For hitters, I also adjusted for position, and for pitchers, I looked at starters and relievers separately. I then entered one statistic at a time into the regression to see whether being strong with respect to that statistic was associated with being paid more than would have been expected based on WAR.

Retrospective Analysis: I looked at all contracts after their completion to discover which statistics correlated with more valuable production than the deals cost. To do this, I utilized my previously established framework for Cost per WAR that adjusts for draft-pick compensation differences between players (hence, "Cost per WAR" rather than "Pay per WAR," since I include the "draft pick tax") and is different for each season. I also developed the average Cost per WAR separately for 1B/OF/DH, C/2B/3B/SS, SP, and RP. This analysis required looking at completed contracts, so I used all contracts that ended between 2007 and 2011.

I decided to remove two groups of players from both analyses for better accuracy. First, I removed all players who re-signed with their old teams before August 1st during their last year before free agency. This is because players who re-signed earlier cost even less than players who re-signed near the offseason.

Next, I removed all players who cost less than $2 million above the league minimum salary. Even though cost per WAR is actually very constant, the smallest contracts seemed to be better bargains. However, since many small contracts include unreported incentives, I am skeptical that small contracts actually cost less per WAR.

Additionally, if we were able to aggregate all of the guaranteed and non-guaranteed contracts under $2 million, we probably would have a lot of money spent on players who were released before playing that would bring up the average cost of signing a player to a deal under $2 million. This next table shows the relatively consistent 2007-2011 Cost per WAR for players at different salary levels, once you get past $2 million.

Salary Range	Cost
$0-2M	$3.70
$2-5M	$4.90
$5-10M	$5.80
$10-15M	$5.40
$15+M	$5.70
All	**$5.40**

Position Players

The story of *Moneyball* is that players with high on-base percentages turned out to be underpaid, while teams overvalued RBI, stolen bases, and defense. Teams began targeting high-OBP players soon after the book was published. In recent years, some have suggested that defense would become the "New Moneyball," and that teams would find that new fielding measures, such as Ultimate Zone Rating (UZR), would be an underrated way of acquiring defensive talents who would provide more value per dollar than other players.

The 2009 Seattle Mariners serve as a prime example. General Manager Jack Zduriencik built a great defensive team that managed to surprise everyone and win 85 games just a year after winning only 61, despite having a very weak offense. The subsequent 101-loss season in 2010 cast a lot of doubt on these methods, and many analysts began pointing to the limits in constructing defensive statistics.

So where do we stand now? It turns out that we may have shifted back too far towards overvaluing offense. Players with strong fielding and baserunning numbers going into free agency were better bargains than comparably costly players whose WAR values were backed by offensive numbers.

This is an important result, and it should be highlighted. There has been much controversy about the value of more subjective fielding and baserunning stats, and many have asserted that their subjectivity and inherent biases call into question their value. However, the following analysis is compelling proof that the value of these noisily measured metrics exceeds the cost of their biases.

Does that mean we should stop innovating when it comes to fielding and baserunning metrics? Absolutely not—but it does tell us that in the absence of superior metrics, targeting players with better UZRs is better than targeting players with better batting numbers, even though those batting numbers are better measured.

However, it appears that the overvaluation of offense is very different than it was before *Moneyball*. Before Billy Beane was constructing 100-win teams, teams were not placing enough weight on on-base skill and were focusing too much on home runs, contact and speed. Below, I will show that home runs, contact, and speed are actually somewhat under-compensated, while players with good OBPs tend to be neutral bargains.

Fielding and Baserunning

Players with strong fielding and baserunning skills are the best bargains on the position-player-free-agent market. They are paid less than players with similar WAR going into free agency, and they subsequently produce more WAR per dollar than players who have more offense-based WAR. The only caveat is that good defensive outfielders do not appear to produce all that much more per dollar than other outfielders (though they still produce more).

This is a significant finding, because one of the biggest critiques of UZR is that players who switch teams see far larger annual changes to their UZR than players who stay on the same team, which would potentially indicate bias. However, even though players who reach free agency and change teams are very overrepresented in this sample (70 percent of analyzed hitters), UZR appears to be very useful despite its inherent biases.

The fact that players with strong baserunning skills also appear underpaid suggests that it may be athletic players in general that are underrated. While it may be that some of their relative value in the retrospective analysis may come from aging better, the prospective analysis also shows that players with good baserunning numbers are paid less than other players with similar WAR.

In retrospect, the five contracts that were the most valuable were Scott Rolen (2003-10), Chipper Jones (2006-09), Alex Rodriguez (2001-07—yes, actually), Carlos Beltran (2005-11) and Placido Polanco (2006-09). It is clear when you look at this list that three elite infield defenders are included in the mix (not including Jones, but yes, including A-Rod, who was an elite defender at the time).

The next table will be the standard one I use in all prospective analyses. In each case, I ran regressions of the cost of the player (conditional on previous WAR), age, if a player was re-signed, position group and the statistic in question. The "Coef. Sign" column shows whether the coefficient on that statistic is positive or negative in the regression using that row's statistic.

When the coefficient is positive, it means that the player was paid more than other players were, given the same WAR, position, age, and re-signed/newly-signed status. When it's negative, the player was underpaid. This does not mean that overpaid is good or that underpaid is bad—that requires a retrospective analysis. The prospective analysis just shows how much teams are weighting those skills relative to how WAR weights them.

The "p-stat" column shows the statistical significance of the coefficient on that statistic. A good rule of thumb is that when the p-stat is less than .050, the finding is significant, p-stats between .050 and .100 are considered weakly significant; they are judgment calls. Anything larger than .100 is probably just a fluke.

In the table below, we see that when UZR/PA or BSR/PA (BSR stands for baserunning runs) is higher, the player is paid less than other players with the same WAR, etc., and we see that the coefficient is statistically significant for both statistics.

Statistic	Coef. Sign	P-stat
UZR/PA	-	0.000
BSR/PA	-	0.035

In the retrospective analysis, I separated the lower-paid positions from the higher-paid positions, rather than looking at all position players. This allows us to avoid confusing positional under/overpayment with the effect of the individual statistic. The table below will be the standard one I use in all retrospective analyses.

The first column shows the statistical threshold being considered, the second and fourth columns show the number of players who reached that threshold in each position group and the third and fifth columns show the difference in net value in millions of dollars relative to cost.

For example, players at 2B/3B/SS/C with positive UZR provided $8.35 million of "value" at $7.79 million of cost, where "value" is defined as the yearly average of Cost per WAR for players at these positions multiplied by their WAR. This made their "net value" equal to $0.55 million. Since players with negative UZR had $6.98 million of value at $7.63 million of cost, they had a net value of -$0.65 million. The difference in net value for players with positive UZR is the $1.20 million in the table.

In the table below, I separated each statistic into a comparison of positive vs. negative UZR the previous season, and supplemented this with great fielders and great baserunners. These were defined by looking at a little more than the top 10 percent of players in terms of UZR and BSR in the previous season, or more specifically, having at least 10 UZR and three BSR. As stated above, better fielders—particularly better infielders—end up underpaid, and better baserunners end up underpaid as well. Combining this with the findings of the table above, we see that teams are not factoring in fielding and baserunning sufficiently when signing free agents, and it is costing them later.

Statistic Threshold?	2B/3B/SS/C		1B/OF/DH	
	#Yes/ #No	Difference in Net Value	#Yes/ #No	Difference in Net Value
UZR>0	121/83	$1.20	91/117	$0.56
UZR>=10	42/162	$2.47	13/195	$0.26
BSR>0	89/115	$0.20	84/124	$3.26
BSR>=3	17/187	$2.84	27/181	$7.11

Critical readers may note that persistently biased UZRs (or BSRs) may be behind this finding. However, they may be relieved by the fact that 70 percent of the players in this analysis switched teams, and these are often the players with the largest swings in UZR (which is often attributed as a demonstration of its bias).

On top of this, looking only at retrospective analysis with WAR adjusted during the contract with UZR and BSR set to 0, these players were still net neutral—even though they are being compared with other players with high WAR in seasons leading into the contract. This means that the athletic types' hitting probably aged more gracefully than the less athletic types, even if those players were not actually playing better defense in the first place. In short, teams are better off targeting players with good UZR, regardless of its limits.

Sabermetric stats: Plate Appearances, Batting Average, On-Base Percentage and Slugging Percentage

Although position players are more valuable when they also possess non-hitting skills, there are definitely differences amongst hitting statistics. These different types of hitting statistics are compensated differently.

Using the prospective analysis, we can see that position players with higher batting averages, on-base percentages, and slugging percentages were all paid more than other position players with similar WARs, naturally because position players whose value came mainly from fielding and baserunning were undervalued. However, we can see that OBP is only weakly significant (with a p-stat of .095), but average and slugging are very significant.

Statistic	Coef. Sign	P-stat
AVG	+	0.023
OBP	+	0.095
SLG	+	0.000
PA	+	0.001

Transitioning to the retrospective analysis, we see that hitters with high averages also appear to be overpaid after the fact. Outfielders with averages of .300 the year before reaching free agency had average salaries of $13.27 million, while only producing $11.60 million of value. Outfielders with averages below .300 got paid $8.68 million for $8.21 million of value. While the difference was much smaller, infielders with .300 averages going into free agency were overpaid, too.

On the other hand, OBP seems to be reasonably paid. Hitters with .500 slugging averages are actually paid fairly, too, when we look at retrospective analysis, despite the fact that the prospective analysis suggested they were paid more than other players with higher WAR going into free agency. As we will see below, the source of power matters and explains some of this.

Statistic Threshold?	2B/3B/SS/C		1B/OF/DH	
	#Yes/ #No	Difference in Net Value	#Yes/ #No	Difference in Net Value
AVG>=.300	45/159	-$0.63	68/140	-$1.21
OBP>=.360	59/145	-$0.36	119/89	$1.00
SLG>=.500	56/148	-$0.41	92/116	-$0.15
PA>=500	131/73	$0.63	154/54	-$2.17

Classic Fantasy Counting Stats: Home Runs, RBI, Stolen Bases and Runs

When I set out to write this article, I was fairly convinced that I was going to find that teams were still overpaying for RBI, despite all that we have learned from sabermetric analysis. When you think about the classic "overpays" in recent free agent history, you cannot help but recall players with 100 RBIs getting nine-figure contracts and failing to produce. I was surprised to find that "RBI men" actually do not appear to be overpaid at all.

On the one hand, the prospective analysis shows that players who had more RBI received higher salaries than comparable players with the same WAR, but this turned out to be because RBI were actually a reasonable predictor of future WAR. The reason is that RBI are correlated with home runs, which were also "overpaid" when looking at the prospective analysis (i.e. players with more HR generated bigger contracts than other players with similar WAR), but home run hitters actually produced slightly more WAR per dollar than other players at the same positions once the contracts actually got underway.

What is happening? It appears that power hitters seem to be either aging a little bit better, or at least power hitters' WAR is more reflective of their talent than their luck. Either way, even though they are getting paid more than other players with similar WAR going into their contracts, they seem to produce more WAR than those players during the length of their contracts.

Players with more runs or more stolen bases going into free agency do not get paid more than other players with the same WAR, and they also do not produce more once the contracts get underway. The few infielders with 20 stolen bases or more did produce only $8.20 million of value for $10.37 million of cost, but this deficit was likely just the result of a small sample size. When removing the four years of Julio Lugo, the net value of the high-SB infielder contracts is $0.91. The rarity of infielders who steal bases makes that number difficult to interpret.

Statistic	Coef. Sign	P-stat
HR/AB	+	0.010
RBI/AB	+	0.007
R/PA	+	0.161
SB/PA	-	0.217

Statistic Threshold?	2B/3B/SS/C		1B/OF/DH	
	#Yes/ #No	Difference in Net Value	#Yes/ #No	Difference in Net Value
HR>=30	31/173	$0.55	62/146	$0.79
RBI>=100	33/171	-$0.12	68/140	$0.89
R>=100	21/183	-$0.51	54/154	-$0.66
SB>=20	13/191	-$2.44	30/178	$0.19

Other Classic Statistics: Doubles, Triples, Walks, and Strikeouts

Basic rate statistics and fantasy baseball statistics tell most of the story, but when we consider some of the less obvious statistics on a baseball card, we can start to see which types of players are improperly valued.

We saw above that players with high slugging averages are paid more than other players with similar WAR, but the analysis of doubles and triples shows the high slugging average pay is pretty much due to home runs. Players with lots of doubles have no significant difference in pay than comparably productive players with few doubles, and players with lots of triples have statistically significant lower salaries than comparably productive players with few triples.

The retrospective analysis shows that players with more doubles are actually more productive anyway (at least outfielders with more doubles are), but not nearly as much as players with more triples. Players with at least five triples are fantastically underpaid. Of course, these are also the players with better baserunning and fielding overall, meaning that speed is actually a somewhat underrated skill. This runs contrary to the findings of *Moneyball*, which suggested that the market had exaggerated the importance of speed. Speed is once again an underrated skill.

Another lesson from *Moneyball* was that walks were undervalued, but it seems that the market has really adjusted on this front. The prospective analysis shows no effect, and the relatively superior net value once the contracts began is mostly just residue from the correlation between walks and power.

Yet another sabermetric mantra has been that strikeouts are not worse than other outs. Both strikeouts and outs on balls in play cost teams about 0.3 runs on average.

Naturally, teams appear to have taken this to heart (if they weren't already), because players with more strikeouts do not get paid any differently than players with similar WAR but fewer whiffs.

However, players with strikeouts in fewer than 18 percent of plate appearances (roughly league average) produce more WAR per dollar once the contracts actually start. Some of this could be related to having more power, but recall that power was not actually that well paid in its retrospective analysis. Instead, it appears that contact is an important skill for which the market has not quite paid enough. This shows the importance of separating past WAR into skill (contact) and luck.

Statistic	Coef. Sign	P-stat
2B/AB	+	0.696
3B/AB	-	0.031
BB/PA	+	0.835
SO/PA	-	0.291

Statistic Threshold?	2B/3B/SS/C		1B/OF/DH	
	#Yes/ #No	Difference in Net Value	#Yes/ #No	Difference in Net Value
2B>=30	84/120	-$0.3	92/116	$1.47
3B>=5	31/173	$1.4	49/159	$4.73
BB>=75	7/197	$0.3	74/134	$1.61
SO/PA<18%	178/26	$1.8	133/75	$0.54

Summary of Hitter Analysis

Putting all of this together, we see that traditional scouting measures of players may actually be valuable in finding bargains in modern baseball. Skills like defense, baserunning, contact, and raw home run power were the skills I identified as being undervalued, while skills like drawing walks and having a high average are less informative of future value. While players who avoided strikeouts were more productive per dollar once their contracts began, players with higher batting averages were not. Overall, though, the real bargain with position players seems to be in finding strong infield defense and baserunning.

However, these differences are actually rather small compared to the differences in value per dollar from players at different positions. The cost per WAR of 2B, 3B, SS, and C was an average of $4.92 million, while OF, 1B, and DH cost an average of $7.15 million per WAR. This difference dwarfs some of the findings above and suggests that the best way for teams to spend their money on the free agent market is to develop their own outfielders and bring in athletic, slick-fielding infielders from other teams. When considering how much pitchers from other teams cost on the free agent market (see above), it seems like an even better idea to seek out these infielders.

Pitchers

While I used fWAR, the construction of WAR used at FanGraphs.com, for the analysis of hitters, I ended up deciding to use rWAR, the construction of WAR at Baseball-Reference.com, when analyzing pitchers. This is not because of superior methodology, but because it shows teams' valuation decisions more clearly.

The primary difference in the construction of WAR at the two websites is that FanGraphs uses FIP to approximate the pitcher effect on run scoring, while Baseball Reference using Runs Allowed per nine innings (RA9). FIP is an estimate of a defense-neutral version of a pitcher's ERA; it assumes a pitcher only controls his strikeouts, walks, and home runs, and that any deviations from runs allowed due to what happens on balls in play is out of the pitcher's control.

On the other hand, rWAR uses runs allowed, adjusting for the average effect of a team's defense overall on each pitcher. Thus, the difference comes from who gets "credit" when a pitcher allows more hits per balls in play than the average pitcher on his team. Pitchers get credit using fWAR, while the defense gets credit using rWAR. The result is that fWAR is more stable year-to-year and is a clearer estimate of pitcher's performance, while rWAR tends to be less biased in large sample sizes. In other words, fWAR is relatively more illuminating in smaller samples, while rWAR is more informative about larger samples.

When I originally began doing the following analysis using fWAR, I found that teams were not paying based on fWAR, despite the fact that it was a better approximation of their value going forward. Although teams have done a good job at following the early sabermetric findings about hitting, they seem to be underestimating the importance of Defense Independent Pitching Statistics, or DIPS Theory. Pitchers who had ERAs that were greater than the value of their ERA estimators, regardless of whether you use FIP, xFIP, tERA, or SIERA, were underpaid. Teams instead have focused on antiquated statistics like wins and saves.

Staple Stats: Wins, Saves, Holds, ERA and Innings Pitched

Despite all of the evidence that wins and saves are poor measures for evaluating pitching, teams still use them to determine how much to pay pitchers. The prospective analysis shows that teams paid pitchers with a higher win total more than they paid other pitchers with similar WAR totals going into free agency. Unsurprisingly, those pitchers with more wins under-produced during their contracts, because wins are not a good way to evaluate pitching.

Teams also paid more to relievers who had more saves going into free agency, paying for the "proven closer" label. This is true even among other relievers, a group that is already paid far more per WAR than hitters and starting pitchers. This is true even if we remove relievers with contracts below $2 million, already limiting the analysis to a group of relievers that is likely overpaid.

On the other hand, holds appear to be underpaid using the prospective analysis. Conditional on being a reliever who makes more than $2 million with a given amount of WAR, relievers with more holds get paid less than others. This is obviously because pitchers who have holds don't have many saves. Interestingly, though, they actually produce less once the contracts get started. It seems that being a setup man is indicative of decline, even when adjusting for age.

Starting pitchers with more innings pitched during the seasons before free agency earn more money than other starters who achieved equivalent WAR totals in shorter stints. In effect, this means that teams give more credit to quantity, rather than quality.

This turns out to be foolish. Pitchers who threw over 200 innings going into free agency generally fell apart afterwards—they produced only $5.45 million of value for $11.55 million annually. This is probably related to the fact that pitchers who switch teams underperform compared to those who stay on the same team (I established in last year's *Annual* that this was primarily due to extra information possessed by re-signing teams). Clubs probably let their workhorses leave more often when they know they are not durable enough to maintain the same high-inning totals moving forward. Interestingly, relievers with more innings going into free agency were not compensated more than others with the same WAR, but did end up outperforming them.

Although ERA did not appear to be linked with higher pay (beyond that of other pitchers with the same WAR) in the prospective analysis, it turns out that starting pitchers with lower ERAs did outperform their contracts more than those with higher ERAs. Teams that spent money on quality of innings, rather than quantity, did better. The same was not true for relievers, likely due to the correlation between a low ERA and being a "proven closer."

| Statistic | Starters | | Relievers | |
	Coef. Sign	P-stat	Coef. Sign	P-stat
Wins	+	0.020		
Saves			+	0.000
Holds			-	0.000
IP	+	0.026	-	0.295
ERA	+	0.575	-	0.170

	Starters		Relievers	
Statistic Threshold?	#Yes/ #No	Difference in Net Value	#Yes/ #No	Difference in Net Value
Wins>=15	45/124	-0.56		
Saves>=30			47/114	-0.56
Holds>=20			36/125	-0.68
IP>=200	62/107	-4.81		
IP>=70			58/103	1.38
ERA<4.00	79/90	1.81		
ERA<3.00			87/74	-0.09

Peripherals: Strikeouts, Walks, Home Runs and Ground Balls

For starting pitchers with the same WAR, having better peripheral statistics appears to be unrelated to higher pay. Teams did not appear to pay pitchers more if their performance was based on the solid footing of strike zone command and ground balls.

Using the retrospective analysis, we can see that they obviously should have. Elite starting pitchers with at least eight strikeouts per nine innings (K/9) were able to outperform their contracts by $3.28 million per season, while those with fewer strikeouts underperformed their contracts by $4.36 million per season. All five of the top starting pitcher contracts in the retrospective analysis went to pitchers who had at least 8.00 K/9 in their platform season: John Smoltz (2005-07), A.J. Burnett (2006-08), Ryan Dempster (2006-08), Derek Lowe (2005-08) and CC Sabathia (2009-11). The sixth most valuable starter contract went to Ted Lilly—he had 7.93 K/9.

Relievers with higher strikeout rates also appeared to be underpaid using the retrospective analysis, but the prospective analysis for relievers at least showed that higher-strikeout relievers were paid more than others with similar WAR.

The "listen to DIPS" mantra should not be limited just to strikeouts. Walks, home runs and ground balls were all largely ignored by teams in awarding contracts to pitchers (at least relative to their rWAR), but pitchers who excelled in these statistics provided much better values once their contracts started. Relievers mostly showed a similar trend, though teams actually did seem to pay attention to relievers' home run rates; perhaps too much, as relievers with more home runs but similar WAR seemed to be underpaid relative to their contracts.

	Starters		Relievers	
Statistic	Coef. Sign	P-stat	Coef. Sign	P-stat
SO/9	+	0.244	+	0.000
BB/9	-	0.394	-	0.072
HR/9	-	0.944	-	0.004
GB%	+	0.985	+	0.876

	Starters		Relievers	
Statistic Threshold?	#Yes/ #No	Difference in Net Value	#Yes/ #No	Difference in Net Value
SO/9 >=8	29/140	$7.64	84/77	$0.91
BB/9 < 3	92/77	$2.16	70/91	$2.67
HR/9 < 1	93/76	$1.18	126/35	-$1.77
GB% >= 50	28/141	$2.88	30/131	$1.56

Luck Stats: Batting Average on Balls in Play, Home Runs per Fly Ball

Batting Average on Balls in Play (BABIP) and Home Runs per Fly Ball (HR/FB) are both traditionally cited by sabermetricians as "luck"-based statistics that do not reflect pitcher skill. The fact that teams do not bid more for pitchers when these figures are high reinforces the fact that teams are not using the correct statistics to evaluate pitchers. This becomes more apparent when you consider that starting pitchers with lower BABIPs and lower HR/FB were much weaker values once their contracts began, as seen by the retrospective analysis.

Interestingly, this pattern did not hold for relievers, though it may be obscured by a biased sample. After all, relievers may have low BABIPs due to usage patterns—for instance, because teams use them against same-handed batters, and will often continue to do so once the contract begins.

	Starters		Relievers	
Statistic	Coef. Sign	P-stat	Coef. Sign	P-stat
BABIP	-	0.575	-	0.983
HR/FB	-	0.167	-	0.084

	Starters		Relievers	
Statistic Threshold?	#Yes/ #No	Difference in Net Value	#Yes/ #No	Difference in Net Value
BABIP<.290	74/95	-$3.28	102/59	-$0.72
HR/FB<9%	47/122	-$1.12	105/56	$0.36

Characteristics: Handedness and Velocity

I tested two other characteristics of pitchers that do not quite count as performance statistics. One of them, handedness, showed little difference in pay based on past performance and did not seem to have a discernible effect on future performance. The other, velocity, most certainly did. Pitchers who threw faster than others with the same WAR were not paid more, at least not amongst starters. However, starting pitchers with more velocity did produce far superior value. This is not a fluke, but rather a result of the underrated importance of velocity in predicting future performance.

In December, 2011, I published an article at hardballtimes.com called "You Shall Know Our Velocity," in which I tested the importance of velocity on future performance. In this article, I showed that even after adjusting for previous season's SIERA, those pitchers who threw 2.9 miles per hour faster than others had ERAs 0.10 lower than others on average. Velocity predicts future performance extremely well, something that also has been reinforced by the success of the new Steamer Projections' in predicting pitcher performance.

| Statistic | Starters | | Relievers | |
	Coef. Sign	P-stat	Coef. Sign	P-stat
LHP	+	0.151	+	0.697
Velocity	+	0.324	+	0.092

| Statistic Threshold? | Starters | | Relievers | |
	#Yes/ #No	Difference in Net Value	#Yes/ #No	Difference in Net Value
LHP	49/120	-$0.47	45/116	$0.16
FBv>=92	46/123	$w4.84		
FBv>=93			46/115	$0.71

Summary of Pitchers

Teams continue to pay pitchers based on traditional performance and ignore DIPS stats. While there are always exceptions to the rule, strikeouts, walks, and ground balls are far better indicators of future ERA than any other pitching statistics. Teams are already not careful enough when picking up each others' discarded free agents. They should be extra careful to at least focus on DIPS and velocity when looking for the rare values on the pitcher free-agent market.

Relievers appear to be compensated more when their DIPS are stronger, but, unfortunately, this is because of the association between strike zone command and the opportunity to close games. As a result, the effect is muted. Relievers in general tend to be overpaid, but if a team is committing to spend a fixed amount of money on relievers, it should look for pitchers who induce a lot of ground balls, a group that is relatively underpaid compared to other relievers (though still more than starters).

Sabermetric findings have been more surprising when it comes to pitchers than hitters. The controversy between sabermetricians and traditionalists surrounding DIPS metrics is more pronounced than any disagreement about hitting value. However, teams appear to be listening to sabermetric research less when it comes to the group of players for whom sabermetric findings are more relevant. Teams do a far better job of paying hitters, as sabermetricians would suggest.

By far, the most significant finding from this analysis is that teams do not pay enough attention to DIPS. In the *2012 Annual*, I showed that signing free-agent pitchers from other teams often provided terrible value. This shows that a safe way around this is to pay attention to their strikeouts, walks and ground balls.

Leaderboard: Total Defensive Value, 2010-12

Measuring defensive value in baseball isn't the final frontier—that's space, obviously—but it's still pretty frontier-y. At FanGraphs, we host both Defensive Runs Saved (DRS) and Ultimate Zone Rating (UZR), the latter of which we include in our Wins Above Replacement (WAR) formula. Drawing strong conclusions about a player's true-talent fielding ability from just a single-season UZR isn't particularly responsible. According to Mitchel Lichtman, who's responsible for the creation of UZR, a three-year sample is required to derive something meaningful from the metric.

Assessing a player's overall defensive ability doesn't stop there, however. We have to recognize that some positions are more demanding than others. A shortstop with a league-average UZR is considerably more valuable than a first baseman with the same total. As such, to create a leaderboard of the best fielders, we also have to consider the positional adjustments with which WAR is calculated.

Below is a leaderboard that does just that. It's the top 10 fielders over the last three years by UZR and positional adjustment combined.

Name	Team	Pos	G	Pos	Fld	Fld + Pos	Def/150
Matt Wieters	Orioles	C	413	27.6	29.5	57.1	20.7
Yadier Molina	Cardinals	C	413	29.4	27.0	56.4	20.5
Brendan Ryan	- - -	SS	403	17.3	33.8	51.1	19.0
Alexei Ramirez	White Sox	SS	472	21.2	28.8	50.0	15.9
J.J. Hardy	- - -	SS	388	17.6	30.2	47.9	18.5
Peter Bourjos	Angels	CF	299	3.5	40.0	43.5	21.8
Michael Bourn	- - -	CF	454	6.7	35.3	42.0	13.9
Brian McCann	Braves	C	392	26.6	15.2	41.8	16.0
Brett Gardner	Yankees	LF	325	-10.6	51.2	40.6	18.7
Clint Barmes	- - -	SS	400	14.3	25.9	40.3	15.1

Notes

Baltimore's Matt Wieters and St. Louis's Yadier Molina illustrate what sort of advantage a talented catcher can give a team. At +12.5 runs per 162 defensive games, catchers receive the largest run-value adjustment of all the positions, a full 25 runs (or 2.5 wins) more than a first baseman, for example. That being the case, even an average-fielding catcher with a league-average bat makes for an above-average player. If, like Wieters and Molina, that catcher is above-average all the way around, that adds a lot to a team. The pair were worth over 10 wins combined in 2012.

To what degree can defensive acumen justify a spot in the lineup for an offensively limited player? That appears to be the question that Brendan Ryan, who's played for St. Louis and Seattle in recent years, is constantly trying to answer. In 2012, Ryan slashed .194/.277/.278 in 470 plate appearances—about 40 percent below league average, even after adjusting for Safeco's park effect. Meanwhile, Ryan still managed to post a 1.7 WAR and has been, in fact, almost a three-win player for every 600 plate appearances over the course of his six-year career.

The Yankees' Brett Gardner is the only player on this list whose positional adjustment is a net negative. That's because he's played the majority of his games in New York as a left fielder. Why he's on this list, however, is because he plays left field much like an above-average center fielder would. Nor is this entirely unheard of elsewhere in the game. Before signing with Boston, Carl Crawford routinely posted double-digit UZRs in left for Tampa Bay. More recently, the athletic Gregor Blanco has parlayed above-average defensive skills into a left-field job with San Francisco, and he made several impressive plays during the 2012 postseason.

- Carson Cistulli

Case Study: Alfonso Soriano

On April 8, 2012, Adam LaRoche, Washington's left-handed hitting first baseman, stepped to the plate against Cubs starter Jeff Samardzija. LaRoche hit a 2-0 fastball the opposite way, a looping fly ball. The ball appeared destined to plop in front of the outfielders for a two-out single, but from the left side of television sets came left fielder Alfonso Soriano, a blur of diving white and blue.

"And a—catch by Soriano!" Cubs play-by-play man Len Kasper yelled as Wrigley ascended to its feet in applause.

Soriano had a great year at age 36. In the parlance of some, he "was worth his money." He hit like a younger self, and—more surprisingly—he snared fly balls like a version of himself not yet seen.

On Nov. 20, 2006, Soriano signed a behemoth eight-year, $136 million contract with the Chicago Cubs. But after hamstring problems in 2009 forever sapped his base-stealing abilities and as his calling-card power began to fizzle, it appeared the Cubs had saddled themselves with an unenviable outfielder. Add to that: His defense at second base had become a liability with the Yankees, and so the Nationals had shuffled him, against his will, to left field, where he struggled too.

In his one season in the outfield with the Nationals, Soriano played 1,373.2 innings—all in left field—and collected an impressive 22 outfield assists and 326 putouts. Both those figures still stand as his career-best numbers. He finished the season with a range factor (putouts plus assists) of 2.20 per nine innings—well ahead of the league average 1.97 for left fielders. According to the advanced fielding metric Ultimate Zone Rating (UZR), he had range worth 3.3 runs above average and an arm worth 4.9 runs above average.

The only problem? He had 11 errors in just 359 chances. His untrustworthy glove and his unorthodox last-second-hop under fly balls left him with a .969 fielding percentage—well beneath acceptable for an outfielder.

As the years passed, Soriano's arm got a little weaker—even when we assign him credit for the baserunners who chose not to advance because of his reputation for starting double plays—and his aggressiveness waned as his range numbers fluctuated. It seemed like the more balls he reached, the more he misplayed.

In 2012, a season in which many expected the Cubs would either trade or release Soriano, he posted his best range factor numbers since 2007. He collected 253 putouts and 12 assists over 1,183 innings for a 2.02 range factor (league average for left fielders was 1.83). UZR said his arm was 1.3 runs below average, but that his range was 12.5 runs above average. And, for the first time in his career, Soriano had an above-average fielding rate. In fact, it was near perfect.

In 266 fielding chances in 2012, Soriano misplayed one ball: On Sept. 6, 2012, Nationals outfielder Bryce Harper hit a looping fly ball to left field. Soriano reached it at full sprint, but then it kicked off the heel of his glove. He recovered quickly, but Harper wound up on second base.

That is it. Soriano's one error. It was by no means his only mistake in the field, but it was his only error—which is amazing for the man who had at least four fielding errors and one throwing error every year of his outfield career. And his lone 2012 error did not even lead to any opposing runs (though the Cubs lost 9-2 that day).

So how has his defense improved in just one offseason? Compare, for an anecdote's sake, Mr. Soriano's aforementioned catch on April 8, 2012, to one he made on July 16, 2010—a pair of catches selected essentially at random. Both were highlight reel catches made on fly balls at Wrigley Field in an afternoon game. Both catches involved Soriano running a great distance, charging a fly ball, and diving forward to make the catch. The 2012 fly ball hung in the air for 3.89 seconds, the 2010 ball was airborne for 4.55 seconds.

In 2010, Soriano stretches out, catches the ball, and then explodes onto the turf like a toddler losing his balance for the first time in his life. His chest hits the outfield grass with all the momentum of his long run as well as all the weight of his body. His feet kick clear above his head and then he rolls—as if a stuntman diving from a moving car—two full rotations. He raises to his knees, tosses the ball away, and then pushes off his legs to stand up. His face says, "Ouch."

The whole affair looks painful, slow, and unnecessarily dramatic. Nothing about Soriano's catch looks repeatable.

In the 2012 catch, Soriano does not have to run as fast or far to get to the ball, which passes alongside the sun. When he finally reaches the point of no return, where he must either sell out and dive or pull up and catch it on a bounce, he leans low over his legs, extends himself parallel to the ground, and makes the catch. He then spreads out, hitting the ground with his hips first, not his knees, and then glides over the grass.

In 2004, ESPN's Buster Olney dissected the diving catches of Gold Glove center fielder Andruw Jones. Olney almost exactly describes one of the key differences in Soriano's defensive game:

> "... [A]s Braves center fielder Andruw Jones pursues a looping fly ball, he swoops in low, dropping his whole body toward the ground—so that when he dives, his body is almost parallel to the playing surface." (ESPN. com, 4/15/04)

In the 2010 fly ball, when Soriano hit the ground, he plummeted with such violence he may have even knocked the wind out of himself. And he was lucky the ball did not join the wind. But in 2012, his chest was only about a foot and a half from the ground before he left his feet. When he hit the ground, he slid; he didn't roll. He not only saw the ball from a better angle through the dive, he also lessened the impact of when he finally hit the ground.

This change in his diving approach allowed him to act more aggressively on fly balls all season. He transitioned from a haphazard charging method based largely on instincts to the practiced efficiency of a true outfielder. He had nowhere near the same speed as his younger self, but he got quicker jumps, took better routes, and dove with greater confidence and consistency.

How did Soriano kick a six-season habit? In the simplest terms, he practiced. According to Sahadev Sharma of ESPN Chicago, when the Nationals moved Soriano into the outfield, they never trained the then-30-year-old slugger how to play the position:

> *"Soriano admitted that this year was the first time he's ever gotten instruction on how to play the outfield. First base coach Dave McKay routinely coaches all the outfielders on how to play defense. That revelation is all the more surprising considering that Soriano moved from second base to left field in spring training of 2006, his only season with the Washington Nationals. Soriano said that the only "coaching" he got at that time and prior to this season was shagging fly balls during batting practice."* (ESPNChicago.com, 9/23/12)

For a laugh, visit the MLB video archive and look at the highlight reel titles from Soriano's catches in every year but 2012. They tell the story just as well: "Soriano's tumbling catch" (5/28/10), "Soriano's falling grab" (3/27/11), and "Cubs' defensive misfortunes" (8/28/09).

Of course, there are many videos quite generously titled "diving grab" and "sliding catch"—as well as an under-appreciated wealth of "strong throws"—but those three titles offer perhaps the most honest analysis of Soriano's first six years in left field. He made some plays, messed up some plays and altogether was a mixed bag.

But in 2012, he was excellent. Among full time left fielders, Soriano's 11.8 UZR ranked him second in the majors—ahead of Desmond Jennings (10.4 UZR) and behind the laser-rocket-armed Alex Gordon (14.1 UZR). Moreover, Soriano led the league in range with 12.5 runs above average. The next closest among qualified left fielders was David Murphy with 9.1 runs above average. Over the previous four seasons, Soriano's 2012 range numbers were bested only by Brett Gardner, Carl Crawford and Juan Pierre.

Soriano played 151 games with the Cubs in 2012—the most he has played since his final season in Washington. Not only did he stay healthy in 2012, not only did he hit 32 home runs, and not only did he provide an above-average .262/.322/.499 slash, but he also positioned himself in the outfield Gold Glove conversation.

Armed with a youth-restoring lighter bat and some transforming defensive chops, Soriano accumulated 4.3 wins above replacement, and given that free agent wins typically are worth at least $5 million, he would have been worth more than $20 million on the free-agent market. For a team paying $18 million for that production—a team believed to be on the brink of eating the contract and releasing him heading into the season—that is some welcome news.

The man is well worth his money.

- Bradley Woodrum

Cat and Mouse with a Runner on First

by Dave Allen

With a runner on base, the pitcher's job becomes much harder. He has to pitch from the stretch, he has to worry about the running game, and, if the first baseman is holding the runner at first base, the defense behind him is compromised. In *The Book: Playing the Percentages in Baseball*, Tom Tango, Mitchel Lichtman and Andrew Dolphin quantified this effect and found that, with a runner on first and fewer than two outs, the batter gains 14 points of wOBA compared to when the bases are empty. What's more, they found that this effect was even more pronounced for left-handed batters—20 points of extra wOBA—than right-handed batters, who gained just 10 points.

Tango et al. didn't drill down into the exact mechanism behind this boost, but we can take a good guess. With a runner on first base, the first baseman is likely to be covering the bag to hold the runner close to it. This opens up a larger hole on the right side of the field, and a left-handed batter typically will hit more grounders to that side of the field than a right-handed batter will.

Now, with the advent of ball tracking—both pitches and batted balls in the field—we actually can test this hypothesis. And once we know the exact mechanism for the runner-on advantage, we can see how batters and pitchers respond to it. That is, we can see how well they take advantage of it (for the batter) or mitigate its consequences (for the pitcher).

So, with a runner on first, we know that batters—and particularly left-handed batters—do better. Where does this advantage come from? First, let's look at how often different batting events occur with a runner on first, compared to having no one on base (for a full discussion of the data and its limitations, see the methods section at the end of this article).

Event	Bases empty	Runner on first
Walks	7.6%	7.7%
Strikeouts	18.9%	17.4%
Home runs	2.7%	2.5%
BABIP	.294	.312

The batter's advantage shows up in two places: strikeouts and batting average on balls in play (BABIP). We will return to the drop in strikeouts when we look at batter behavior, but for now let's consider balls in play. This 22-point increase in BABIP suggests that the defensive concession of holding the runner on at first probably plays a big role in the runner-on advantage.

We can test this even more explicitly by looking at how BABIP changes with a runner on, split by where the ball is hit (to the left of second base or to the right of second base).

Ball is hit:	No runners on	Runner on first
Right of second	.280	.311
Left of second	.312	.313

As you can see, the increase in BABIP with runners on is only seen on balls hit to the right side of the field, which is what we would expect if the defensive positioning of the first baseman is indeed behind the increase in BABIP.

This helps explain the difference between right-handed and left-handed batters in the runner-on advantage. Batters generally pull ground balls, while they generally hit balls in the air to the opposite field. Matt Lentzner presented a great physics-based explanation for why this occurs on The Hardball Times website (you can find the link at the end of this article), and the data bear it out very well.

Here is a graph of the direction ground balls head when hit off the bats of left-handed and right-handed batters:

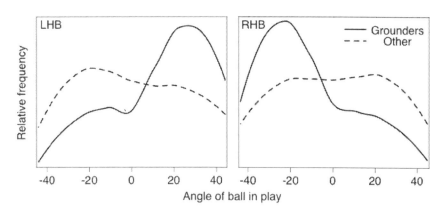

You can see that for both right-handed and left-handed batters, the peak frequency of grounders is over 20 degrees to the left (for right-handed) or right (for left-handed) of second base. The frequency of grounders going toward the middle of the field drops off fairly rapidly and then slowly declines in the opposite field. For balls in the air, the pattern is the mirror opposite of this one, though not nearly as extreme.

The upshot of all this is that left-handed batters are much better suited to take advantage of the larger hole on the right side of the infield (probably between about 35 and 20 degrees on the graph). We can actually test this explicitly by looking at the BABIP of ground balls based on the angle of the ball in play and the base state.

The gray bands in the graph below show the error around the estimated BABIP curves (again, see the methods section for a full description).

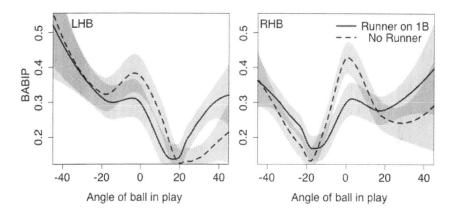

There is some strange behavior here. Grounders up the middle actually have a lower BABIP when a runner is on base. It is not clear why this happens, and it would be an interesting avenue to study further. Is a middle infielder more likely to cover the middle on stolen-base attempts or hit-and-runs? Is the pitcher a better defender pitching from the stretch? Is the second baseman positioned differently with runners on base?

But for the purpose of our study, the important fact is that a left-handed batter has a much higher BABIP on a grounder between 20 degrees and 40 degrees when a runner is on first than on a grounder between those angles when no runner is on. This is just as we suspected and, since this is the same place a left-handed batter is most likely to hit a grounder, it is largely responsible for the higher BABIP when lefties bat with a runner on.

Although the results aren't surprising, we have been able to nail down the major reason for the BABIP increase with a runner on—and thus the wOBA increase with a runner on—for left-handed batters. And this is a little bit intriguing.

Baseball is a cat-and-mouse game; it is a game of actions and counter-actions. The pitcher, the batter and the fielders all adopt strategies that create the most evenly balanced outcome among the three of them. If anything, we've learned that the sport of baseball suffers when its components become unbalanced. A marked imbalance in the game requires a response.

So let's ask the question: Based on what we now know, how do pitchers and batters respond when there is a runner on first?

Going forward, I'm going to examine only left-handed batters. As we saw above, the increased production with a runner on is largely due to hits getting through the larger hole on the right side of the infield. So you would think the pitcher has to deal with this and potentially shift his strategy to reduce such hits.

The first thing to know is that the likelihood of a pitch being pulled depends on the type of pitch thrown. Inside pitches are pulled more often, and slower pitches—particularly curveballs and change-ups—are also pulled more frequently than fast-balls and sliders. Evidence for this can be seen in two posts I wrote at the Baseball Analysts blog (links listed at the end of this article).

Let's look at some pitching graphs. In this, and all other graphs showing the horizontal location of pitches, the plot is from the catcher's perspective. This means that the left side of the graph is outside for the left-handed batter and the right side of the graph is inside.

Below is a graph showing the BABIP of a pitch based on its horizontal location (left-handed batters only). The solid line shows BABIP when a runner is on first; the dotted line shows BABIP in all situations.

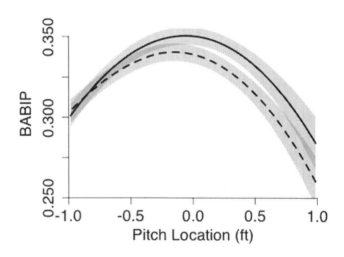

Most of the BABIP increase occurs in the center of the plate. You can see there is a jump in BABIP around the middle, and the difference between the two situations remains about the same as pitches move to the inside. This is a little surprising—we might have expected a bigger difference in the pitches furthest inside—but the result probably speaks to the notion that batters can better control pitches that are in the middle of the plate instead of either too far inside or outside.

Overall, this suggests that the pitcher should avoid the middle of the plate, which is something pitchers always try to do, of course. But since the entire middle and inside portions of the plate become more favorable for the batter, you would think that with a runner on first, the pitcher would pitch slightly more away to a left-handed batter than when the bases are empty. Does he do so?

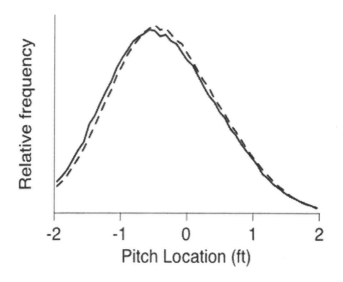

Once again, the solid line represents at-bats with a runner on first; the dotted line represents all other at-bats. You can see that there is a slight difference, but only very slight. Overall, pitchers throw the ball just over half an inch farther to the outside of the plate when a runner is on first compared to when the bases are empty. So, at least for horizontal location, there is just a small adjustment by pitchers.

Now let's turn our attention to pitch height. Since most of the runner-on advantage comes from grounders, we might expect a higher BABIP on pitches that are more likely to be grounders with a runner on first than when the bases are empty. Since lower pitches are more likely to be grounders, they should show the runner-on advantage more than high pitches.

Here's the graph, in which the left side of the graph is low in the strike zone; the right side is high. Again, the analysis is restricted to left-handed batters.

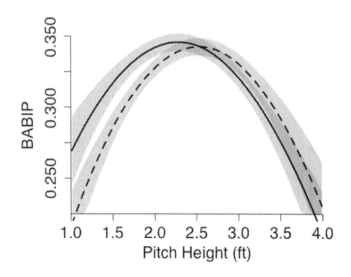

Here, the effect is very strong and consistent with the expectation. From about 1.4 feet to 2.3 feet (for reference, the strike zone typically goes from 1.5 to 3.5 feet) pitches have a higher BABIP when a runner is on first than when the bases are empty. The difference is as high as 0.025, quite an increase.

So, do pitchers respond by throwing higher in the strike zone with a man on first? The graph, please…

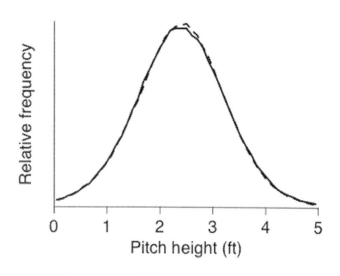

No. Pitchers are not throwing the ball at different heights based on base state. Pitchers in the face of this runner-on advantage to hitters are not changing their pitch location very much at all. A little to the side, not at all up and down.

Let's take a break from all the graphs. As a general rule, pitchers like ground balls and batters don't. Ground balls are rarely extra-base hits, and although fly balls are more often caught for outs, they also more often result in extra-base hits—particularly home runs. As was noted a long time ago—in *The Hardball Times Annual 2006*—an outfield fly ball generates .035 runs more than average. A ground ball generates .101 runs *fewer* than average.

With a runner on first, this dynamic changes. Holding the runner on at first increases the chance for an infield hit, but it also increases the chances of a double play. This may be the reason that pitchers don't really change their approach with a runner on first.

Do batters?

We know that the batter has this big hole offered to him on the right side of the field. Does he change his approach at the plate? Let's start by looking at the swing rate by horizontal location broken down by base state (left-handed batters only).

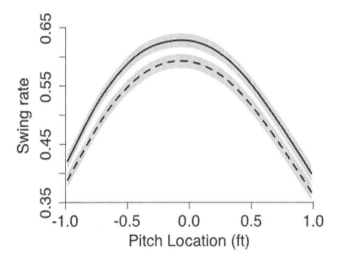

Really, the only difference here is that when the runner is on, the batter swings more often across the entire zone. There is no real consistent pattern for this difference; batters just swing more often. This behavior explains why strikeouts decrease with a runner on first. More swings mean slightly more whiffs, but they also mean more contact. More contact means that at-bats will end before the batter strikes out.

The bottom line is that left-handed batters, as a whole, are not actively trying to take advantage of the hole by swinging more often at inside pitches. What about pitch height?

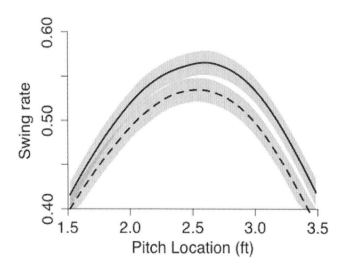

Here you see the additional swings as well, but they are relegated to part of the zone, from roughly the middle of the zone (vertically) to the top of the zone. In other words, with a runner on first, left-handed batters are not looking to hit extra grounders to take advantage of the hole given by the defense. Just the opposite, in fact. Batters are actively avoiding ground balls by swinging more often at high pitches. Why might this happen?

With a runner on first, the possibility of a double play comes into play. So the batter is dealing with two conflicting issues: (1) a ground ball with a runner on first has a higher BABIP than without the runner on first, but (2) there is the possibility of a double play eliminating both the batter and the base runner. For right-handed batters who see little BABIP benefit on grounders, (2) surely outweighs (1).

For left-handed batters, the difference is not as clear. In fact, going back to the data, ground balls from left-handed batters have slightly higher—actually less negative—run value with a runner on, -0.08, compared to -0.10 with no runners on. So the impact of the higher BABIP is greater than the impact of the double plays.

Left-handed batters are following the wrong strategy. They are too concerned about the impact of a double play and foregoing the possible incremental gain from the hole on the right side of the infield. They should not be trying to hit more fly balls with a runner on first. Most likely, they should continue to follow the pattern that works best for them but, if anything, they should be trying to hit more grounders.

I began this research because I was interested in knowing if pitchers change their approach at the plate with a runner on first. The answer turned out to be that, no, pitchers don't, but batters do. Despite a greater potential for a base hit, left-handed batters swing more often at high pitches and actively avoid ground balls. This makes intuitive sense, but it isn't the right approach. For left-handed batters, when the first baseman is holding the runner on first, the added BABIP on a grounder outweighs the impact of a possible double play.

It may be the case that select players do change their approach, and that would be a very interesting next step. Pitchers most likely to take advantage would be those with good control, who could routinely pitch away to decrease balls in play to the right side of the field. On the flip side, batters with good bat control may try to take advantage by getting additional balls in play to that half of the field. There is always more to learn about baseball.

Methods

In this article, I used the PITCHf/x data for pitch tracking and the Major League Baseball Advanced Media (MLBAM) Gameday data for ball tracking. Neither of these data sources is perfect, as no data source is, but they represent the best source of publicly available ball-tracking data. The PITCHf/x data (described in the *2009 Annual*) is based on a system of cameras installed in every baseball park that tracks each pitch. It has been shown to be highly accurate. More questionable is ball-in-play data, which records where each batted ball was fielded and is released with the Gameday data set. Stringers working for MLBAM mark these positions. There has been some discussion about systematic biases in these data. Here, I used the data to get angles of the ball in play, and for my purpose I think they adequately show the broad patterns.

I restricted my analysis to data from the 2009 to 2011 regular seasons (2012 data was not completely available by press time). The comparisons, unless stated otherwise, are between at-bats with a runner on first base only and fewer than two outs compared to those with the bases empty and fewer than two outs.

There are two types of plots in the article, those that show relative frequencies and those that show rates. The relative frequency graphs are histograms showing how often events fell into bins (e.g., how often balls in play were to different angles). The rate graphs look at the rate of something happening based on an independent variable (e.g., the rate a batter swings at the ball based on the horizontal location of that ball). I estimate that rate by fitting a LOESS curve to the data to predict the fraction of time the event happens. Around each curve, I also plot the error, in gray, to show how confident the prediction of the rate is based on that data.

References:

1. Find Matt Lentzner's article at: http://www.hardballtimes.com/main/article/why-flies-go-one-way-and-grounders-go-the-other

2. Find my article on hitters' tendencies to pull pitches at: http://baseballanalysts.com/archives/2009/06/last_week_i_too.php

3. Find my article on the angle of ball in play by pitch type and speed at: http://baseballanalysts.com/archives/2009/07/angle_of_ball_i.php

4. Find discussions about stringer biases, and much more, at *The Book* blog: http://www.insidethebook.com/ee

What Happens after Tommy John Surgery?

by Brian Cartwright and Jeff Zimmerman

The Nationals shut down Stephen Strasburg early this year. They did it because he had pitched 160 innings, and the team didn't want to put further strain on his young arm—an arm that already had been surgically repaired once via Tommy John Surgery.

You all know the tale by now. Back in July of 1974, Tommy John's pitching elbow stopped him cold. At the time, he was 13-3, and his 2.74 FIP was the best mark of his career, but his elbow suddenly felt utterly dead. Though he didn't know it, the ulnar collateral ligament in his elbow had torn. Not content to call it a career, John went to Dr. Frank Jobe to see if his elbow could be resuscitated. When Jobe weaved one of John's forearm tendons into a figure-eight pattern through his humerus and ulna bones, he created a procedure that is still resurrecting careers nearly 40 years later.

It wasn't all Jobe, of course. John put in the work to make this newly planted thing a functioning part of his body through hours, days and months of grueling rehabilitation work—18 months in all. But the payoff was more than worth it, as John pitched for 13 more years, posting a FIP better than league average in eight of them, and nabbing four All-Star nods, as well. In short, he became a medical miracle.

Today, Tommy John surgery (also known as TJS) is ubiquitous. Young pitchers, such as Strasburg and Josh Johnson, have it done at the first sign of a relatively mild elbow injury instead of waiting until after a serious one occurs. Heck, Jason Isringhausen has had it three times. The procedure now usually takes only an hour, and as we'll show, it works.

In *The Hardball Times Annual 2007*, David Gassko examined pitchers who came back from TJS. He found that pitchers who had successfully returned to the major leagues after the surgery showed no decrease in performance; they returned to their former level of performance.

Some pitchers have said the velocity of their fastball even increased after the surgery. Although Dr. Jobe doubts this, it may be that the wear and tear on these pitchers' elbows had been affecting their velocity, and the subsequent surgery restored the few miles per hour they would normally possess. Dr. Jobe and others, such as Dr. Christopher Ahmad, who is the Yankees' team physician, have had healthy pitchers ask if they could get the surgery, just to see if they can improve their performance.

The good news is that enough data are now available that we can examine how pitchers will produce after returning from TJS, as well as the chance they will head back to the infirmary. Let's take a look.

Rehab Time

In the beginning, the success rate of TJS was unpredictable. It took a while for pitchers to come back from the procedure. As a comparison, it took John 639 days after his last start to pitch again. Strasburg was able to return in just over half that time (381 days). The reasons for the faster return include quicker diagnosis, better rehab and just plain better knowledge of how to help pitchers recover from the surgery.

The timetable for players returning from TJS is now just over a year. For instance, here are the return dates for five pitchers who came back after having surgery during the 2011 season:

Name	Date of Surgery	Date of Return	Days
Joba Chamberlain	6/16/2011	8/1/2012	412
Brett Anderson	7/14/2011	8/21/2012	404
Rubby De La Rosa	8/9/2011	8/22/2012	379
Daisuke Matsuzaka	6/10/2011	6/9/2012	365
Rich Hill	6/9/2011	4/29/2012	325

Most pitchers return in a bit over a year, some sooner. However, not all pitchers make it back within the one-year mark. It took Ben Sheets two years to return from 2010 surgery to pitch for the Braves this past season. Generally, if a pitcher is not back on the mound within 400 days, he has experienced some form of setback.

Performance

Everyone is anxious to see how a pitcher will perform when he returns from surgery. Will he still be able to strike out batters? Will his pitches still have the same movement? Will he be better? Worse? Thanks to the depth of baseball data now available, we can directly answer some of these questions.

Our first analysis is a comparison of each pitcher's projected ERA and home run, walk and strikeout rates (per nine innings) from before the injury to the actual results after each pitcher returned. In the table below, we compare the performance of 180 pitchers who returned from TJS to a performance projection that was based on their stats from before the surgery. The projections were created by Brian Cartwright's Oliver system, which has been the centerpiece of THT Forecasts for the past three years.

Here are the results for all pitchers in the three seasons after their return, showing the percentage difference between their pre-surgery projected performance and their actual performance.

Season	ERA	HR/9	BB/9	K/9
One	5.8%	7.2%	5.0%	-4.4%
Two	0.6%	-2.0%	0.7%	-1.6%
Three	0.2%	2.1%	0.7%	-0.9%

Not surprisingly, the first season back is the worst for pitchers. Most of their stats underperform by around five percent. With home runs, walks, and strikeouts all heading in the wrong direction, ERA is six percent worse than projected. In the second season back, however, almost all those differences are wiped out; the strikeout rate is the only value with a percentage change over one percent. By the third season, there is no significant difference in the stats; the pitchers are right where they were expected to be.

To put those values into perspective, let's look at a comparison of how Tommy John and Nationals teammates Strasburg and Jordan Zimmermann each performed before and after their surgeries, remembering that it took John twice as long to recover:

Player	Season	ERA	K/9	BB/9	HR/9
Tommy John	Season Before	2.59	4.6	2.5	0.2
	First Season After	3.09	4.0	2.7	0.3
	Second Season After	2.78	5.0	2.0	0.5
Stephen Strasburg	Season Before	2.91	12.2	2.3	0.7
	First Season After	1.50	9.0	0.8	0.0
	Second Season After	3.16	11.1	2.7	0.8
Jordan Zimmermann	Season Before	4.63	9.1	2.9	1.0
	First Season After	4.94	7.8	2.9	2.3
	Second Season After	3.18	6.9	1.7	0.7

John fits the pattern almost perfectly. In his first season back, his basic rates were all worse, resulting in an ERA that was half a run higher. In his second season back, all of his stats had recovered. In fact, his strikeout and walk rates were better. The only stat that didn't follow the pattern was his home run rate, which actually rose after the surgery. Home run rates can be fluky, however, so we shouldn't read too much into this trend.

It's a different story with Zimmermann and Strasburg. Zimmermann struggled in all four categories during his first season back. In his second season back, he improved in all rates except strikeouts. In Strasburg's first season back, the young pitcher posted remarkable numbers, but he only pitched 24 innings, so no reasonable conclusion can be drawn from the data. In his second season back, all of his basic stats were in line with his performance before the surgery.

Another factor that can be measured is the change in a pitcher's fastball velocity from before to after the surgery. Using Baseball Info Solutions' fastball data from 2002 to 2011, we compared fastball speeds for 46 pitchers from the season before the injury to the next three seasons. Seasons Two and Three data were not always present because some pitchers spent the entire two seasons recovering. Season Four was the first complete season back for all pitchers.

The data were examined two ways. First, the change in speed was weighted by each pitcher's innings pitched. This approach essentially gave greater weight to some pitchers, however, which can cause some problems with interpretation of the results. Pitchers who experience an increase in speed are going to have better results and pitch more, and this will bias the results.

For the second method, therefore, we averaged the fastball speeds for all the pitchers evenly. Fastball speeds stabilize within two to three pitches, so a small sample size is usable. Here is how much the average pitcher's fastball speed varied between the four seasons, where Season One is the pitcher's last full season, Season Two is the season of injury, Season Three is the season back from injury and Season Four is the first full season back:

Season	Weighted	Non-weighted
Season 1 to 2	-0.10	-0.37
Season 1 to 3	0.14	0.05
Season 1 to 4	-0.07	-0.60

The results are reasonable. In Season Two, pitchers were unknowingly headed towards surgery, and their velocities were down significantly. In their first seasons back, pitchers actually improved their velocity from their season of injury. Finally, in the fourth season, the pitchers' velocities dropped, but the drop was less than expected.

Let us explain. Normally, pitchers will lose just a little more than 0.25 mph on their fastball each year, using the weighted method. (Data are not available on non-weighted values.) In general, pitchers would be expected to lose 0.75 miles per hours over three seasons—from Season One to Season Four in our sample. Instead, our pitchers only experienced a 0.60 decline in fastball speed. Pitchers who have had the surgery seem to be defying the normal aging patterns of pitchers.

Some pitchers can expect to retain the same fastball speed, while others will see it drop. Most, however, will not see much change at all. Here are a few examples:

Name	Year of TJS	Year Before Injury	Year of Surgery	First Partial Season Back	First Full Season Back
Francisco Liriano	2006	94.8	94.7	-	90.9
B.J. Ryan	2007	90.7	89.9	88.9	87.2
Randy Wolf	2005	86.3	87.6	88.3	87.4
Tim Hudson	2008	90.9	90.3	91.2	90.5
Edinson Volquez	2009	93.6	93.7	93.6	93.6
Josh Johnson	2007	91.8	92.4	93.5	95.0
Chris Carpenter	2007	91.4	90.5	91.9	93.0

Tim Hudson fits the mold of the data well, as he showed some decline in his speed from Year One to Year Two. But when he returned, he experienced a small bump in speed and then began the downward trend again.

Bottom line: It normally takes a pitcher one year of pitching to completely recover from Tommy John surgery. Once he has recovered, the pitcher has a very good chance of returning to his previous level of performance in terms of stats and basic fastball velocity.

Determining Surgery Failure

One of the greatest controversies of the past season was the innings limit the Nationals put on Strasburg in an attempt to prevent further injury to his arm. There is no science behind the 160-inning limit. Even if a theoretical ideal number of innings was known, every pitcher is different.

With different ways to measure the success of TJS, this section will focus on the other end of the spectrum: failures. Two types of failures will be examined, one short-term and one long-term.

1. The number of times pitchers were not able to return from surgery.
2. The time frame in which the pitcher may begin to lose his usefulness and require a second session with the surgeon.

Between 1999 and 2010, there were 86 pitchers who underwent Tommy John surgery and had pitched at least 100 innings in the majors. Eleven of them did not pitch in the majors again, and another 13 pitched fewer than 50 innings after their return. These results are difficult to interpret, however. Some of these pitchers had the surgery in an attempt to prolong their fading careers. So, the answer to our first question is that while pitchers do sometimes fail to return after surgery, many of those failures probably were doomed to begin with.

We also believe that the success of the surgery will be apparent before the pitcher even pitches in a major league game again. Usually, before any rehab game or just soon after, a failing pitcher will have to return for further tests and possible surgery. Here is a look at several players in our data set who had to be shut down for a second surgery and the number of innings they threw before being shut down.

Name	IP	Seasons	IP/Season
Brian Anderson	0	0	0
Jeff Zimmerman	2	1	2
Tim Spooneybarger	7	1	7
Jose Rijo	94	3	31
Darren Dreifot	110	2	55
Chad Fox	117	5	23
Scott Williamson	165	3	55
Shawn Hill	271	4	68
Matt Riley	282	3	94

These pitchers were never able to come back and pitch close to anything that resembled a full season.

Here's a good rule of thumb: If a post-surgery pitcher is able to reach 100 innings pitched in a season as a starter or 40 innings pitched as a reliever, it is reasonable to say that he won't need an immediate repeat of the surgery. However, if the pitcher is able to make it back pitching regularly, he then falls into the group of pitchers who begin to wear out their elbows again and need a second TJS.

The time frame for a second surgery, after pitching at full capacity, starts at approximately 400 innings. Here is a list of pitchers who pitched after one Tommy John surgery and were able to return to the majors yet eventually needed a second time under the knife.

Name	IP between 1st and 2nd TJS	IP after 2nd TJS
Joakim Soria	315	N/A
Doug Brocail	667	334
Chris Capuano	884	432
Jason Isringhausen	694	107
Tyler Yates	394	0
Victor Zambrano	1,021	0

These two-time Tommy John pitchers averaged around 650 innings between their first and the second surgeries. After undergoing the second procedure, Yates and

Zambrano never were able to make it to the majors again, while Brocail, Capuano and Isringhausen were able to return (the book is still out on Soria, as he had surgery in April, 2012, but at press time he was throwing and was on track to return from his surgery in the one-year time frame).

Given these data, it seems reasonable for the Nationals to have been worried about Strasburg's innings count. They currently control him through 2016, or four more seasons, so he will almost certainly reach the 400-inning mark while he is still under their control.

Strasburg may seem to have youth on his side, but youth doesn't necessarily carry an advantage. Examples are scarce since so few pitchers have both reached the majors before their 25th birthday and have required TJS, but history has not been kind to young starting pitchers who have had Tommy John surgery. Kerry Wood (22), Josh Johnson (23), and Francisco Liriano (23) were all good young starters when they had TJS, each was somewhat limited in innings pitched his first year back, and each had injury issues later in his career.

	Kerry Wood	Francisco Liriano	Josh Johnson
1st Season Back	137	76	91
2nd Season Back	174	136	184
IP before 2nd major arm injury	876	404	495

Each of the three starters was eased back into the rotation then threw between 400 and 900 innings before finding himself back on the disabled list. Many young pitchers have not been able to come back as starters and spent their careers in the bullpen instead. Jason Frasor, Jason Isringhausen and Kerry Wood are examples of starters who eventually ended up in the bullpen.

Each pitcher is different and will wear down differently. Using some historic numbers, it looks like Strasburg has about three full seasons left before he may begin to experience serious arm troubles again.

Conclusion

Tommy John surgery transforms a pitcher's unusable arm, and most pitchers who receive the surgery return to the mound in fine shape. The rehab time for the surgery has been cut in half, and pitchers now regularly return to action a year after surgery.

We also know that the season pitchers see a return to normalcy is generally not their first season back but their second. What's more, the velocity of pitchers who have had TJS degrades at a less steep rate than pitchers who haven't. Finally, we are now able to assess the benchmarks a pitcher needs to hit in order to have had a successful return, as well as the danger zone for when a second TJS may be on the horizon. With so few samples, and with those samples spread out over long periods of time, the data for Tommy John surgery can be difficult to corral, but we know a great deal more than we did five years ago, and our understanding undoubtedly will continue to evolve.

References

- http://static.espn.go.com/mlb/columns/bp/1431308.html
- http://www.hardballtimes.com/main/article/lose-a-tick-gain-a-tick/
- http://www.insidethebook.com/ee/index.php/site/comments/fastball_speeds_reliability/
- http://www.fangraphs.com/blogs/index.php/pitcher-aging-curves-introduction/

Et Cetera

Glossary

BABIP: Batting Average on Balls in Play. This is a measure of the number of batted balls that safely fall in for hits (not including home runs). The exact formula we use is (H-HR)/(AB-K-HR+SF).

Batted ball statistics: When a batter hits a ball, he hits either a ground ball, fly ball or line drive. The resulting ground ball, fly ball and line drive percentages make up a player's mix of statistics, with infield fly balls, or pop-ups, being tracked as a percentage of a player's total number of fly balls.

BB%: Walk rate measures how often a position player walks—or how often a pitcher walks a batter—per plate appearance. It is measured in percentage form.

BB/9: Walks allowed per nine innings

BSR: Paul not smart enough to know proper definition.

ChampAdded: The proportion of a world championship contributed by a player or team, based on the impact of a play on a team's winning a game, and the value of that game within the context of winning the world championship. Please refer to [insert title of Brad's article] for more information.

ERA: A pitcher's total number of earned runs allowed divided by his total number of innings pitched, multiplied by nine.

ERA+: ERA measured against the league average and adjusted for ballpark factors. An ERA+ over 100 is better than average, less than 100 is below average.

FIP: Fielding Independent Pitching, a measure of all those things for which a pitcher is specifically responsible. The formula is (HR*13+(BB+HBP)*3-K*2)/IP, plus a league-specific factor (usually around 3.2) to round out the number to an equivalent ERA number. FIP helps you understand how well a pitcher pitched, regardless of how well his fielders fielded. FIP was invented by Tom M. Tango.

K%: Strikeout rate measures how often a position player strikes out—or how often a pitcher strikes out a batter—per plate appearance. It is measured in percentage form.

K/9: Strikeouts per nine innings

kwERA: An ERA estimator that works similar to FIP, but takes home runs out of the equation. The formula is: 5.40-12*(K-BB)/PA.

LI: Leverage Index. Invented by Tom M. Tango, LI measures the criticality of a play or plate appearance. It is based on the range of potential WPA outcomes of a play, compared to all other plays. 1.0 is an average Index.

MLEs: Major League Equivalencies is the concept of translating a player's statistics across leagues, be it the Japenese leagues to Major League Baseball, the American League to the National League, or a Double-A league to the majors.

OBP: On-base percentage, an essential tool, measures how frequently a batter reaches base safely. The formula is: (hits+walks+hit-by-pitch) divided by (at-bats+walks+hit-by-pitch+sacrifice flys).

OPS: On Base plus Slugging Percentage, a crude but quick measure of a batter's true contribution to his team's offense. See wOBA for a better approach.

Pythagorean Formula: A formula for converting a team's Run Differential into a projected win-loss record. The formula is $RS^2/(RS^2+RA^2)$. Teams' actual win-loss records tend to mirror their Pythagorean records, and variances usually can be attributed to luck.

You can improve the accuracy of the Pythagorean formula by using a different exponent (the 2 in the formula). In particular, a sabermetrician named US Patriot discovered that the best exponent can be calculated this way: $(RS/G+RA/G)^{.285}$, where RS/G is Runs Scored per Game and RA/G is Runs Allowed per Game. This is called the PythagoPat formula.

SIERA: Skill-Interactive Earned Run Average estimates ERA through walk rate, strikeout rate and ground ball rate, eliminating the effects of park, defense and luck.

Slash Line: Everyone once in a while, one of our writers may refer to a batter's "slash line." He means something like this: .287/.345/.443. The numbers between those slashes are the batter's batting average, on-base average and slugging percentage.

tERA: True Runs Allowed is a defense-independent ERA estimator designed as an alternative to FIP and xFIP that includes variables for balls in play.

UZR: A fielding system invented by Mitchel Lichtman, similar to John Dewan's Defensive Runs Saved system. Both systems calculate a fielder's range by comparing his plays made in various "vectors" across the baseball diamond to the major league average rate of plays made in those vectors. Both systems also look at other factors such as the effectiveness of outfield throwing, handling bunts and turning double plays.

WAR: Wins Above Replacement. A "win stat" that calculates the number of wins a player contributed to his team above a certain replacement level. WAR is calculated at FanGraphs and Baseball Reference. Though the two implementations vary a bit, they share a common framework that includes a "linear weights" approach to runs created, advanced fielding metrics, leverage for relievers and replacement levels that vary by position. The methodology was established over time at the Book Blog (www.insidethebook.com).

wOBA: Introduced in The Book: Playing the Percentages in Baseball, by Tom Tango and friends, this is a "linear weight" offensive rating system that is similar to OPS, except that it's better and is set to the scale of on-base percentage.

WPA: Win Probability Added is a system in which each player is given credit toward helping his team win, based on play-by-play data and the impact each specific play has on the team's probability of winning. Read "This Game Is Rigged: The Orioles' Amazing Bullpen" for more details.

wRC+: Like OPS+ and ERA+, wRC+ is scaled so that 100 is average and a higher number is positive. The "RC" stands for Runs Created, but it's not Bill James' Runs Created. It's a "linear weights" version derived from wOBA.

xFIP: Expected Fielding Independent Pitching. This is an experimental stat that adjusts FIP and "normalizes" the home run component according to the number of fly balls a pitcher allowed.

For more information on these and other statistics, visit: hardballtimes.com/main/statpages/glossary or fangraphs.com/library.

Who Was That?

Dave Allen teaches biology at Middlebury College. In his spare time, which is becoming increasingly limited, he likes to think and write about baseball. He is particularly interested using pitch-tracking data (PITCHf/x) to answer questions about the game.

Evan Brunell is a long-suffering Red Sox blogger, blogging at firebrandal.com since 2003. He has written for CBS Sports and currently freelances while attending graduate school and being involved in charity endeavors. He has contributed to The Hardball Times since 2008.

Craig Calcaterra is the Blogger-in-Chief for HardballTalk at NBC Sports.com. He is also appears from time to time on the NBC Sports Network, where he is one of the three baldest sports commentators allowed on basic cable television. Craig lives in a fortified compound in New Albany, Ohio, with his daughter Mookie and his son Carlo.

Dave Cameron is the managing editor of FanGraphs, and he also contributes regularly to ESPN and the *Wall Street Journal.* More importantly, he's a leukemia survivor, and will take any opportunity given to shamelessly suggest that you donate both blood and platelets. He's happy to still be writing about trivial things like baseball.

Brian Cartwright started reading Bill James more than 30 years ago while spending his summers as the statistician and head scorer for the host league of the All-American Amateur Baseball Association in Johnstown, Pa. He created the Oliver projection system, which became The Hardball Times Forecasts. Before coming to THT, Brian wrote for Seamheads, StatSpeak and FanGraphs. For the past 25 years he was worked as a photogrammetrist, compiling digital map products from 3D aerial photography.

Carson Cistulli has been hurting FanGraphs' credibility, in one way or another, since 2009.

Chris Cwik is a blogger for CBSSports.com's MLB Rumors Blog and writes for both FanGraphs and RotoGraphs. He has also contributed to ESPN. Originally from Chicago, he currently lives in Alexandria, Va., with his fiancee, and is looking forward to the Rick Hahn era.

Joe Distelheim, The Hardball Times' chief copy editor, is a lifelong Cubs fan and a lifelong newspaperman. Despite overwhelming evidence that both institutions are in decline, he continues to believe in them.

Adam Dorhauer is a third-generation Cardinal fan now living in Arizona. He has contributed to *The Hardball Times Annual* and the Baseball ProGuestus series, and occasionally blogs at 3-DBaseball.net.

Glenn DuPaul is currently an economics major at Lehigh University. He writes about sabermetrics for The Hardball Times, Beyond the Box Score and Bugs and Cranks.

Ben Duronio is a Braves fan exiled in the New York City-area, and writes about baseball for both FanGraphs and the Capitol Avenue Club. He formerly worked for the ESPN Stats & Info Group, and is currently an MBA student who focuses his studies on finance.

A student at Syracuse University, **Matt Filippi** loves sabermetrics as well as scouting and player development. He has contributed to other sites like Beyond the Box Score, Penn League Report, and The Stirring Straw (a Yankees blog).

Vince Gennaro is the president of the Society of American Baseball Research (SABR), the author of *Diamond Dollars: The Economics of Winning in Baseball*, a consultant to MLB teams, and he appears regularly on MLB Network's show, *Clubhouse Confidential*. He also teaches at Columbia University and Manhattanville College in the graduate sports management programs.

Marc Hulet has been writing about baseball—mostly prospects—for the past 10 years. He currently writes for FanGraphs and produces the site's annual Top 15 prospects lists. His work has also appeared at ESPN.com. Rotoworld, NBCsports. com, *Heater Magazine*, *The Graphical Player*, the *Toronto Sun* and BaseballAnalysts.com, among others. He has a background in print and broadcast journalism and spent five years as a newspaper reporter and editor.

Ranked by pay, **Brandon Isleib** is a lawyer and columnist. By any other ranking, he is a columnist and lawyer. He lives south of Seattle which, when you think about it, is true of most of the world.

Chris Jaffe is a history professor, Cubs fan, and author of the award-winning book, *Evaluating Baseball's Managers*.

Brad Johnson is a baseball addict and a statistics junkie who currently resides in Atlanta, Ga. He played four seasons of injury-plagued baseball at Macalester College from 2006-2009, and has since made the transition to a purely off-the-field existence. Baseball has and always will be the unifying principle of his life.

Matt Klaassen reads and writes obituaries from his cult compound in quasi-exurban Ontario.

David Laurila grew up in Michigan's Upper Peninsula and now writes about baseball from his home in Cambridge, Mass. He authors the Q&A series at FanGraphs and is a regular contributor to several publications, including *Red Sox Magazine* and *New England Baseball Journal*. He is co-chair of the Boston chapter of SABR.

Dan Lependorf is a Bay Area native and a recent chemical physics graduate from the University of California-San Diego. He might be able to answer any question about the chemical composition of the infield dirt off of the top of his head.

Jack Marshall is a professional ethicist and lawyer. He is president of the ethics training and consulting firm ProEthics, and writes about all manner of ethical issues, including baseball, on his blog Ethics Alarms (www.ethicsalarms.com).

Jeff Moore is a regular contributor to The Hardball Times and is the creator of MLB Prospect Watch (www.mlbprospectwatch.com). A former college baseball player and college coach, he still holds three NCAA records from his playing days. He currently resides in Delray Beach, Fla.

Though he's a freelancer, most of the pieces **Eno Sarris** writes find a home at FanGraphs specifically. As a German-Jamaican-American who has lived around the world, he's found himself most at home in front of a baseball game, generally.

Eric Seidman is an accountant from Philadelphia who works closely with contractors, athletes and entertainers. One of the original three Fangraphs bloggers, Eric also covers the Phillies at the popular site, Phillies Nation. Eric has previously written for *The Hardball Times Annual*, as well as SABR's quarterly newsletter By the Numbers, and the *Historical Baseball Research Journal*. Eric has consulted for major league teams and players, and co-created the ERA estimator SIERA.

Greg Simons has been an editor and occasional writer for The Hardball Times since 2010, and he has been producing baseball content for various entities since creating his own geocities web site way back in 1999. Game Six of the 2011 World Series is probably his all-time favorite sports memory.

Sean Smith is a consultant to a major league team. He lives in Maryland with his wife, two daughters and two cats.

Dave Studenmund is still trying to get the hang of Twitter.

Matt Swartz is an economist who finished his Ph.D. at UPenn in 2009. His recent work can be found at FanGraphs, The Hardball Times, and MLB Trade Rumors. He lives in Philadelphia with his wife, Laura.

In the drafting of the poets, **Paul Swydan** was the number-seven pick. This is his first contribution to *The Hardball Times Annual*. While he is a regular contributor to both FanGraphs and ESPN, Paul's most important job is being a stay-at-home dad.

Steve Treder has been a writer for The Hardball Times since its founding in 2004. He's also been a frequent contributor/presenter in other forums, such as the SABR national convention, the NINE Spring Training Conference, and the Cooperstown Symposium. He roots for the Giants from his home in Santa Clara, Calif.

Bradley Woodrum is a freelance writer from Chicago with a master's degree in economics and a penchant for lumberjackian facial hair. His writing credits include FanGraphs, DRaysBay and Cubs Stats.

Jeff Zimmerman currently writes for RoyalsReview.com and Fangraphs. He and his brother Darrell also maintain the baseball injury data website—BaseballHeatMaps.com. Currently he resides out in the sticks near Wichita, Kan., with his lovely wife Kristen and their two ornery kids, Ruby and Cole.

Made in the USA
Lexington, KY
27 December 2012